SEA

THERLANDS

els

Milan Soncino
• Mantua Venice
• Cremona
Po River
Genoa • Bologna
• Pisa
• Florence
• Livorno

ITALY

Rome

Naples

TYRRHENIAN SEA

Palermo
Sicily
Paierno

MEDITERRANEAN SEA

LONGWOOD
LIBRARY

Longwood College, Farmville, Virginia 23901

A center for learning. A window to the world.

SOFONISBA ANGUISSOLA

The First Great Woman Artist of the Renaissance

SOFONISBA ANGUISSOLA

The First Great Woman Artist of the Renaissance

Ilya Sandra Perlingieri

RIZZOLI
NEW YORK

First published in the United States of America in 1992
by Rizzoli International Publications, Inc.
300 Park Avenue South, New York, NY 10010

Library of Congress Cataloging-in-Publication Data

Perlingieri, Ilya Sandra.
    Sofonisba Anguissola: the first great woman artist of the Renaissance / Ilya
Sandra Perlingieri
        p.   cm.
    Includes bibliographical references and index.
    ISBN 0-8478-1544-7
    1. Anguissola. Sofonisba. 1532–1625.   2. Painters—Italy—
Biography.   3. Painting, Renaissance—Italy.   I. Title
ND623. A5395P4   1992
759.5—dc20   91-38245
    [B]   CIP

Editor: Stephanie Salomon
Designer: Abigail Sturges

Printed in Italy

Endpapers, Anguissola family tree, Anguissola and Gazzola family coats of arms,
and Renaissance textile motifs designed and drawn by Blake Andrew Perlingieri

This book is dedicated to the memory of
Dr. George V. Gallenkamp
and
"la bella pittrice."

PATRONS

CONTENTS

ACKNOWLEDGMENTS

There is not any primary sixteenth-century research that can be undertaken without the help of scholars in the field. My many research trips to Europe were made immeasurably easier by the assistance of many scholars to whom I am most grateful. Dr. Maria Teresa Binaghi Olivari, director, History of Art, Pinacoteca di Brera, Milan, graciously shared her own research files on Anguissola with me, and was tremendously supportive and enthusiastic from the beginning. The countless hours we spent together discussing sixteenth-century esoterica and her numerous contacts opened many doors all over Italy. Dr. Gino Corti, Villa I Tatti, Florence (also visiting scholar, UCLA and the J. Paul Getty Museum, Malibu), over many years kindly helped in and out of his graduate Paleography classes in the herculean task of deciphering numerous obscure documents. Our discussions on grammar and handwriting were tremendously helpful.

Costume scholars Grazietta Butazzi, Castello Sforzesco, Milan, and Carmen Bernis, Madrid, discussed dating paintings via sixteenth-century fashions.

In Rome, Dr. Giulia Barberini offered her friendship and scholarship to help unravel the puzzle of Anguissola's life. The assistance of Monsignor Charles Burns, Archivio Segreto, the Vatican, and Isabel Aguirre, archivist, Castle Simancas, through the maze of Philip II's correspondence deserve special thanks.

Dr. Alessandra Mottola Molfino, director, Poldi Pezzoli Museum, Milan, encouraged me and helped in various aspects of my research. Art historians Drs. Frederick Hartt and Federico Zeri gave their time, advice, and historical perspectives that also proved extremely beneficial.

Dr. Winifred Higgins, professor emeritus, San Diego State University, was of tremendous assistance through many phases of my research both in graduate school and after. Her friendship and guidance, as well as that of Drs. Steven Schaber, Department of Oriental Languages, and Tom Cox and Graziella Kehrenberg, Department of French and Italian, San Diego State University, through the labyrinth of academic bureaucracy confirmed my faith in what teaching excellence is all about.

Discussions about Anguissola's medical diagnosis came from ophthalmologist, Dr. Milton Lincoff. Even across the centuries, it is possible to make a medical diagnosis when the art work has been anatomically accurate.

In Madrid, Don José Manuel Calderón, archivist, Palacio Liria, Señora Doña Maria Carmen Crespo, director, Archivo Historico Nacional, and Ernesto and Alicia Belanger were of great assistance with the period of Anguissola's twenty-year stay at Philip's court.

In London, I am very thankful for the gracious assistance of John Somerville, Department of Old Master Paintings, Sotheby's, Dr. Joanna Woodall at the Courtauld Institute of Art, and Christopher Lloyd, Surveyor, the Queen's Royal Collection. I am deeply appreciative to Her Majesty Queen Elizabeth II, for giving me special permission to view the *Portrait of the Infantas Isabella Clara Eugenia and Catalina Micaela* at Buckingham Palace.

I am very grateful, too, for a Samuel H. Kress Foundation award during the final stages of completing my manuscript; to editor Jeffrey Schaire for having the vision to do my 1988 cover story for *Art and Antiques;* and for the assistance of Stephanie Salomon, my editor at Rizzoli, who saw me through a difficult transition with both a keen eye and a special understanding of women's issues that have eluded others.

Madeline Scott's patience and friendship through numerous drafts of both my thesis and this monograph are graciously acknowledged and appreciated.

To the Anguissola family: Victor di Suvero and Liana and Ferrante Anguissola d'Altoè for their kindness and help during the last two years. It has meant a great deal to me.

A tremendous thanks to Carol Coller Vaiuso, Oneil Cormier, Jr., Johanne Landry, Dr. Susan Foley, Dr. Rose Graf-Taylor, Karen Spurgin, Dr. Patsy Boyer, and Lilla Sweatt for their on-going help here and in Europe. Dear friends Jane Richmond, John Finch, Kathleen Butler Kolk, John Noble, Jodi Shagg, Rebecca Busby, Jill and Tony Spurgin, Marsha and Bill Speckmann, and Gaynor and Peter Nelson kept me going through the bleakest of moments, and to Dr. Marina Sparaci and Denise Paccione, for their special last-minute help. Their gifts of love and caring sustained me. To GJP chi è molto lontano da me.

In 1976, I went to see the pioneering exhibit "Women Artists: 1550–1950" at the Los Angeles County Museum. It was my six-year-old daughter who noticed Anguissola's portrait first. Looking at her marvelous work changed my life. I took up the gauntlet that Linda Nochlin and Ann Sutherland Harris threw down in their important exhibition catalogue: I tracked Anguissola down, through countless archives, museums, and libraries. Three years later, when Germaine Greer's *The Obstacle Race* was published, I knew that my desire to research Anguissola's life was vital. I am indebted to them for their vision.

To my brother, Larry, who also has given me his long-distance encouragement and help from the very beginning, my deepest thanks.

To my dearest daughter, Chemynne Alida, and my wonderful son, Blake Andrew, who drew the sixteenth-century map, the original sixteenth-century-inspired textile designs that decorate each chapter, the Anguissola family tree, ancient coat of arms, and Gazzola crest, my heartfelt appreciation for their loving care, editorial assistance, enthusiasm over these sixteen-and-a-half years, and general help in working through my ideas on Anguissola.

Finally, to the memory of my first mentor, New York University art history professor, George V. Gallenkamp. It was his friendship and brilliant scholarship that has been my beacon through a lifetime of delving into the joys of studying art history. His teaching was done with a great deal of love. I have endeavored to continue to pass that torch on to my students.

FOREWORD

A few years ago, when with the help of some scholarly Italian friends we embarked upon the project "Sofonisba and Her Sisters" with the objective of promoting their lives and works of art in a museum exhibition, I could not have imagined that Ilya Sandra Perlingieri had been doing the same work, on the same subject—with a grand passion—for the previous sixteen years.

In this book, Professor Perlingieri presents a broad picture of Sofonisba's surroundings in context of the customs and culture in which she and her sisters lived and worked. Additionally, beyond the actual importance of each artist, I believe that it is also necessary to view the problems and historical situation with which artists, and above all a woman artist, would be confronted.

The Renaissance was a period of great painters, but it omitted the contributions of women, no matter how good their work might have been. Despite this, Sofonisba was successful and became a first-rate painter, as witnessed by the testimony of Vasari, Michelangelo, and Van Dyck. Later her name fell into oblivion.

Sofonisba's works have been scattered throughout the world, some attributed to more famous contemporaries, while others have been destroyed in the fires at the Pardo Palace in Madrid. Now, however, research and identification of her masterpieces and the study of our family archives have come together to comprise an important page of Italian art history and give Sofonisba Anguissola her proper place in this history.

Thus, Ilya Sandra Perlingieri's diligent work, the fruits of her shining research in museums and archives in Italy and Spain, now give a pioneering and valuable contribution to Sofonisba's work. Thanks to this work, the years of Sofonisba's oblivion are finished. Now we can begin a new era in art history where we can look forward to this book initiating a new period of study and research about her life and works.

Count Ferrante Anguissola d'Altoè
Milan

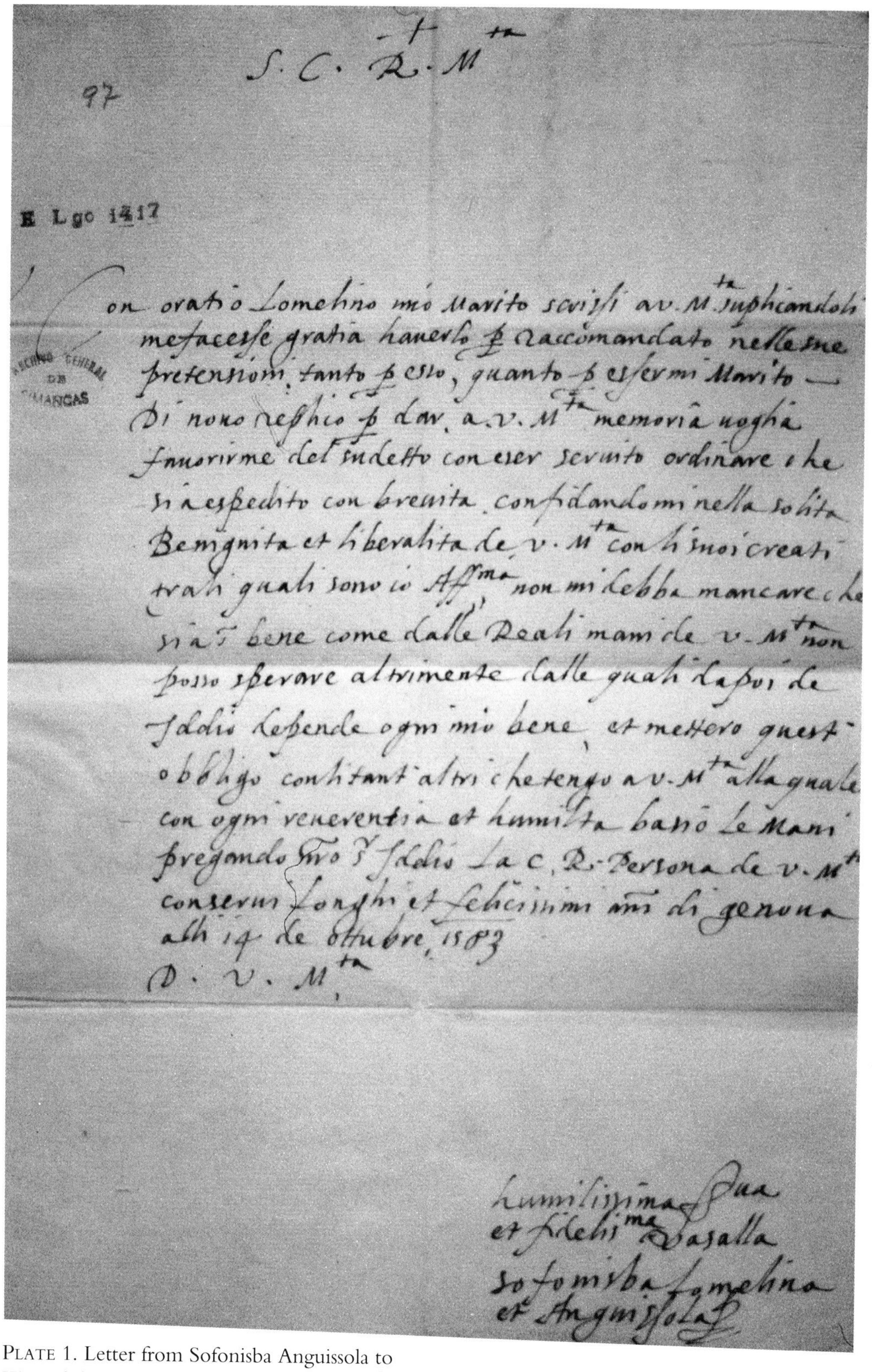

S. C. R. M.ta

97

E Lgo 1417

Con oratio Lomellino mio Marito scrissi a V. M.ta suplicandoli
me facesse gratia haverlo per raccomandato nelle sue
pretensioni, tanto per esso, quanto per essermi Marito —
Di novo replico per dar a V. M.ta memoria voglia
favorirme del sudetto con eser servito ordinare che
sia espedito con brevita. confidandomi nella solita
Benignita et liberalita de V. M.ta con li suoi creati
tra li quali sono io Aff.ma non mi debba mancare che
sia bene come dalle Reali mani de V. M.ta non
posso sperare altrimente dalle quali dapoi de
Iddio depende ogni mio bene, et mettero quest'
obbligo con li tant' altri che tengo a V. M.ta alla quale
con ogni reverentia et humilta basio le Mani
pregando Nro Sr Iddio la C. R. Persona de V. M.ta
conservi longhi et felicissimi anni di genova
alli 14 de ottubre, 1583
D. V. M.ta

humilissima sua
et fidelis.ma vasalla
Sofonisba Lomelina
et Anguissola

PLATE 1. Letter from Sofonisba Anguissola to
King Philip of Spain, 1583. (Translated on p 174.)

INTRODUCTION

Who *was* Sofonisba Anguissola? This was the question that I would ask myself frequently in 1976, after I had seen one of her exquisite self-portraits at the major art exhibition "Women Artists: 1550–1950" at the Los Angeles County Museum of Art. In this painting, Anguissola's expressive eyes were haunting. What lay behind them? Her work was striking and it was all the more inexplicable that her name was not in any of the art history books and known only to a few art historians. Why had this artist—internationally famous in her own lifetime, a student of Michelangelo and court painter to King Philip II of Spain—been forgotten over the next four-and-a-half centuries? The more I delved into her fascinating life, the more intrigued I became about this obscure Renaissance painter. I became hooked on the search, and thus began a sixteen-and-a-half year research odyssey. In the process, I slowly saw the transformation in myself from art historian to detective. The rewards were continuously gratifying as I discovered important documents and paintings.

The next logical question then was, "Should I write a book on an unknown woman painter?" It was more than just the issue of writing about another forgotten artist. As I researched in out-of-the-way European archives and struggled with saving funds for my many trips, it seemed increasingly important to bring this information to a wider audience than just other art historians. It also became more of an issue to balance the art history scales a bit more through my own Renaissance research.

I remembered a conversation in the 1960s with Horst Janson, who was head of the art history department at New York University where I was studying as an undergraduate. He had said to me, "Women's contribution to art was very minor. They did not amount to very much." It still burns in my memory, and it was perhaps then that the seeds were sown for my interest in women artists and writing about them. However, it took looking at Anguissola's self-portrait in the following decade until those seeds began to take root and flower.

Art and art history, I have been told frequently by many a male art historian, were a man's domain. Certainly, that was evident. Men were in control of the field. Even the majority of art historians, up until fairly recently, have been men: they have written most of the art history books and criticism and still are the arbiters of "who's important" and "who's omitted." For centuries, the pervasive attitude has been that artistic talent is a male prerogative and the few women who "made it" were the exception. Further, even for those gifted and courageous women, avenues of artistic study were extremely limited, and until this century women generally were denied access to sketching the nude male model.

I had hoped that there would be an interest in academic circles to uncover new information on unknown artists, as is the case in other disciplines. However, there still is a great deal of resistance, and the majority of art history courses taught today in the United States still reflect a male bias. So, the issues expanded as I researched this period: historical and sociological aspects kept cropping up. In what capacity did women participate, as the humanistic "rebirth" of the sixteenth century made its way north from Italy to other cultural centers in Europe? What, in fact, was women's status? Were they really part of what we call the Renaissance? How did Anguissola's exceptional position—as a talented artist, role model, and pioneer of genre painting—figure in the period?

Generally speaking, most art history until fairly recently has been written in a vacuum: discussions of artists and their works are compared and contrasted, but rarely in the context of the period in which works were created. This is the way much of art history is taught and the way much of it is still written. However, artists did not work in a vacuum. Their oeuvre is their personal expression of the sociological, political, and economic signs of their times. It is in this context that I have written about Anguissola's life and work: as she fits into the ever-expanding pieces of the marvelous puzzle of Renaissance art history.

The sixteenth century was a turbulent yet fascinating time. It was a time of heated passions and passionate people. What time of great change isn't? The blossoming of Italian Renaissance art had taken hold in the previous century; and its message had spread to northern Europe with artists such as Dürer and Holbein going to that source and the Italians, in turn, bringing their discoveries north. Although the artistic energy flowed in both directions, it was heavily weighted in favor of Italy.

Artists were dependent for their livelihood upon aristocratic patronage and whim and/or the Catholic Church. In an era of constant political instability, survival for many creative souls was tenuous, at best. A handful managed well, but many—including Leonardo, Michelangelo, and Titian—often had to badger their patrons for payment which frequently came late.

The European scene was a game of political chess, with each ruler vying for control. For almost the entire first half of the sixteenth century, three men ruled most of Europe: Henry VIII (r. 1508–47) was secure on England's throne; Francis I (r. 1515–47) ruled France; and Charles V (r. 1516–55) oversaw the running of the Holy Roman Empire. When Charles abdicated, his son, Philip II—Anguissola's patron for twenty years—became Spain's ruler. Italy, on the other hand, was fragmented into rival city-states, ruled by various noble families: the Medici in Florence; the Gonzaga in Mantua; the Sforza in Milan; and the d'Este in Ferrara. The popes, in Rome, and the doges, in Venice, also came from Italy's aristocracy.

Both Henry VIII and Francis I had tremendous egos and opulent tastes in the arts to match. In June 1520—twelve years before Sofonisba Anguissola's birth—the two rulers met at the Field of the Cloth of Gold, near Calais, in an extravaganza staged so that each monarch could outshine the other. Bejeweled and clothed in the most exquisite of costumes, it was a political and social contest of one-upmanship, where artists and artisans had a feast day preparing for this gathering. Here, as Will Durant has written, "medieval art and chivalry displayed themselves in sunset magnificence."

At the same time, northern Europe (of which Spain artistically was considered a part) was going through a transitional period between the Middle Ages and the early Renaissance. It was not without its birth pangs. Three years earlier, in 1517, events took a serious turn which would echo down the rest of the century. From the highest to the lowest position in the clergy, the Catholic Church was in a state of chaos. There had been rumblings for a long time. Petrarch, Machiavelli, Savonarola, and Erasmus all had written about the Church's excesses—to no avail. In fact, criticism of the Church could bring down the wrath of the Inquisition on many an innocent soul. Events finally came to a head. Political and religious events coalesced in the figure of Martin Luther who, on 31 October, tacked his 95 Theses to the castle church in Wittenberg. By the following decade, northern Europe (especially Germany and England) had broken with the Church, and the Reformation was born.

Italy, too, while extremely tolerant of artistic creativity and basking in the beauty of Botticelli, Leonardo, and Perugino, had its own religious and political upheavals. The Inquisition brought a reign of terror to all of Europe. The Catholic Church absolved its inquisitors of any wrong-doing and forced the secular branches of governments to carry out mass executions of thousands of innocent people—most of whom were women and children. No one was free of suspicion. Added to this on-going travesty of justice, there were frequent wars. The toll was a heavy one for the sixteenth century to bear.

Unrest is not always conducive to creativity. Art often suffers—witness Botticelli, in 1494, placing his paintings on the pyre in Florence's Piazza della Signoria at the urging of Savonarola. Despite the questioning of the Church's corruption, no serious attempt at internal reform was contemplated for several decades, until the Council of Trent (1545–65).

The fragmentation of Italy—without one political ruler, although the pope was the spiritual one—enhanced the role that art played, as there were more rulers who paid the price for paintings, sculpture, decorative arts, textiles, and buildings.

Into this period of splendor and squalor, magnificent artistic achievements and the most horrifying brutalities of the Inquisition, Sofonisba Anguissola was born. She was fortunate and blessed to have had an aristocratic and supportive family and managed to overcome enormous obstacles that Renaissance patriarchal society imposed on its creative women. While her achievements were lauded during her own lifetime, she was obliterated from the annals of art history over the next four centuries.

However, the past sixteen years of research have demonstrated that—despite these more than four hundred years since Anguissola's birth—much still can be discovered in European archives. It just takes tenacity and vision. Another picture also has emerged from this research: women artists and important issues concerning them have been ignored in much of the art history literature. Even Anguissola, as a well-educated Renaissance woman, would have been extremely aware of the obstacles, inconsistencies, and unfair—written and unwritten—rules of behavior expected of women. There was no women's movement then; but she was part of a system that she, no doubt, struggled with—even if she may not have voiced her concerns. We are all products of the time in which we live, and Anguissola was no exception. Yet, she broke new ground and offered new directions in an age when women were considered decorative objects. She triumphed.

There are many issues that still require much discussion, research, and reevaluation, some of which have not changed significantly since Anguissola's day: a language that is heavily weighted to patriarchal nomenclature (witness, for example, "old masters" vs. "old mistresses"); double standards for men and women; and, today, thousands of art history courses and texts that only mention a few "token" women. Women's contributions to the history of art still are not part of the mainstream. What is now required is an open-mindedness to reexamine the male bias, negativity, and conflicting messages that women artists have received and which have permeated art studies and writing. Art should be enjoyed for its intrinsic beauty, not for the gender which produced it.

Some final notes. Throughout most of the sixteenth century, the "old style" Julian calendar was in use; it was ten days behind the Gregorian (known as the "new style") calendar. Spain and the Netherlands adopted the Gregorian calendar (which is now used universally) in 1582; England was still using the "old style" Julian calendar in 1588. Since many archival documents were in poor reading condition—and sometimes words and dates were indecipherable—I have chosen to keep the old style dates. I also have kept the various monetary values. The complexity of trying to convert fluctuating Italian and Spanish sixteenth- and seventeenth-century monetary values to twentieth-century equivalents was not attempted. For me, it also has been a way to maintain the flavor of sixteenth-century financial exchanges.

This book has been written (in a less academic fashion) with the general reader in mind—although for those interested readers, sources are cited. I have intentionally written in an informal manner to make this important story more accessible to those who love art history. For those who are not art history scholars and, therefore, not familiar with certain esoteric early sources, a word about them. Giorgio Vasari was the first to write about Anguissola in his *Vite* (the abbreviated Italian term for his *Lives of the Most Excellent Painters, Sculptors, and Architects*), which was published in an expanded version in 1568. Most later sources—including Soprani (1674), Baldinucci (1681), Zaist (1774), and Sacchi (1872)—based their writings on Vasari's work. None of these authors did any archival research in Spain to elucidate for their readers Anguissola's important twenty-year stay at King Philip II's court. This is the first book to do so.

While it has been permissible to use given names for male artists—Leonardo, Michelangelo, and Titian, etc.—for women, it has been a mechanism for denigrating their hard-won status. In an effort to balance the scales, many art historians now use patronyms. I have chosen a combination: when talking of Anguissola as a child or in intimate, family settings, I have used her given name; otherwise, her surname has been used.

Not every one of Anguissola's paintings that I either tracked down or discovered is discussed here. Rather, I have chosen to focus on a sampling of her major works. A catalogue raisonné is planned to go with an international exhibition that I hope to curate in the future.

I have also discussed textiles and costumes in Anguissola's paintings in detail. They are some of the great glories of Renaissance art. However, generally, they only receive a passing reference—if at all—by very few art historians. Yet, a knowledge of costume history is vital for dating portraits—and it was important in tracking down Anguissola at the Spanish court.

The Renaissance was a moment of splendor. However, much more research needs to be undertaken in order to explore the importance of women's contributions. It is my hope that this book will spark both graduate art history and women's studies programs to encourage more primary research of women artists in the archives and museums of Europe and the United States. Then, a more balanced art historical view will take place.

On a personal level, it has been a wonderful labor of love to bring Sofonisba Anguissola back to life: to give her her rightful place in the history of art.

SOFONISBA ANGUISSOLA
The First Great Woman Artist of the Renaissance

THE ANGUISSOLAS:
A NOBLE FAMILY'S BEGINNINGS

Anguis sola fecit victoriam.(The lone snake became victorious.)
—*Anguissola family motto*

Despite the passage of more than four and a half centuries since Sofonisba Anguissola's birth, the provincial city of Cremona, about seventy-five miles southeast of Milan, is much the same today as it was in the sixteenth century: cobblestoned, narrow streets, the large Piazza Comunale, and Il Torrazzo, the thirteenth-century *campanile* that dominates the landscape. It is this bell tower—the tallest in Italy at 387 feet—that one sees miles in the distance as one approaches the city. The Cremonese countryside still maintains its thriving agriculture, and the air is redolent with smells of farming.

Cremona's history dates back two millennia. It was founded in 212 B.C.E. as one of Rome's first colonies. Over the centuries, because of its rich farmland and ties to Milan, the city was a pawn in the political vicissitudes of the Po Valley. It survived a siege by Hannibal during the Punic Wars and then was sacked periodically during the Middle Ages. By the Renaissance, the city had regained its economic prominence. Cremona also has had its share of illustrious citizens dating back to the time when Virgil studied there. Within a span of a little less than a century, both composer Claudio Monteverdi (1567) and violin maker Antonio Stradivari (1644) were born there.

At the beginning of the sixteenth century, Cremona was a small city with a population of about forty thousand and an abundance of medieval and Renaissance churches, many of which are still in use today. Churches were open for early morning prayers and were used throughout the day for social gatherings. For rich and poor, daily routines had some similarities, among them: regular church attendance and shopping trips to purchase locally made textiles in the big open-air market in the Piazza Comunale, where farmers also sold their produce, flowers, medicinal and culinary herbs.

Agriculture was an important part of Cremona's economy with cereal grains grown and harvested in the surrounding countryside, but a substantial part of the city's considerable wealth during the fifteenth and sixteenth centuries came from its

PLATE 2. Visconti family coat of arms, San Sigismondo, Cremona.

textile production. It was Cremona's most important industry, and in the Lombardy region it ranked second only to armaments. Mulberry trees, used to feed silkworms for Venice's thriving silk trade, were grown. Cremona also specialized in the production of fustian, a cloth that was made by weaving a cotton weft with a linen or wool warp. The division of labor in this industry—controlled by the craft guilds—was one of the most complex and, according to contemporary sources, could include "a specialized occupation"[1] for each step. Since the production process could require up to twenty different occupations, there were an abundance of jobs.

As Cremona was a tributary for the duchy of Milan, the land owned by the nobility was taxed according to the output of its production. Under Charles V, Holy Roman emperor from 1519 [defacto from 1516] to 1555, Cremona's prosperity was taxed, thus penalizing the city "heavily for her comparative success."[2]

The city's fortunes had been tied to the Pallavicini family until 1344. It went through considerable upheaval during the following century, often due to the political machinations of France and Spain and their alliances with various Italian city-states: Cremona fell to Milan and was controlled first by the Visconti and then by the Sforza families; from 1499 to 1509, the Venetians held it; and from 1535 until the early eighteenth century, it was under Spanish rule.

A century before Anguissola's birth, Cremona was part of the dowry of Bianca Maria Visconti, the only child and heir of Filippo Maria Visconti, duke of Milan, and his wife, Agnes del Maiano. The Maianos and Visconti were two of Milan's most powerful families. Filippo Visconti's adept *condottiere* (mercenary general) Francesco Sforza, was rewarded for his allegiance to the family by receiving in marriage Bianca Maria and her considerable dowry. They were married in Cremona's San Sigismondo. The church, built in 1253 and today still carrying the Visconti coat of arms over its main doors (see plate 2), would figure later in Anguissola's family history.

At the end of the fifteenth century, Italy became the battlefield for what has become known collectively as the Italian Wars. The wars began in 1494—the year in which Amilcare Anguissola, Sofonisba's father, probably was born—with the invasion of France's King Charles VIII and lasted sixty-four years. Italy was not then the cohesive whole that it is today. Rather, it was made up of rival city-states ruled by a number of powerful noble families. This fragmentation of the peninsula exacerbated the greed of the French royal house of Valois and the Spanish imperial Hapsburg house, whose rival dynastic claims fed on the ambitions of the leaders of the various Italian city-states and encouraged among them constantly shifting alliances and virtually unending wars.

Despite the frequent wars, it was a glorious age. Since the days of Giotto, Italy had built up an incredible artistic momentum, and the arts, including sculpture, literature, music, magnificent textiles, and paintings flourished. By 1500 Leonardo, Raphael, Titian, and Michelangelo all were creating masterpieces. Even in the provincial towns and cities, the impact of these great Renaissance artists was keenly felt. Cremona, a few day's journey from the Sforza's Milanese court, was tied historically to Milan, its powerful neighbor, but was actually governed by the *comune* (the city's fathers), a group of aristocrats and wealthy merchants—including the Anguissolas—who were fast becoming part of the new middle class.

The Anguissola family was among Cremona's minor nobility. One branch of the family, in Piacenza, dates back to the tenth century. The Società degli Anguissola were international bankers in France and Italy from 1100, but by 1200 they had to liquidate because of a political crisis. Sofonisba's paternal grandparents came from the Gazzola and Pigazzano branch of the family. Annibale (son of Lazzaro and brother of Marsilio), Sofonisba's paternal grandfather, was born in 1479 and died in 1510. He lived in the parish of San Giorgio and earned his living selling medicinal herbs. His father, Lazzaro, sold perfumes. Annibale married Elena de Filisgradis, daughter of Giacomo. No date for her birth, marriage (which probably took place in the early 1490s), or death are recorded, which is not unusual because such records generally were not kept prior to the Council of Trent in 1565.[3]

The small provincial parishes, such as those of Cremona, were the last to partic-

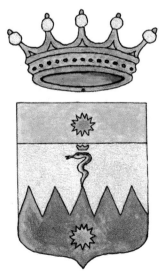

PLATE 3. Anguissola family ancient coat of arms.

PLATE 4. Gazzola branch of Anguissola family coat of arms.

ipate in the council's sweeping changes, and so these new regulations were implemented rather erratically until 1585. Thus, many events in the Anguissola family were not incorporated into the council's rulings. Evidence for these rites of passage, when they are found prior to 1565, usually come from tangential documents, such as monetary exchange (for a dowry) or legitimization of a nobleman's birth (which happened frequently), as in the case of Sofonisba's father.[4]

While married to Elena de Filisgradis, Annibale Anguissola had a liaison when he was fifteen with one Bianca Crivella. Bianca later gave birth to Amilcare, Sofonisba's father, in about 1494, and later to a daughter, Elena.[5] Again, no records remain. Teenage marriages were customary during the Renaissance as the average life expectancy was about thirty.

In 1499, the Anguissolas were given their patent of nobility, and they became counts. Having a noble surname also entitled them to display a coat of arms. The ancient Anguissola coat of arms had a bird of prey rising from an urn out of which flowed ornate leaves (see plate 3). At the bottom of the urn were four red points. By the time the Cremonese Gazzola branch received its patent of nobility, the coat of arms had a crown above it (see plate 4). The red points remained at the bottom, but a fifth point was added. Above the center point is an undulating serpent (*anguis* means serpent or asp in Latin), above which is a golden sun. The solitary serpent was then incorporated into their motto, *Anguis Sola Fecit Victoriam* (The Lone Snake Became Victorious). The Anguissolas now had a title of nobility and a coat of arms. There was the possibility of social mobility in sixteenth-century Italy, and it worked to the Anguissolas' advantage. Although they had an ancient lineage, they were relative newcomers to the nobility by others' standards. Yet within a few short years, they had made important family connections.

Amilcare entered the service of the Marchese Galeazzo Pallavicini in 1509, the same year that the French army took Cremona. It was quite common for a sixteenth-century nobleman to send his eldest son to another nobleman's palace for his upbringing, which included education, military training, and service to the family. Usually the son was sent off at a fairly young age (generally about ten). However, Amilcare was about fifteen when he went to live with the Pallavicini.

The Pallavicini were a great feudal family whose origins dated back to the twelfth century in Lombardy. By the fifteenth century, they were distinguished and well-connected aristocrats who had served under the Visconti, Sforza, and King Louis XII of France. Seven of them also became cardinals, including Sforza Pallavicini, who was famous as the author of *The Story of the Council of Trent,* which documented the proceedings.

Apparently Amilcare proved himself to his father's satisfaction while he was with the Pallavicini because two years later, in 1511, Annibale legitimized his son. In sixteenth-century Italy, illegitimacy did not hold the same stigma it was to have in later centuries. The aristocracy—including many of the popes—was notorious for its abundance of illegitimate offspring and so legitimization was a common practice, especially if a son proved worthy in the eyes of his father. Galeazzo was also pleased with his charge, for at some unknown date (probably somewhere between 1510 and 1515) a marriage was arranged between the marchese's daughter, Bianca, and Amilcare. Bianca Pallavicini's dowry was drawn up on 18 May 1510, and listed many bolts of fabric in gold, brocades, and velvets; pieces of silver, including candlesticks; and the property of Monticello that included twenty-seven cows.[6] In the early years of their marriage, war visited its horrors on Cremona. The French occupied the city in 1520, and the Germans entered it in 1525, leaving the countryside "barren of both food and inhabitants."[7] However, some semblance of order continued during these foreign occupations.

Although Bianca and Amilcare's marriage lasted until about 1530, they did not have any children. A male heir was a most important consideration for any aristocratic Renaissance marriage. It is not known whether Bianca died (perhaps in childbirth, which was very common) or the marriage was annulled because there were no heirs. Carlo Bonetti, who discovered several documents in 1928, states that Bianca was "barren," but does not provide any evidence.[8]

About 1531 Amilcare remarried, this time to Bianca Ponzone, daughter of Count Ponzino Ponzone, son of Ruberto, of the parish of San Bartolomeo in Cremona. A dowry contract was drawn up by notary Jacopo Pietro Comenducci on 15 September 1533.

The Ponzone family, whose wealth came in part from cattle, received their patent of nobility in the previous century when Filippo Maria L'Anglo Visconti, duke of Milan, bestowed it on the family on 8 October 1416. It was then periodically reconfirmed: first in 1455 by Francesco Sforza, who extended jurisdiction of Cremona to the Ponzone descendants; then in 1470, 1482, and 1500. Their coat of arms was a shield divided into four quarters decorated with opposite sides of red stripes and gold dots. Their motto was *Virtus ad Alta Volat* (Virtue Soars Above All Things). Francis I of France, who claimed the duchy of Milan for himself, also confirmed the Ponzone title, stating that "his imperial majesty . . . beyond the confirmation of jurisdiction, gives the title of Count"[9] to the Ponzone family.

Although much information about the early years of the Anguissola family is fragmentary, it has been possible to piece together, through notary documents discovered by this author, some of Amilcare's business dealings. Investing family money into new business ventures became more popular as the century progressed, and Amilcare was one of the new breed of titled merchants. He and his father-in-law, Count Ponzino Ponzone, went into business together as silent partners with a Cremonese bookseller, Giacomo Zavarisi, investing six hundred imperial lire with the latter. The partnership agreement was drawn up on 21 June 1533, and renewed the following year on 31 July.[10] The bookshop had "sole rights to print books" and also sold handmade paper and art supplies.

On 4 May 1536, Amilcare bought a piece of land on the outskirts of Cremona.[11] The following year, business was doing well, and he lent three hundred lire to one Jacopo Francesco Barosi to set the latter up in a cheese shop business in Cremona.[12] By 1537, Amilcare was receiving installment payments from two Cremonese brothers, Matteo and Francesco da Asti, from their business in grains and produce.[13] Over a thirteen-year period, Amilcare's investments grew, enabling him to buy another piece of land in 1546.[14]

Between his investments in land and business, Amilcare was doing quite well in the 1530s and 1540s. In addition, he had married into another distinguished family, the Ponzones. It was a promising second start for the forty-year-old nobleman.

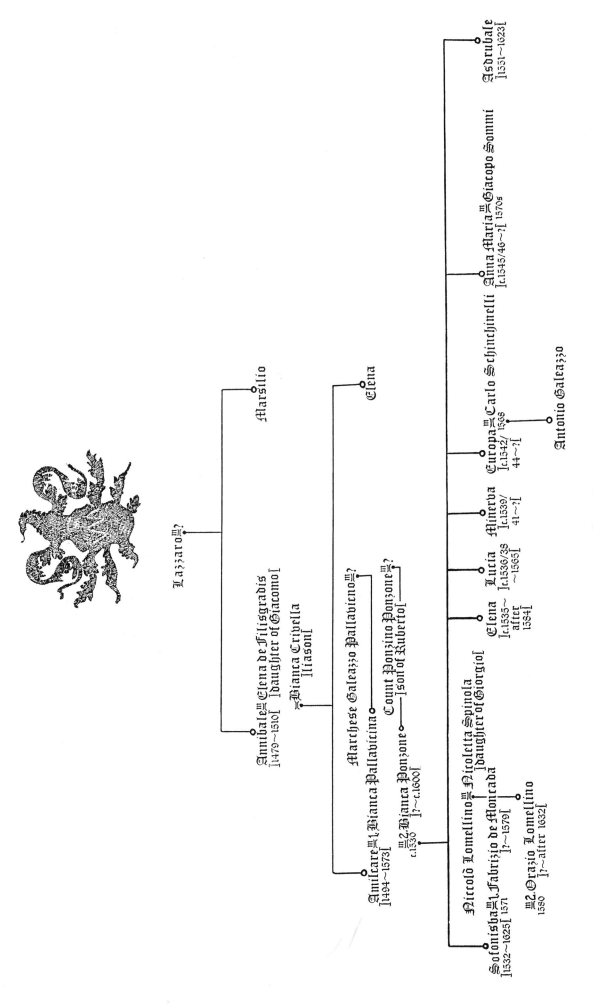

Lazzaro^m?

Annibale^m Elena de Filisgradis
[1470~1510] [daughter of Giacomo]

Marsilio

^m Bianca Cribella
[Iiason]

Marchese Galeazzo Pallavicino^m?

Amilcare^m1. Bianca Pallavicina
[1494~1573] ^m2. Bianca Ponzone
c.1530 [?~c.1600]

Elena

Count Ponzino Ponzone^m?
[son of Ruberto]

Niccolò Lomellino^m Nicoletta Spinola
[daughter of Giorgio]

Sofonisba^m1. Fabrizio de Moncada
[1532~1625] 1571 [?~1579]
^m2. Orazio Lomellino
1580 [?~after 1632]

Elena
[c.1535~
after
1584]

Lucia
[c.1536/38
~1565]

Minerva
[c.1539/
41~?]

Europa
[c.1542/
44~?]

Carlo Schinchinelli
1568

Anna Maria^m Giacopo Sommi
[c.1545/46~?] 1570s

Asdrubale
[1551~1623]

Antonio Galeazzo

Gazzola e Pigazzano Branch of the Anguissola family

PLATE 5. Anguissola family tree.

A CHILD AT LAST

Art is very much alien to the mind of woman, and
these things cannot be accomplished without a great deal
of talent, which in women is usually very scarce.
—Boccaccio. De claris mulieribus, 1370

There has been scholarly debate for several hundred years about the date of Sofonisba Anguissola's birth, which occurred before the Council of Trent required parishes to keep records. Conjectural dates have ranged from 1527 to 1540, but 1532 seems the most plausible.[1] It would also explain the later date of 1632 that was celebrated as the centenary of her birth, when her second husband, Orazio Lomellino (who was probably much younger, although no birth record has been found for him), dedicated her tombstone. Further, on her *Self-Portrait* now found in the Uffizi Gallery in Florence (see plate 31), she notes on the canvas in her own hand that it had been done when she "was twenty years old." If Anguissola had been born as late as 1540, this self-portrait would have been done in 1560, when she was already at the Spanish court. By that time, her technique was far more polished than is evident in this self-portrait, which was probably done in 1552.

Over three generations, the Anguissola family had a strong connection to ancient Carthaginian history, and it appears more than coincidence that they named their offspring after relatives of the great General Hannibal (247–183/82 B.C.E.) who had laid siege to Cremona centuries before. The story is worth relating in some detail, as it has bearing on Sofonisba's life.

Hannibal was the son of Hamilcar Barca, who was known for his great loyalty to his family and whose guerilla tactics and military strategy were a source of harassment to the Romans during the First Punic War (264–41 B.C.E.). Rome was Carthage's sworn enemy. Hamilcar Barca commanded Carthaginian forces in Sicily. While Hannibal was growing up, he and his brother, Hasdrubal, went on many of their father's campaigns, including a long trip to Spain (when Hannibal was nine), where Carthage was carving out a new part of its empire. By the time he was twenty-five, Hannibal was a commander in Spain, and in 218 B. C. E. he led a daring expedition with sixty thousand troops—which included a large contingent mounted on elephants—from Spain, through France, and across the Alps into Italy, in order to attack Rome. Hasdrubal stayed behind to raise funds for the war and to recruit mercenary troops. He, too, later crossed the Alps to join Hannibal, but he was assassinated before he could reach his brother.

In 220 B. C. E., Rome had established one of the first Latin colonies in Cremona in order to consolidate her hold on northern Italy against Gallic raids. The Cremonese were extremely resentful and revolted on several occasions, despite the maintenance of a Roman legion which was garrisoned there. Then, in 218 B. C. E., Hannibal laid siege to Cremona in an unsuccessful attempt to conquer Rome.

Hannibal's brother-in-law was also named Hasdrubal. When Hamilcar Barca died in 229 B.C.E., he was succeeded in Spain by his son-in-law, Hasdrubal. It was this Hasdrubal, son of Gisgo, who had a daughter named Sophonisba. She came from one of the most prestigious families in Carthage and was "conspicuous for her beauty, had received an excellent literary and musical education, and was clever, ingratiating, and so charming that the mere sight of her, or even the sound of her voice, sufficed to vanquish everyone, even the most indifferent."[2]

There are several different versions of Sophonisba's life as political pawn and queen to two Numidian kings. Hasdrubal Gisgo arranged a marriage between Sophonisba and Masinissa, the son of the king of Massaylia (a Numidian ally of Carthage). Masinissa had been sent to Carthage to be educated, and it was there that he met Sophonisba and they fell in love. The king of Massaylia (present-day western Tunisia and eastern Algeria) was the sworn enemy of Syphax, another Numidian king.

Syphax, too, was in love with Sophonisba. When Hasdrubal and Masinissa left Carthage to fight in Spain, Syphax contrived to marry Sophonisba and she became queen of Numidia. Tragedy ensued. When Syphax discovered that Sophonisba was betrothed to Masinissa, he led his troops against Carthage. "Lacking an army itself, the Carthaginian senate acted in desperation: without consulting with Hasdrubal or Masinissa, it gave Sophonisba in marriage to Syphax."[3] When Masinissa returned, he received word from Sophonisba that she had been forced to marry Syphax. Subsequently, Syphax and Masinissa met in combat, and Syphax was taken prisoner. He was then sent to Rome, where he died. Masinissa then married Sophonisba, but he was ordered to turn his wife over to Rome, as the Romans feared that she would never show allegiance to any country but her own. Rather than give his wife to Rome, Masinissa gave Sophonisba poison to drink.

The fourteenth-century humanist and poet, Boccaccio (1313–75) wrote about Sophonisba in his Latin tome, *De claris mulieribus (Concerning Famous Women)*. In this first collection of women's biographies, he painted a rather negative picture of Queen Sophonisba, and that was in keeping with the moralizing, patriarchal tone of the early Renaissance, as well as his own antipathy toward women.

These ancient stories were most probably told in the Anguissola family. With their strong ties to Cremona, the Anguissolas no doubt felt resentful that their city was besieged first by one foreign power and then another—just as Hannibal felt the constant threat from Rome. Following the family's tradition of naming some of their offspring after the great Carthaginian family, Lazzaro Anguissola named his son Annibale (probably after Hannibal), who, in turn, named his son Amilcare (probably after

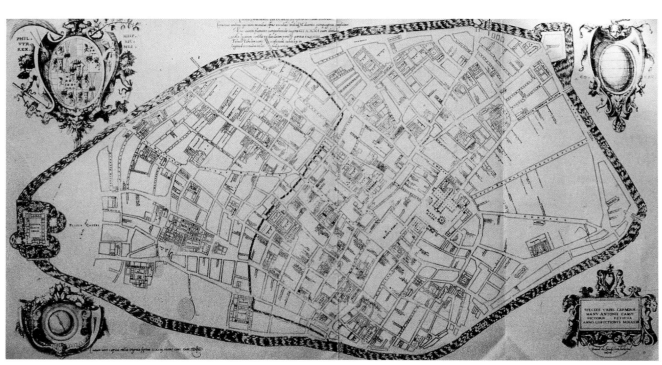

PLATE 6. Antonio Campi. Map of Cremona, c. 1582.

Hamilcar Barca). When Amilcare and Bianca Anguissola had their seven children, they continued the family tradition and also added their own penchant for mythological names, which were fashionable in Renaissance Italy. Bianca probably had her girls a year and a half to two or three years apart: Sofonisba, 1532; Elena, c. 1535; Lucia, c. 1536–38; Minerva, c. 1539–41; Europa, c. 1542–44; and Anna Maria, c. 1545–46. Although no dated documents have been found, later family portraits done by Sofonisba of her sisters show that the girls were fairly close to one another in age. Asdrubale, the long-awaited son, was born in 1551 and was probably named after both Hasdrubal Gisgo and Hannibal's brother (see Anguissola family tree, plate 5).

During the 1530s, Amilcare Anguissola was just beginning to invest in several businesses as his second marriage was starting. His home, perhaps a small palazzo, was conveniently located next to his parish church of San Giorgio, where the family went for morning and evening prayers. The building, on via Gaetano Tibaldi, no longer in existence (and known through a sixteenth-century map of the city, see plate 6), was probably two stories high with a central courtyard, stables, and kitchen below, and living quarters above.

The Anguissola household must have expanded to accommodate the additional staff required—probably including wet nurses (aristocratic ladies did not nurse their own infants), cooks, scullery maids, grooms, and attendants for the children. Generally, children did not mingle with the adults. When small, they spent the days with their servants, and later they had private tutors or were sent to live with another aristocratic family. Young Sofonisba certainly was attached to one servant and later sketched her and also painted her portrait as part of *The Chess Game,* done in 1555 (see plate 49).

Amilcare was far ahead of his time when he gave his daughters the same Renaissance education usually accorded only to the sons of the aristocracy. (Perhaps he did so in part because he remembered the brilliance of his daughter's Carthaginian namesake.) However, this practice was not unprecedented. Sir Thomas More (1477/78–1535) gave his daughter, Margaret (1504–44), an outstanding education under the brilliant English academician Roger Ascham. She was considered the match of any Tudor scholar. After the death of her husband in 1525, Vittoria Colonna (1490–1547) devoted the remaining twenty-two years of her ascetic life to writing poetry. As the granddaughter of Federico da Montefeltro, duke of Urbino, she, too, had been well educated. Colonna kept up a correspondence with Baldassare Castiglione, Pietro Aretino, and Bernardo Tasso; after 1538, she became a very close friend of Michelangelo.

Recent scholarly research by Christiane Klapish-Zuber, Margaret King, and Joan Kelly-Gadol[4] has documented the extremely limited education for the majority of sixteenth-century women; that, in fact, most women did not have a Renaissance education. For the poor of both sexes, formal education was nonexistent. Sometimes a middle-class or aristocratic young woman would be given instruction in the arts—music, needlework, and reading, but not many Latin and Greek texts, which might prove too risqué—to be more eligible for a better marriage. Women in the sixteenth century even had lost some of the freedom that they had enjoyed during the Middle Ages, such as inheriting or owning property. They were the chattels first of their fathers and then their husbands; and they had no say in their own futures. Betrothals took place in childhood: Vittoria Colonna was betrothed at four. Daughters were excluded from a share of a father's estate, as they were dowered. The only other alternative to marriage was entering a convent, and that option was always considered when a child was still young. Usually, it was the second child (son or daughter) who was earmarked for the religious life. A dowry was required when entering a convent, but it "might only be twenty percent of what husbands expected."[5]

It was a patrilineal society. Even when a father decided it might prove advantageous to his financial or political needs, a Renaissance education for an aristocratic young girl was limited: singing and learning to play a musical instrument (Queen Elizabeth I was noted for her ability to play the virginals, and Sofonisba painted two self-portraits memorializing her own capability at the clavichord), and being skilled at embroidery (Mary Queen of Scots was denied quill, paper, and ink during her eighteen-year captivity, but was allowed needles and silk threads for her many needlework projects).

By the mid-sixteenth century needlework, which decorated many a gown or accessory, had been elevated to a high art. Most courts had full-time embroideresses to embellish a silk or velvet gown or doublet. Dressing elegantly and fashionably was also a part of a noble lady's polish. Italian velvets, silks, and fustians were the envy of the rest of Europe. Of course, Cremona's textile industry supplied beautiful bolts of fabric. Today they also provide the costume and art historian with ample material to document and date one of the sixteenth century's most important sources of wealth. Later, Sofonisba would excel at painting all the magnificent details of sixteenth-century costume.

Modern languages, rhetoric, and letters were not as frequently taught to six-

PLATE 7. Raphael. *Baldassare Castiglione*,
c. 1515. The Louvre, Paris.

teenth-century aristocratic ladies as to their predecessors. Even under the best of circumstances, the negative view held by the majority of men regarding the education of women, the severe restrictions imposed by the century's fashions, and the institutionalization of women's total dependency on family (which thereby limited their social options), all placed rigorous limitations on women.

Count Baldassare Castiglione's *The Book of the Courtier*, generally known by its abbreviated title, *The Courtier*, was required reading. Castiglione (1478–1529) belonged to the aristocracy: his father was a count and his mother was a Gonzaga. He spent his life as a diplomat, man of letters (both in Italian and Latin), and courtier (see plate 7). His book was written as a treatise in four parts and it describes evenings at the court of Elisabetta Gonzaga, duchess of Urbino. It was written between 1509 and 1518 but not published until 1528. The book describes in detail what constitutes the ideal courtier. It also points out the enormous gulf between what was expected of men and women.

Books One and Two are devoted to the courtly attributes to which a noble gentleman should strive: bravery and loyalty. He should have a good education, be a good horseman, and be adept at music, dancing, and games. Finally, he also should know how to behave properly in a lady's company and act with ease and grace.

Book Three deals with the qualities of a noble lady. Whereas both men and women were expected to be educated and civilized, foremost for aristocratic women were chastity and charm. According to Castiglione, women were "imperfect" and "nature seeks perfection in all her creatures, and would, if she could, produce nothing but men." This misogynistic view was prevalent. Nonetheless, *The Courtier* became a bestseller, going through forty editions in the sixteenth century, and was the benchmark by which courtiers conducted themselves. It was, therefore, even more to Amilcare and Bianca Anguissola's credit that their daughters were well educated.

Some authors[6] have felt that Amilcare and Bianca had an ulterior motive, since dowries had to be found for all of the girls and that Amilcare was not very enlightened, but instead rather shrewd. His personal letters, if he wrote any on the subject, have not survived. Certainly Sofonisba's portraits of her father show a warm and kind face. Her family portraits leave a picture of love and a strong bond of kinship.

In 1566, Giorgio Vasari went out of his way to visit the Anguissola household when he heard of all the "marvels" of the six sisters' accomplishments. By that time, however, Sofonisba was already in Spain at King Philip's court. All subsequent biographical references by historians Raffaelo Soprani (1674), Filippo Baldinucci (1681), and Giambattista Zaist (1774) stem from Vasari's visit. All these writers were lavish in their praise of the talents of the Anguissola sisters: "excellent in painting, music, and *belles lettres*";[7] "Amilcare gave them the opportunity to study the best in the arts and sciences";[8] and "their parents [Bianca and Amilcare], were inclined to be liberal, and had them instructed in letters, music, and successfully in painting."[9] In sum, the Anguissolas have had an historical reputation as generous and liberal, and their daughters were known as Renaissance *wunderkinder* whose renown spread. Those who did not believe that women were capable of learning viewed with amazement those rare women who, when given the opportunity, proved it.

If Amilcare did have any ulterior motive for educating his daughters, it might have been that there were gaps in his own education.[10] His Italian spelling and grammar were quite poor (as evidenced in his later letters to Michelangelo in 1557 and 1558), and he was probably well aware of it. Since he had been legitimized at seventeen, after only two years of service to Marchese Galeazzo Pallavicini, he may have started his education late and never completed it.

Before her own academic studies began, young Sofonisba must have shown an aptitude for drawing at a very early age. One could imagine an elegantly attired little girl of four or five dressed, as was the custom, as a miniature adult. She would have worn her auburn brown hair parted down the center (as she did in all her self-portraits), loose and flowing, with a circular jeweled hair piece (worn as a ribbon to keep her long hair from falling in her face).

Her gown would have been made in two parts: a silk or velvet bodice that laced up the back, with detachable sleeves and a skirt or kirtle in a bell shape with a whalebone farthingale (a wired-hooped skirt) underneath to keep the stiff shape. Under the bodice, she would have worn a soft linen chemise embroidered with Spanish blackwork[11] that had a drawstring tie at the neckline. Under the chemise, a whalebone corset covered in linen was laced tightly up the back of her gown. This corset severely restricted both breathing and movement. A woman walked slowly not so much because of grace, but rather due to being so tightly and fashionably corseted.

One could imagine little Sofonisba toddling around in an elegant gown—perhaps an embroidered velvet or lavish brocade, which she would later paint her sisters wearing in *The Chess Game*. Perhaps with quill in hand or chalk and handmade paper, she would have done her first scribblings or tentative sketches. Considering the tight corseting required even for a small child, it is all the more amazing that she had the tenacity to continue her sketching and drawing. In short, the physical restrictions of sixteenth-century fashion did not squelch her budding creativity. It is no wonder that Vasari went out of his way to see these unusual sisters.

PLATE 18. Sofonisba Anguissola. *Self-Portrait*, c. 1548.
Chalk sketch. 138 3/16 x 103 15/16 in. (351 x 264 cm).
Gabinetto dei Disegni, Uffizi Gallery, Florence.

EARLY ART STUDIES

But above all others, Sofonisba Anguissola honored him
[her teacher Campi] by the excellence of her paintings.

—*Giorgio Vasari*

Despite any early talent that Anguissola showed, she was, nevertheless, a product of her time. Women—even of the aristocracy—were not accorded the same privileges as their male counterparts. As historian Peter Burke has written, a "talented but well-born child might be unable to become a painter or sculptor because these occupations were considered beneath them."[1] Even Michelangelo's father, who was a gentleman, did not want his son to become an artist. Burke, of course, was referring only to men. It was unheard of for a woman to become a painter and infringe upon what had always been a man's profession. Certainly the popularity of Castiglione's *The Courtier* did nothing to improve an aristocratic lady's situation.

Most art training took about thirteen years. The usual procedure for a promising male artist was to be apprenticed for five to seven years in the studio of a "master," as the young Leonardo had been in Verrocchio's studio. Andrea del Sarto was seven when he began his apprenticeship; Titian was nine; Mantegna was ten. Amilcare Anguissola faced two problems regarding Sofonisba's artistic training: she was a woman, and she was a member of the nobility. The solution was found when Amilcare sent fourteen-year-old Sofonisba and her next younger sister, Elena, to study with Bernardino Campi.

Campi, who was born in Cremona in 1522 to Barbara Vaghi and Pietro Campi, was one of the most prolific Cremonese painters. His father, Pietro, was a well-known goldsmith who furnished his young son with the basics in design and techniques of relief work. Bernardino was sent to apprentice in the workshop of Giulio Campi, another Cremonese painter. Although there were other artists with the name Campi—Galeazzo and his sons, Giulio (with whom Bernardino studied), Antonio, and Vincenzo—they were not related to Pietro and Bernardino.

Bernardino apparently was not happy at Giulio's studio, and so his father sent him to Mantua to work with Ippolito Costa, a student of the Mannerist artist Giulio

Romano. Costa and Pietro Campi were old friends and corresponded regularly. While he was in Mantua, Campi learned from Costa and Romano about the Mannerist style that was sweeping northern Italy. He continued his studies with Costa until 1541.

Campi's style is a reflection of what became known as northern Italian Mannerism, which began appearing in the 1520s and 1530s. Prior to that, for a brief twenty-five years, there was a blossoming of Italian High Renaissance art. While acknowledging a debt to antiquity, the art of the High Renaissance was the embodiment of a new vision—in painting, sculpture, and architecture—characterized by an idealized type of religious painting and portraiture in which space was organized in a controlled, symmetrical, and harmonious fashion. Instead of concentrating solely on religious themes, artists at the beginning of the sixteenth century added, as Vasari stated, a newly discovered "appeal and vigor of living flesh" where "roundness and fullness derived from good judgment and design."[2] Figures were portrayed in a balanced and natural way, as in Titian's *Sacred and Profane Love* of 1515 (see plate 8), or his *Portrait of a Bearded Man*, c. 1511–15 (see plate 9), or Raphael's 1515 *Portrait of Baldassare Castiglione* (see plate 7).

By the 1520s, several artists began experimenting in architecture, sculpture, and painting with elongating the human figure and changing proportions, as Parmigianino—one of the foremost northern Italian Mannerist painters—did with his *Madonna of the Long Neck,* 1534–40 (see plate 10). Here, Mary's body appears to have been stretched lengthwise, and the Christ child sits precariously on his mother's lap.

Parmigianino's other interesting Mannerist work is his *Self-Portrait in a Convex Mirror,* 1524 (see plate 11), in which distortions are again present. Vasari said of it that the artist was "fascinated by his own reflection in a barber's convex mirror [and] he decided to reproduce it exactly."[3] So he "had a carpenter turn a wooden sphere on a lathe and then saw off one section as the base for his painting."[4] What he painted shows a normal face, but there is distortion of his oversized left hand and sleeve as well as the tilted studio skylight at the upper left of the oval.

PLATE 8. Titian. *Sacred and Profane Love,*
c. 1515. Borghese Gallery, Rome.

PLATE 9. Titian. *Portrait of a Bearded Man*, c. 1511–15. National Gallery, London.

Michelangelo, too, was experimenting with disjointed and tensely posed figures that were another expression of Mannerist art. His allegorical Carrara marble sculptures for the tomb of Giuliano de' Medici, *Night* and *Day* (see plate 12) in Florence's Medici Chapel (1519–34) show two *contrapposto* figures that appear to be ready to slide off the tomb on which they are insecurely sitting. *Contrapposto,* meaning "set against," was a method of representing the human body in which its individual parts were set in opposition, often in a twisted fashion; this technique was characteristic of Mannerism.

Giulio Romano (c. 1499–1546), a pupil of Raphael, was applying Mannerist concepts to his architectural designs. Romano worked with Raphael (as a painter and architect) until the latter's death in 1520, and then inherited his studio. Between 1527 and 1534, at almost breakneck speed, he built the Palazzo del Tè, an imposing pleasure villa for Federico Gonzaga, in Mantua.[5] Romano was introduced to Gonzaga by Castiglione in 1524. Romano changed the usual architectural motifs, creating enormous pediments above the first-story windows, which are very heavily rusticated, in sharp contrast to the smooth second-story windows. There is also "a decorative frieze with every third triglyph out of place." Romano knew the classical architectural rules that Leon Battista Alberti had set down in his great treatise a century earlier.

Alberti believed in the architectural harmony of the classical ideal as embodied in the Roman Pantheon. He felt that if one understood, as art historian Frederick

PLATE 10. Parmigianino. *Madonna with the Long Neck*, 1534–40. Uffizi Gallery, Florence/Art Resource.

PLATE 11. Parmigianino. *Self-Portrait in a Convex Mirror*, 1524. Kunsthistoriches Museum, Vienna.

Hartt has stated, "the grammar of ancient architecture well enough, one could at times devise one's own vocabulary."[6] Alberti not only wrote the first treatise on painting, *Della Pittura* (1436), but also ten books on architecture. In his treatise he laid down the principles of proportion, elegance, order, perspective, simplicity, and decoration, all of which would culminate in a unified whole.

Understanding this, Romano broke new ground in the Palazzo del Tè. Inside is the Sala dei Giganti, a room covered (including the doors and ceiling) with an enormous fresco depicting the Greek myth of the Giants who tried to assault Mount Olympus (see plate 13). The imagery is full of tension and destruction; and entering the room, one feels totally dwarfed by the huge, frescoed figures twisting and turning in every direction. Even over the fireplace, the Giants are tumbling downward; when the fire was lit, they appeared to be hurtling into the flames. Federico Gonzaga entertained Charles V in this room in 1530 and again in 1532 when the emperor of the Holy Roman Empire visited the duke. The opulent festivities held against this backdrop of *contrapposto* figures certainly must have been quite a sight.

Bernardino Campi is also known to have worked for a time painting in Mantua's Ducal Palace, a five-hundred-room structure to which Romano added many rooms. Between 1536 and 1538, Romano and Titian, who was a close friend, collaborated on some of the additions. It is not known when Campi was there, but it is conceiv-

PLATE 12. Michelangelo. *Night* and *Day*, 1519–34. Tomb of Giuliano de' Medici, Medici Chapel, San Lorenzo, Florence/Art Resource.

able that his studies coincided with Titian's visit. That certainly would explain his adoption of Titian's marvelous Venetian colors directly, as it were, from the great master.

There is also an interesting link between Romano, Lavina Teerlinc, and Sofonisba Anguissola. Teerlinc (1510/20–76), a rare exception to the all-male artists' domain, was appointed court painter by Henry VIII in 1546 (four years after the death of the king's previous court painter, Hans Holbein, and the same year that Anguissola began her studies with Campi).[7] A portrait by Anguissola, c. 1578 (Zeri Collection, Rome) of the miniaturist Giorgio Giulio Clovio (1498–1578) shows Clovio holding a miniature portrait thought to be of Teerlinc, who probably studied with Clovio between 1540 and 1546, before she was appointed miniaturist to the court of Henry VIII (see plate 14). Clovio, in turn, is thought to have studied with Romano.

By the time Bernardino Campi went to Mantua, Romano's Palazzo del Tè had been built for several years. Artists came to see the impressive Mannerist structure, and those who were anxious to expand their own horizons with these new concepts in proportion (both in architecture and painting) absorbed and adapted them to their own needs. So, despite the provincial atmosphere of Cremona, the artists working there were in touch with the significant trends and changes that Mannerism was bringing to art. Bernardino Campi assimilated these elements as well as those of Venetian coloring—marvelous, soft hues of red, blue, and gold. His religious figures are attenuated; faces are often gaunt and ascetic, but bodies show the influence of Michelangelo in his realistic portrayal of anatomy.

Campi was also influenced by another Cremonese artist, Camillo Boccaccino (1501/04–46), whose father, Boccaccio, was a painter. Camillo went to Parma to work with Correggio, the other great northern Italian Mannerist artist, from 1522 to

PLATE 13. Giulio Romano. *Sala dei Giganti*, 1530–32. Palazzo del Tè, Mantua.

PLATE 14. Sofonisba Anguissola. *Portrait of Giorgio Giulio Clovio*, 1578. Oil on canvas, 39 3/8 x 32 5/16 in. (100 x 79.5 cm). Zeri Collection, Mentana.

1524, and the latter's influence—softer colors, play of light, and sinuous lines—was lasting. In 1546, the year Anguissola began studying with Campi, he was commissioned to do the fresco vault of the Chapel of Saints Filippo and Giacomo for Cremona's San Sigismondo (see plate 15). The attenuated, *contrapposto* figures and coloring show how closely Campi followed Camillo's style. So Anguissola's early studies with Campi also indirectly exposed her to Correggio's coloring.

When Campi completed his studies, he returned to Cremona about 1541, and received commissions to paint several large religious paintings for a number of the city's churches. His earliest work, signed and dated 1542 (when Anguissola was ten years old), is an *Ascension,* done for the church of Sant'Agata. The church was not far from Anguissola's own church, and it is conceivable that she may have gone with a chaperone to watch Campi at work.

One particular religious painting sums up much of what Campi had learned from his teachers and then passed on to Anguissola. It is a *Pietà* (Pinacoteca di Brera, Milan, see plate 22) with six elongated figures huddled together around the dead Christ. There is a calmness about this composition, which is characteristic of many Italian Renaissance works, despite the pain and sorrow. Standing out vividly is a serene Saint Catherine of Alexandria, richly dressed in Venetian-colored reds and golds. The other figures, including Saints Elia and Eliseo, and Father Gabriele Pizzamigli (a Carmelite brother, who commissioned the work), all are limned in muted colors that blend in with the rocky landscape. Only the background shows any hint

41

PLATE 15. Bernardino Campi. *Saints Filippo and Giacomo*, 1546. San Sigismondo, Cremona.

of the great drama: a craggy cliff, with trees (reminiscent of Perugino's stylized ones) tilting and windblown; and the sky filled with stormy gray clouds. The trees, hanging precipitously at the edge of the cliff, seem an ominous portent and lead the eye to the crosses of Calvary in the distance. This painting would later figure into Anguissola's studies with Campi.

Bernardino kept busy with other commissions in Cremona, including the 1546 frescoes for San Sigismondo. Amilcare Anguissola was one of the superintendents of San Sigismondo and one of his responsibilities was to commission artists to decorate the church. It was probably at this time that Amilcare, through his official church duties, met both Campi and Bernardino Gatti (Anguissola's second teacher), and arranged for Sofonisba and Elena to study with Campi, "who was already renowned in Cremona. . . He introduced her to the pleasures of art, sometimes correcting her without reproach, sometimes praising her without flattery, to which she responded with affection. The stay lasted several years [three], and she seized with delight the habit of having kind conversations with Bernardino's wife [Anna]."[8]

Sofonisba and Elena stayed with Bernardino and his wife as paying guests. However, "apprentices formed part of the extended family of their master,"[9] and therefore, the girls' stay with the Campi family was not unusual. It also provided supervision for the two unmarried sisters, as Anna Campi acted as their chaperone.

In addition to their daily sketching sessions, which took place around the Campi house, and visits from their private tutor for their academic studies, there were also beginning lessons in oil painting and the mixing of pigments. Drawing taught Sofonisba and Elena to use easier and more fluid lines so that they could concentrate on the intricacies of spatial relationships, perspective, proportion, and light and shadow—something that probably they had only read about in Alberti's treatise, *Della Pittura* [*On Painting*]. Drawing from the nude model or cadavers, as both Leonardo and Michelangelo had done surreptitiously, was of course forbidden. Sofonisba and Elena had to rely on their understanding of their own anatomy. The availability and cooperation of the Anguissola family for sittings made the girls' studies easier. Portraits and religious themes were the typical subject matter for Sofonisba and Elena. They would copy the works of other masters or those of Campi. Since Campi's work decorated many of Cremona's churches, the two sisters would go there to paint, always accompanied by a chaperone.

Under Campi's tutelage, Anguissola learned about the complexity of preparing a canvas or panel, as an artist had a choice of working on either one. Before 1513, painting was only done on panel, with northern European artists preferring to paint on hard woods such as walnut or oak (usually taken from "float wood" coming from old ship hulls), while the Italians usually chose pine or poplar. In 1513, Raphael completed his *Sistine Madonna* (the first known painting to be done on canvas), and it opened up an innovative type of ground for painters. By the time Anguissola began using canvas, in the late 1540s, it had been in use only about thirty-five years, and artists were still experimenting with it.

The preparation, for both panel and canvas, was similar: thin layers of a glue base, using powdered white chalk (calcium carbonate) or gypsum (calcium sulfate), were applied and "covered with one or more fatty layers consisting of a white lead ground in oil and diluted with essence of turpentine."[10] Anguissola had to learn how to make the glue base (from dried rabbit skin) and cook the oil (either linseed or walnut mixed with lead) until it reached the proper consistency and color (called "black oil," it was actually a dark brown). After the oil cooled, it was poured into bottles and sealed tightly. The next step for Anguissola was to learn how to mix the oil with the various colors, all of which derived from natural sources: yellows and browns from iron oxides, earth, and lead; reds from iron oxides mixed with lead for flesh tints; greens from copper; black from various carbon-based sources; and blue from lapis lazuli.

Each process was time-consuming and tedious. Although these procedures were part of the basics in oil painting, each artist had secrets which he imparted only to his disciples. Since Sofonisba and Elena did not study in Campi's workshop, it is most likely that the kitchen in the Campi house was turned into a private workshop. Iron pots were probably brought to the house from Campi's workshop, and in the kitchen he showed the two budding artists how to cook the oil and mix the colors in their proper ratio.

Cooking made way for art. The huge stone fireplace in the kitchen with its blazing, open hearth had several different pots cooking the oils and rabbit skins, with Campi explaining what the final color of the oils should look like. If they were too dark or too light, they would not be suitable. Sofonisba and Elena probably wore some kind of smock, perhaps similar to Parmigianino's *A Painter's Assistant Grinding Pigments*, c. 1535 (Victoria and Albert Museum, London, see plate 16) to protect their elegant gowns from dripping oils and paints.

PLATE 16. Parmigianino. *A Painter's Assistant Grinding Pigments*, c. 1535. Victoria and Albert Museum, London.

There are two early sketches by Anguissola, dating from the mid-1540s (both in the Gabinetto dei Disegni, Uffizi Gallery, Florence) that she may have done for Campi either as examples of her capabilities before she began her studies with him, or possibly shortly thereafter. *Self-Portrait with Old Woman,* c. 1545 (see plate 17), is done in black chalk on a bluish white paper. Here, young Sofonisba portrays herself in her early teens (or possibly at eleven or twelve) wearing a mid-sixteenth-century costume with the typical corseted bodice and sleeves that are puffed and slashed at the shoulders and then fitted to the wrist with lace at the cuff. The linen chemise is gathered at the neckline into a drawstring tie. The full skirt is shown gathered at the waist and the overskirt is pulled back and tied. She faces the viewer, smiling—something rarely seen in Renaissance portraits—in a three-quarter-length pose (a chair is visible to the left of her arm), and she is pointing to an old woman wearing a shawl draped over her head and shoulders. Her bodice laces up the center front, and the sleeves and chemise are quite plain. The old woman's simple gown suggests that she was a servant in the Anguissola household. Her spectacles are precariously worn at the edge of her nose; and she holds a book in her hand. Perhaps the artist is teaching the old woman to read, or she is pointing with emphasis to something of importance in the book.

The second sketch, titled *Self-Portrait,* c. 1548 (see plate 18), is also done in black chalk on bluish white paper. It is a three-quarter-length pose of a teenager with a solemn, almost sad face and the big eyes that were to become the hallmark of the artist's self-portraits. Anguissola's large, melancholy eyes stare out at the viewer and, no doubt, she used a mirror as her left eye is disproportionately larger than her right.

Her face seems to have matured somewhat from the previous sketch: the cheeks are slimmer, and the lips are the same as those in later portraits.

Her hair is parted down the center with a braid wrapped around her head. This was a popular style throughout the century and can be seen in numerous Italian portraits, including Titian's *Isabella of Portugal, Wife of Charles V*, c. 1535 (Prado Museum, Madrid, see plate 19); Bronzino's *Lucrezia Panciatichi*, c. 1540 (Uffizi Gallery, Florence, see plate 20); and Giovanni Battista Moroni's portrait *Pace Rivola Spini*, c. 1570 (Accademia Carrara, Bergamo, see plate 21).

The bodice in Anguissola's *Self-Portrait* is different from the one in the earlier sketch, giving the costume and art historian an opportunity to compare different regional styles. Here she wears a bodice with a high neckline and only the ruffled collar of the linen chemise shows. The sleeves are full at the shoulder and then taper to the lace cuffs at the wrist. She holds a book in her left hand.

Although these two sketches are the earliest extant examples of Anguissola's budding talent, one already can see a particular stylistic feature that continues to appear in most of her portraits over the next six decades. Characteristic of her portraits is the manner in which she positioned and stylized the hands with the thumb and index finger shaped somewhat like a "square-U." This positioning of the fingers became her trademark.

It is obvious from these early sketches that the young artist was still grappling with problems of anatomy: the old woman's left hand is drawn imprecisely as are Anguissola's left thumb and index finger; the self-portrait also shows difficulties with pro-

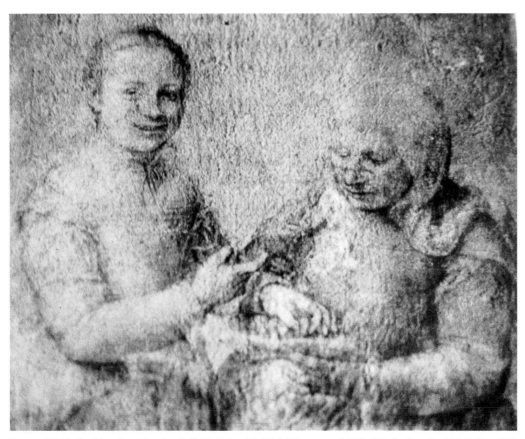

PLATE 17. Sofonisba Anguissola. *Self-Portrait with Old Woman*, c. 1545. Chalk sketch, 118 7/8 x 158 1/4 in. (302 x 402 cm). Gabinetto dei Disegni, Uffizi Gallery, Florence.

19

21

20

PLATE 19. Titian. *Isabella of Portugal, Wife of Charles V,* c. 1535. Prado Museum, Madrid.

PLATE 20. Bronzino. *Lucrezia Panciatichi,* c. 1540. Uffizi Gallery, Florence.

PLATE 21. Giovanni Battista Moroni. *Pace Rivola Spini,* c. 1570. Accademia Carrara, Bergamo.

portion, spatial depth, and the limning of the fingers on both hands. Nonetheless, this is a promising beginning, and there is tenderness and warmth in the depiction of the old woman's face. As an adult, Anguissola would continue to excel in her sensitive portrayals of older people.

One of Anguissola's assignments was copying Campi's *Pietà*, c. 1550s (Pinacoteca di Brera, Milan, see plates 22 and 23). By the time she tackled this, her understanding of anatomy had vastly improved, and she had absorbed some of the Mannerist components that were part of her teacher's style, including the elongation of the figures, *contrapposto* of the bodies, and contrasts of light and shadow (*chiaroscuro*), all of which can be seen in both *Pietàs*. Anguissola's *Pietà*, an oil on wood panel, is a simplified rendition showing just the essence of the event with Mary and the dead Christ in her lap.

The huge folds of Mary's steel-blue-gray gown seems to give added support to the lifeless body of her son. In design, it is reminiscent of Michelangelo's marble *Pietà*, in St. Peter's, which had been sculpted half a century earlier, in 1498. That work had a tremendous impact on how artists subsequently portrayed this scene. Anguissola probably had seen sketches or engravings of Michelangelo's work since any important masterpiece circulated in artistic circles through these sketches.

The background of Anguissola's painting is serene, as if she had chosen to portray Mary's acceptance of her son's death—again, reminiscent of Michelangelo's characterization—without the turbulence in Campi's portrayal. The undulating hills, on the right side of the painting, have a roseate afterglow of sunset, and the clouds, although gray, are not as ominous as those in Campi's work.

Comparing the *Pietàs* of both teacher and student, it is evident that Anguissola not only simplified the composition and muted the colors, but she also chose to portray it in an atmosphere of calm resignation. Her homage to her teacher incorporates only similar facial features (but done more delicately) and the elongation of the figures.

In 1926, Lionello Venturi saw both of these paintings together on exhibition (currently, they are in storage at the Brera) in Milan and wrote:

> In a small room of the same gallery, with a similar background of gloomy cliffs, the central group of Bernardino Campi's *Pietà* was copied by Sofonisba Anguissola. The luminous close-up imagery and *sfumato* [a smoky shading and coloring from light to dark] of the countryside, on the right, is thus enhanced. Her teacher's work is scrupulously and truthfully copied. But Sofonisba shows more signs of Parmigianesque influence than Bernardino, in the pointed hands of the Virgin, in the golden color, in the delicacy of the pointed face and tiny features. The shadows are less severe, Christ's profile is not done so crudely as Campi's, and the stiffened, mortal remains are planed like a tree trunk without leaving a vital trace of muscle flexibility. The Leonardoesque shadows move about on the face of Bernardino's Lady of Sorrow, while that painted by the school girl is presented with a subtle and diffuse visual facility. Everything becomes softer and dimmer.[11]

Anguissola's *Pietà* indeed shows some influence of Leonardo's *sfumato* treatment of the faces, the distant blue mountains, and cliffs. In essence, Anguissola in her early painting had adapted elements not only from her teacher, but also from Michelange-lo, Leonardo, and Correggio. It was a very encouraging beginning for the young artist. The painting recently has been dated after 1560 by Italian art historian Mina Gregori.[12] This dating is open to question, as Anguissola was already in Spain at that time. More likely it was done in the early 1550s when she was still in Italy. Anguisso-la's copying and absorption of Mannerist principles, which she learned from Campi and Bernardino Gatti—especially her attenuated figures—were far more pronounced in the early part of her career than they were after she went to Spain.

In late 1548, Cremona was ablaze with excitement. It was announced that Prince Philip of Spain would be paying a visit to the city. His father, Emperor Charles V, had decided that Philip needed to see the vast territories over which he would rule one day. It was a necessary part of his political education, and it proved fortuitous, as Charles was to abdicate seven years later.

On 1 October 1548, Philip left the security of his palatial abode at Valladolid (where he had been born in 1527) for the arduous two-and-a-half year trip. His en-tourage first traveled by land through Aragon, Catalonia, Saragossa, and Barcelona. He then departed at Rosas with a fleet of fifty-eight galleys headed by the most fa-mous Italian naval commander of the century, Genoese Admiral Andrea Doria (1466–1560), and sailed for Genoa, arriving there on 25 November. The Genoese did not like the taciturn young prince, although Philip tried in his own way to make a pleasing impression.[13] He was a withdrawn person and was not used to long trips and the frequent celebrations that accompanied each stop along the route. The Genoese were glad when he left. From there, he traveled to Milan, arriving there on 18 De-cember 1548, and then went to Cremona.

Months before, when the Cremonese were notified that the Spanish prince would be paying them a royal visit, enormous preparations were made to fête him in regal style. All artists in the city were engaged to design and build canopies under which the prince could view the planned festivities. All the Campis (related or not) were hired to build scenery for the elaborate pageants that would follow. Bernardino was hired by the *comune* to paint pictures of Philip's army. Since Anguissola was still studying with him at this time, it is conceivable that she was asked to help. The prince made his triumphal entrance into Cremona on 9 January 1549.

The Cremonese nobility, including the Pallavicini, Ponzone, and Anguissola families, had the responsibility of providing lodging (at their own expense) and en-tertainment for the several hundred servants and nobility traveling with Philip. Mag-nificent feasts were prepared at each palazzo. In all probability, young Sofonisba was present with her family at one of these elaborate festivities—perhaps she was even in-troduced to the twenty-one-year-old prince. Sofonisba was sixteen at the time, and a shining example of the city's nobility and artistic talent, all combined into one elegant and well-educated lady. Her father, Amilcare, made important contacts during Philip's brief stay that would prove invaluable ten years later when Sofonisba was in-vited to Philip's court.

That same year, 1549, Bernardino Campi went to Milan. He was introduced at the ducal court of the governor of Milan, Ferrante Gonzaga (1507–57, son of March-ese Francesco II and his wife, Isabella d'Este), by Alessandro Sesto. In a letter dated 2

May 1550, Isabella di Capua, princess of Molfetta, Ferrante's wife, requested that Campi paint a portrait of her daughter, Ippolita.[14] Apparently, the portrait was a success, as Ippolita Gonzaga wrote a letter circulating in 1554 that commended "Bernardino Campi for his virtue . . . placing him among the familiars at her household."[15] With his trip to Milan, Bernardino's star was on the rise.

It was about this time that Anguissola painted *Bernardino Campi Painting Sofonisba Anguissola* (Pinacoteca Nazionale, Siena, see plate 24). Most sixteenth-century portraits depicted an elaborately dressed individual seated or standing. Only the aristocracy and the wealthy emerging middle class could afford to be memorialized in this way, and sometimes they were portrayed with a book or a dog as a prop. This painting by Anguissola took sixteenth-century art in a new direction, that of action: the sitter is shown engaged in some kind of activity. The static quality of a portrait thereby is changed into one of movement, memorializing the sitter in a favorite activity. This is one of those rare paintings that has as its theme the teacher-student relationship of artists. What better way for Anguissola to pay homage to her teacher than to show him painting her. This is the only known portrait of Campi and is far more sensitively done—in her own style—than Anguissola's portrayal of herself, which appears much flatter, as if she were painting herself as Campi would have—trying to imitate his style.

Campi is wearing what appears to be a large, black artist's smock with full sleeves. Underneath is a white linen shirt, the plain collar of which is visible at the neck. In his right hand, which is steadied by an *appoggiamano*, a hand rest (made of a long stick at the end of which is a stuffed, covered cloth ball, placed there to avoid smudging the canvas), he holds his paint brush. Anguissola portrays herself on a canvas on an easel. She is wearing the same type of dark gown with puffed sleeves at the cap and, interestingly, the chemise (with the usual lace edging and three ties ending in tassels) appears to be the same one as that in the Uffizi *Self-Portrait*. In her left hand, she is holding a pair of gloves.

Anguissola's hair here is painted a light auburn with touches of blonde, and in her left ear she wears a silver drop earring. She looks at the viewer intently with her large eyes, the left eye appearing somewhat reddish and larger than the right one, an indication of an eye inflammation. She is known to have had ophthalmic problems later in life.

Unfortunately, many of the details of this three-quarter-length dual portrait have been obscured by more than four hundred years of accumulated dirt. The date given for the painting by the museum is 1558.[16] However, on the basis of the costume and Anguissola's own artistic style, an earlier date, c. 1550, would be more appropriate. The face seen here is not a mature one but rather one more in line with Anguissola's *Self-Portrait* at the Uffizi where she is much younger (twenty), with a fuller face. Moreover, the painting of the hands, both Campi's and her own, still are not anatomically correct, something she finally resolved in the mid-to-late 1550s.

Furthermore, her hair seems to be much lighter in this painting. Most of her canvases have not been cleaned and, therefore, it is difficult to tell many of the original colors. However, it would appear that a lighter hair color would be in keeping with Anguissola at a younger age. Even taking into account the darkened canvas,

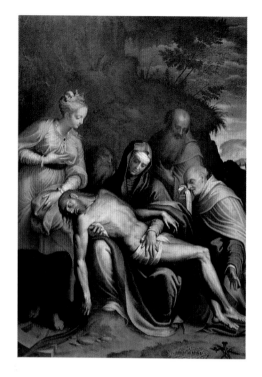

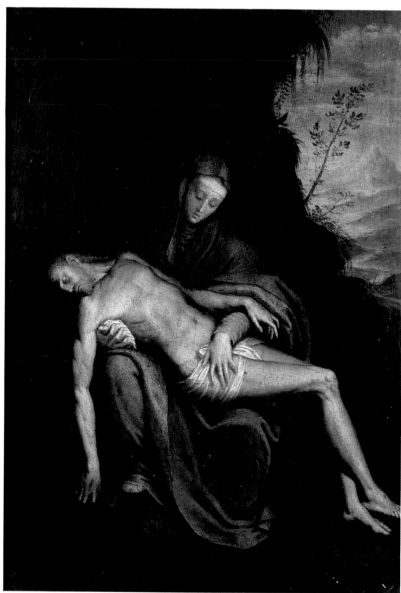

PLATE 22. Bernardino Campi. *Pietà*, c. 1550s.
Pinacoteca di Brera, Milan.

PLATE 23. Sofonisba Anguissola. *Pietà*,
c. 1550s. Oil on canvas, 19 11/16 x 15 3/4 in.
(50 x 40 cm). Pinacoteca di Brera, Milan.

PLATE 24. Sofonisba Anguissola. *Bernardino
Campi Painting Sofonisba Anguissola*, c. 1550.
Oil on canvas, 43 11/16 x 43 5/16 in. (111
x 110 cm). Pinacoteca Nazionale, Siena.

PLATE 25. Bernardino Gatti, *Resurrection,* 1529. The Duomo, Cremona.

there is a definite progression of light to darker hair color. All of this then would support an earlier dating.

Close examination in 1983 and 1988 also revealed part of a faint, but still visible, signature. The word "VIRGO," as she often signed herself, and "…SSOLA" are evident in very pale yellow in the lower right-hand corner of the canvas.

Bernardino Campi's departure left Anguissola and Elena without a teacher. As always, Amilcare proved quite resourceful. His daughters were good students, the eldest showed promise, and so Amilcare arranged for Sofonisba to continue her studies with Bernardino Gatti. Elena apparently did not continue her art studies and entered a convent shortly afterward. Amilcare was still one of the superintendents of San Sigismondo, and his name appears on a church document, discovered in 1983, hiring Gatti to paint a vault.[17]

Bernardino Gatti (c. 1495–1576) was the son of Orlando Gatti of Pavia. It is not known whether he was born in Pavia or in Cremona, or where he grew up. By the time he was about eighteen, he was painting in Cremona, and by then, he was nicknamed Il Sojaro (a kind of wine vat, which his father made). He lived for a while in

PLATE 26. Bernardino Gatti. *Ascension of Christ*, 1549. San Sigismondo, Cremona.

Parma and is believed to have studied with Correggio, who worked for the Gonzaga court at Mantua. In 1529, Gatti completed a signed large fresco rendition of the *Resurrection* for the Duomo in Cremona (see plate 25). By 1550, the Church of San Pietro in Cremona had commissioned him to do a painting in its refectory, and the following year, he did a work for San Sigismondo.

From what is known about Gatti, even though there are considerable gaps, it is possible to connect his work with other trends and stylistic similarities to other artists. In 1548, Gatti returned to Cremona and remained there until 1559, the year that Anguissola left for Madrid. The following year, 1549, he did an *Ascension of Christ* for San Sigismondo (see plate 26) in which he showed a heavy compositional debt to Camillo Boccaccino's *Christ in Glory,* done in 1535 for the same church. Correggio's influence on Boccaccino and Gatti can be seen in the soft coloring and *contrapposto* figures—both the angels and saints—of this fresco. While neither Boccaccino nor Gatti ever reached Correggio's artistic heights, nonetheless, they derived seminal inspiration from him.

Gatti's early religious figures also show the same gentle Mannerist elongation

PLATE 27. Anna Maria Anguissola. *Holy Family with Saint Francis*, Museo Civico ala Ponzone, Cremona.

that is seen in Campi's works. His colors, too, have warm a Venetian glow. Gatti and Correggio were the same age, and if he did study with Correggio, which seems likely from recent research, he probably acquired a "clarity of contour and smooth gemlike color"[18] from his master. Thus, Gatti's work is an amalgam of what he borrowed from other teachers, collaboration with some of the Campi family, as well as Leonardo's work, which so strongly influenced the currents of Italian art.

Dates are uncertain, but Anguissola probably continued her studies under Gatti for about three years (1549–c. 1552/53), in between his heavy load of commissioned works. Whether Anguissola stayed with Gatti or with her parents is not known. Zaist, who was writing in the eighteenth century, states that "above all. . . Sofonisba became such an expert that it was not a small wonder that she could render in sketches original ideas in what she saw with a greater freedom of hand."[19]

Interestingly, Sofonisba's younger sister, Anna Maria, whom Vasari saw as a little girl when he visited the Anguissola home in 1566, appears to have been inspired by Gatti's work, although she did not study with him. Anna Maria's *Holy Family with Saint Francis* (Museo Civico ala Ponzone, Cremona, see plate 27) derives its compositional form and the roundness of its figures from Gatti's *Holy Family with Saints Anne and John* (Museo Civico ala Ponzone, Cremona, see plate 28). It is known that So-

PLATE 28. Bernardino Gatti. *Holy Family with Saints Anne and John*. Museo Civico ala Ponzone, Cremona.

fonisba was Anna Maria's teacher, and they collaborated on a *Madonna with the Christ Child and Saint John* (whereabouts unknown), which they both signed.[20]

By a series of fortuitous circumstances—parents who were willing to encourage an artistic education for their daughter and good teachers—Sofonisba had the beginnings of an apprenticeship (although it was never termed that, since she was a noble lady). Even though her apprenticeship was an unusual one, time was devoted not only to the basics of a young noblewoman's education but art studies as well: sketching, copying, and learning how to mix pigments and apply them to canvas, wood, or copper. Through her teachers and their own artistic studies, she was exposed to and inherited two divergent trends in sixteenth-century art: the High Renaissance, with its controlled, ordered, and graceful poses and balanced colors; and Mannerism, its antithesis, with uncontrolled, agitated, and attenuated figures and compositions with contrasting coloring.

So, by mid- entury, Anguissola was developing her artistic skills and knowledge. It was time for her to explore the rest of Renaissance art outside the confines of Cremona. Rome was the center of artistic activity, and Michelangelo was living there. So, accompanied by a chaperone, Anguissola would soon be off to Rome.

PLATE 39. Sofonisba Anguissola. *Asdrubale Being Bitten by a Crab*. Sketch, 13 1/8 x 15 1/8 in. (33.3 x 38.5 cm). Gabinetto dei Disegni, Museo Nazionale di Capodimonte, Naples.

ROME AND MICHELANGELO

What marvels from the works . . . wonderfully painted by the hand
of the beautiful Cremonese lady painter [Sofonisba Anguissola].

—*Francesco Salviati*

I n 1551, Bianca Ponzone Anguissola gave birth to Asdrubale, her last child and the family's long-awaited son. By now, Sofonisba had become adept in her sketching and painting techniques and continued to use her family frequently as her models. Her artistic capabilities improved with each family portrait. Her brother became her youngest model, and when he was about three, Sofonisba used him in her sketch *Asdrubale Being Bitten by a Crab* (see plate 39).

That same year, Elena Anguissola, as the second-born child of a noble house, followed the usually prescribed path and took her vows in a religious order, instead of continuing her art studies with Sofonisba. Although no documents remain, it would have been expected that Amilcare give a dowry to the Convent of the Holy Virgins at San Vincenzo in Mantua when Elena entered there as a Dominican nun. Little is known about Elena's life thereafter, although Zaist states that she was still living in 1584.[1] It is possible that once Elena was part of convent life, she continued to paint. This would have been in keeping with a tradition of nun-painters that dated back to the tenth century when some of the earliest nunneries were founded by wealthy aristocratic women. Well educated at home and later in the convents they entered, these women spent time embroidering liturgical vestments and copying and decorating manuscripts. Vasari mentions Paolo Uccello's daughter, Antonia (1446–91), a Carmelite nun, whose death certificate notes that she was a *pittoressa* (painter). Earlier, there was Caterina dei Vigri (1413–63), who joined a convent of Franciscan nuns. She was canonized in 1703. Elena may have found time to paint; but cloistered away from any artistic community, her creative capabilities and growth would have been severely hampered. Elena's works have not survived.

To commemorate Elena's taking of her vows, Sofonisba most probably went to Mantua to paint her sister in her novitiate's habit (Southampton Art Gallery, see plate 29). Known as *Portrait of a Nun,* this oil on canvas, three-quarter-length portrait shows Elena holding a Bible that is covered in a burnt siena-colored leather and decorated

PLATE 29. Sofonisba Anguissola. *Portrait of a Nun* (Portrait of Elena Anguissola), c. 1551. Oil on canvas, 29 9/16 x 23 1/4 in. (75 x 59 cm). Southampton Art Gallery, Southampton.

PLATE 30. Sofonisba Anguissola. *Portrait of a Nun* (Portrait of Elena Anguissola), c. 1558. Oil on canvas, 9 7/16 x 7 1/16 in. (24 x 18 cm). Borghese Gallery, Rome.

PLATE 31. Sofonisba Anguissola. *Self-Portrait*,
1552. Oil on canvas, 34 7/8 x 27 3/8 in.
(88.5 x 69 cm). Uffizi Gallery, Florence.

in gold. The delicacy of the painting of Elena's hands and fingers is typical of Anguissola's style. Art historian Eleanor Tufts, writing in 1979, states that there is also a "strong family resemblance in the long nose, arched brows, and large almond eyes."[2] Interesting, too, Elena's face is reminiscent of Mary's face in Sofonisba's *Pietà* (see plate 23); and this would be in keeping with her use of family as models for her paintings.

A second portrait of Elena, done by Sofonisba several years later, shows a more mature nun. It, too, is known as *Portrait of a Nun* (Borghese Gallery, Rome, see plate 30),[3] with no mention of Elena's identity. When these two portraits are viewed together, the facial similarities are quite striking: the eyes, long nose, and lips are almost identical. It seems clear that both these portraits are of the same person, but at different stages of her life. One is the youthful Elena holding a sacred book, while the other shows her as a devout Dominican nun. The face has aged a bit and become fuller, and there is also a heavier symbolism in the later portrait. Instead of a Bible, Elena now holds three lilies in her right hand—symbols of the Trinity, purity, and the Virgin Mary. In her left hand, she holds a crucifix piercing a red heart, which symbolizes "contrition and devotion under conditions of extreme trial"[4]—all of which the older nun has absorbed and embodied, as her sister saw her. What extreme trials she had gone through are unknown, although entering the convent would have been a difficult transition. However, these two portraits together are a documentary of Elena's progress in the convent.

An educated guess on the dating of these two portraits is also possible. No birth date for Elena is known. However, she was Bianca and Amilcare's second child and was probably born about 1535. If Elena and Sofonisba were studying together with Campi until 1549—and Zaist does not mention that she continued her studies with Gatti—then it is likely that she entered San Vincenzo sometime around 1551, when the first portrait was done.[5] The second portrait probably was done at the end of the decade before Sofonisba left for Spain in 1559.

Sofonisba probably kept in touch with Elena by letter, although they did not see each other very often, as was customary after Elena took her final vows. In all likelihood, Sofonisba returned to Mantua to paint the second portrait.

In 1552, Anguissola commemorated her own twentieth birthday with a *Self-Portrait* (Uffizi Gallery, Florence, see plate 31).[6] The dating of this painting, is based on a birthdate of 1532. This particular portrait has not figured in scholarly research, perhaps because it is located in the vast labyrinthian Vasari Corridor (named after its architect), which the museum keeps closed. In Anguissola's self-portrait, the young artist inscribed her painting on the left, "Sofonisba Anguissola, Cremona, painted this at twenty." The writing is very faint, as the canvas has darkened considerably with time.

Anguissola portrays herself in a gown very similar to the one she wears in the oil on copper miniature (Museum of Fine Arts, Boston, see plates 33, 34). This gown, with minor variations, especially in the collar, also can be seen on other portraits that she would paint during the 1550s: a tightly boned V-neck bodice with a small maroon velvet inset; puffed maroon sleeves with small strips at the sleeve cap, and then fitted to the wrist; and underneath the bodice, a chemise with a high stand-up collar edged in lace. In her right hand, she holds a piece of paper and in her left, a paint brush and palette.

PLATE 32. After Sofonisba Anguissola. *Self-Portrait at Easel*. Oil on canvas, 25 x 23 1/4 in. (66 x 59 cm). Zeri Collection, Mentana.

In the Uffizi portrait, Anguissola's hair is parted down the center with a braided crown and velvet band around it. Her face with her large blue-gray eyes looking out at the viewer, is somewhat more somber than in the miniature, and her cheeks are a bit puffy. The shape of her right earlobe is consistent with other self-portraits. Here, she is not wearing earrings, although in other portraits she does.

Anguissola portrays herself with paint brushes in her left hand, which may indicate that she was left-handed. She certainly would be in illustrious company as both Leonardo da Vinci and Hans Holbein were left-handed. Generally, other artists have portrayed themselves with brushes in their right hand. In another copy of a self-portrait (Zeri Collection, Mentana, see plate 32), Anguissola painted herself with a brush in her right hand. Why the switch in hands? Documents later found in Spain, written by Anguissola herself, did not conclusively indicate with which hand she wrote.[7]

There is an exquisite miniature self-portrait done by Anguissola during this same period, about 1552, that she may have started while she was still with Bernardino Gatti or shortly thereafter (as she was about to leave for Rome). This oval, oil on copper miniature (Museum of Fine Arts, Boston, see plate 33), shows her dressed in mid-sixteenth-century fashion and is far more delicately painted than the Uffizi *Self-Portrait*. Unfortunately, sometime after 1983, the miniature was badly damaged, and

33

34

PLATE 33. Sofonisba Anguissola. *Self-Portrait*,
c. 1552. Oil on copper miniature, 3 3/16 x 2
1/2 in. (8.2 x 6.3 cm). Courtesy, Museum of
Fine Arts, Boston, Emma F. Munroe Fund.

PLATE 34. Sofonisba Anguissola. *Self-Portrait*,
c. 1552 (damaged after 1983). Oil on copper
miniature, damaged. 3 3/16 x 2 1/2 in. (8.2
x 6.3 cm). Courtesy, Museum of Fine Arts,
Boston, Emma F. Munroe Fund.

PLATE 35. Mary Queen of Scots. Octagonal
needlework, c. 1570. Monogram: MARIE
STVART, crowned, with thistles. Victoria
and Albert Museum, London.

Anguissola's left hand—with her typical "square-U" delineation—is now missing (see plate 34).

Her hair is parted down the center and braided and wrapped around her head like a ~~tiara~~. She is wearing a tightly boned bodice, although only the standing collar and underchemise (the sixteenth-century term for a blouse), with lace edgings and tie strings, are visible.

She is holding a circle with thumb and index finger (now obliterated) in her "square-U" style, which reads: "Sophonisba Anguissola Vir[go] Ipsius Manu Ex Speculo Depictam Cremonae" (The maiden Sofonisba Anguissola painted this from a mirror by her own hand, Cremona). Interestingly, in both this and the Uffizi *Self-Portrait,* she spells her name So*ph*onisba, which she generally did not do in her other paintings. In spelling her name this way, she may have been making a personal statement connecting herself with her ancient namesake. It is possible that once she arrived in Rome (if this oval was completed there), Anguissola heard many horrendous stories about the Sack of Rome in 1527, and in her own mind may have associated the mercenary troops of Charles V with the ancient Romans who wanted to take Sophonisba prisoner. It was still a topic of discussion; and it is quite possible that she heard the stories directly from Michelangelo.

Inside the circle of the miniature are a series of intertwining letters: E, R, A, C, K, Y, M. The pattern of intertwined letters was a Renaissance device which played upon *double entendre.* Monograms, emblems, and riddles all were popular with Renaissance intellectuals who delighted in hidden meanings. Emblems were popular, and books on the subject were fashionable in France and England in the second half of the sixteenth century. Frequently, there were Latin inscriptions, as in this miniature, or mottos that could have double meanings.

The recognition and solving of emblems was as absorbing to the educated men and women of the period as crossword puzzles are today. In French, as well as in English [and this could also be applicable to Italian], the spoken and written word was becoming more vivid and flexible, so that riddles, puns, and anagrams, especially those translated from the universal Latin to which Italian was extremely close in the sixteenth century, had a freshness and meaning that today can scarcely [be] appreciated.[8]

It is possible that this oval self-portrait was given to the Anguissola family, perhaps as a memento—a popular contemporary gift—before Sofonisba left for Rome or shortly after she arrived. The gift would have been apt, in either case. Presumably, the letters indicate Sofonisba's hidden message, which would have been evident to the person(s) for whom it was intended.

Prominent in the center is the "A," which probably not only stands for Anguissola but for the artist's father's, sister's, and brother's given names: Amilcare, Anna Maria, and Asdrubale. Next to the "A" is a "C" which could stand for Cremona and/or Campi with whom she began her artistic studies.

The "E" on the left could stand for Sofonisba's two sisters, Elena and Europa. The "E" could also be read as an "L"—minus the middle and top strokes—which would then stand for her other sister, Lucia. Intertwined with the "E" and "L" is also a "P/R," perhaps indicating Sofonisba's mother's maiden name, Ponzone. The "R" also could have stood for Rome where she was planning to go or had already arrived.

The other letter, "M," is not so easily decipherable. However, it would be interesting to speculate that this miniature might have been done shortly after Sofonisba's arrival in Rome, after her contact with Michelangelo; and thus, the "M" might then have been a tribute to Michelangelo who had corresponded with her father. Another possibility is that the "M" stands for her other sister, Minerva. Or, in keeping with the fact that emblems oftentimes had more than one meaning, the "M" could have stood for other names. Finally, although a "K" and "Y" are visible to the English-language reader, they are not used in Italian.

Ideas taken from these "new emblem books, which had come from Italy"[9] could be adapted to the needs of the artist's brush or devices in needlework. A similar example is an interesting piece of needlework done by Mary [Stuart], Queen of Scots, c. 1570, during her eighteen-year captivity in England (see plate 35). It is an octagon with intertwining letters, here done as a monogram. It is very similar to Anguissola's device of intertwined letters in her miniature and, therefore, interesting for comparison. Here, clearly, one can see the letters in Mary's and Elizabeth I's names, as well as the "S" for Stuart. Although superimposed on each other, the letters and their hidden meaning—that Mary was seeking a rapprochement with Elizabeth, as well as indicating that the two were cousins—are decipherable to anyone with a knowledge of Tudor history. Nonetheless, it confirms the widespread popularity of the emblematic

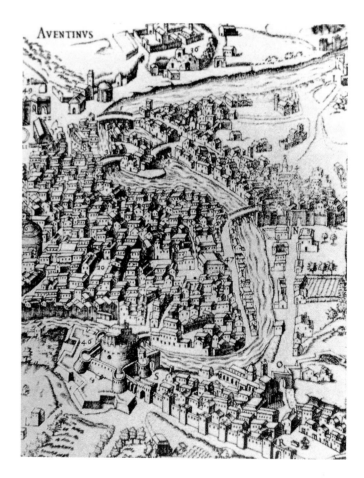

PLATE 36. G.A. Dossio's Plan of Rome, 1561.

device with Renaissance women and shows that the idea could be applied to needle or paintbrush.

As an art form, the self-portrait was only fifty years old when Anguissola began doing her own. It had originated with Albrecht Dürer (1471–1528), who was the first artist to do so many self-portraits and who "kept records of his own appearance."[10] His earliest self-portrait was done in silverpoint in 1484, when the artist was thirteen. The portrait says, "I have copied this of myself in a mirror." Anguissola, as part of her education as a noblewoman, very possibly was familiar with various kinds of mirror-image self-portraits and miniatures, and she may have seen a copy of Dürer's through engravings that circulated.

Dürer had traveled to Italy, absorbed much of the Italian Renaissance in his art, and left his own stamp on northern Italy. North Italian Renaissance artists, such as the Campis, Lorenzo Lotto, Giovanni Battista Moroni, the Venetian painters, and Anguissola, maintained artistic links between Italy and northern Europe. By midcentury, north Italian Renaissance art was a blend of Venetian coloring, Mannerist principles, and, because of its proximity, German and Flemish art. This exchange between Renaissance artists which led to shared influences was vital to the evolution of sixteenth-century art in Europe.

Sometime about 1554 Anguissola left for Rome. The approximately two hundred sixty-mile journey from Cremona to Rome probably took about three weeks. Traveling by coach, on unpaved roads, she had with her a small entourage which included a chaperone, a few servants, and possibly her sister, Lucia. Most likely, she stayed with family or friends.

Once in Rome, Anguissola settled down to an artistic routine that included visiting (with a chaperone) the ancient ruins and medieval churches that were still in use, painting portraits in oil, and continuing to improve her sketching abilities. Since she was working outside the *bottega* (workshop) that was available only to male artists, portraiture became her most important vehicle during this decade.

Mid-century Rome was the seat of the Papal States, the vast territory over which the Church claimed temporal authority, including Bologna, Ravenna, Rimini, Urbino, Perugia, Assisi, Orvieto, Spoleto, and Rome itself. Visually, Renaissance Rome, with a population of about fifty thousand, was far different from the ancient city (see plate 36). Rusticity pervaded: sheep and cattle grazed among the ruins; vineyards grew on the Palatine Hill; and the city, which was divided into districts, had very few well-paved cobblestoned streets. Many of the splendors now associated with the city had not yet been built. Even the dome that Michelangelo designed for St. Peter's had not yet been completed.[11]

Just twenty-seven years before, in 1527, the German mercenary troops of Charles V's Imperial Hapsburg army had laid siege to the city: about ten thousand lost their lives during the devastation. Plague and famine ensued for most of the following year, and Michelangelo and other artists fled, along with another ten percent of the city's population. Pope Clement VII (Giulio de' Medici, elected in 1523), besieged in Castel Sant'Angelo, had to hand over several hostages, including Cardinal Ciocchi del Monte.

PLATE 37. Caravaggio. *Boy Being Bitten by a Lizard*, c. 1597. Fondazione Roberto Longhi, Florence.

It was this Cardinal Ciocchi who was elected the new pope in 1550, taking the name Julius III. He and Rome's citizenry never forgot the brutality of Charles' troops, and as the new decade began, they maintained an uneasy peace with the aging, gout-ridden emperor. Over the next five years, the Papal States lost their independence and much of the rest of Italy changed hands.

Despite constant political tension, the arts flourished and the city's vitality returned. At the hub of this creativity was Michelangelo, at seventy-five still working for the Church at an ambitious pace. In the spring of 1550, a few months after Pope Paul III's death, he finished two frescoes for the Pauline Chapel in the Vatican.

Michelangelo's impact was enormous. His sketches were copied, discussed, passed around in artistic circles, sent off to many other artists all over Italy, and subsequently reinterpreted. As Charles de Tolnay, the late twentieth-century art historian and former director of Casa Buonarroti in Florence, stated, "Michelangelism dominated the sixteenth century . . . however, his message (at least as far as representational art is concerned) was not understood in its entirety. Each artist drew his inspiration from a single aspect of the Master's art, transforming it and integrating it within the scope of his own tendencies."[12]

Artists working in Michelangelo's style included Vasari, Bronzino, members of the Campi families, Pontormo, Sebastiano del Piombo, and later Caravaggio, one of whose paintings, *Boy Being Bitten by a Lizard,* c. 1597 (see plate 37), was inspired by Anguissola's earlier sketch (c. 1554), *Asdrubale Being Bitten by a Crab* (see plate 39). According to de Tolnay, "the origins of Caravaggio's style have been traced back to Lombard local tradition (in Bergamo, Cremona, and Brescia), and in particular to the milieu of Antonio and Vicenzo Campi."[13] Therefore, it is possible to trace the absorption of Mannerism and, of course, Michelangelo's tremendous impact through these other artists to Cremona and Anguissola's teachers there.

It has been known for some time that Anguissola stayed in Rome. Two Michelangelo scholars, E. H. Ramsden and J. A. Symonds, mention Anguissola's stay in Rome, although they do not give a date. Ramsden states that "Sofonisba Anguissola was the child of enlightened parents, to whom Michelangelo showed great kindness and offered every encouragement during her two years in Rome, prior to her appointment to Queen Isabella of Spain."[14] Symonds says that "Sofonisba was studying design in Rome" with Michelangelo.[15]

These statements are based upon two letters written in 1557 and 1558 from Amilcare Anguissola to Michelangelo, preserved in the Buonarroti Archives (and now housed in the Medeceo Laurenziana Library in Florence, see plate 38).

My Most Honorable Sir,

Your most excellent, virtuous, and good natured soul (all that is given by God) made me keep that memory of you which duly has to be given to such an important and extraordinary gentleman. And what makes me and my whole family obliged to you is having understood the honorable and thoughtful affection that you have shown to Sofonisba, my daughter, to whom you introduced to practice the most honorable art of painting. I assure you that I am more grateful for the favor I receive for your most honorable affection [towards my daughter] than all the riches that any Prince could give, because I find myself very obliged for the virtuous and liberal actions that you granted me and Antonio Anselmi, above all the dignity and gifts which could be given in this world. Therefore, I am asking you, as in the past you were kind enough by your gracious courtesy, to talk to her and encourage my daughter, once again in the future to share your divine thoughts with her. I promise you, when she knows the honorable favor you are bestowing on her, she will direct her mind with great devotion in such a way that I would hope for the best results. We could not receive that with more honor and happiness. This would be all the more if you would be kind enough to send her a sketch so that she can paint it in oil, obliging her to send it back duly finished by her own hand. If you would do this, to compensate my obligation to you, I would dedicate my daughter, Sofonisba, the dearest thing that I have in this world, as your servant. From Cremona, 7 May [15]57.

Your most obedient servant,
Amilcare Anguissola[16]

A year later, on 15 May, Amilcare wrote to Michelangelo again:

Most Magnificent and Honorable Michelangelo,

Your friendly *letters* [italics added] are much dearer to me than those which I could receive from our king [Philip II]. Assuring you that among the many obligations I have to God, that such a great and talented gentleman—beyond any other man—such as you, was kind enough to examine, judge, and praise the paintings done by my daughter, Sofonisba. I hope that God's divine majesty permits her, who is so virtuous in paint-

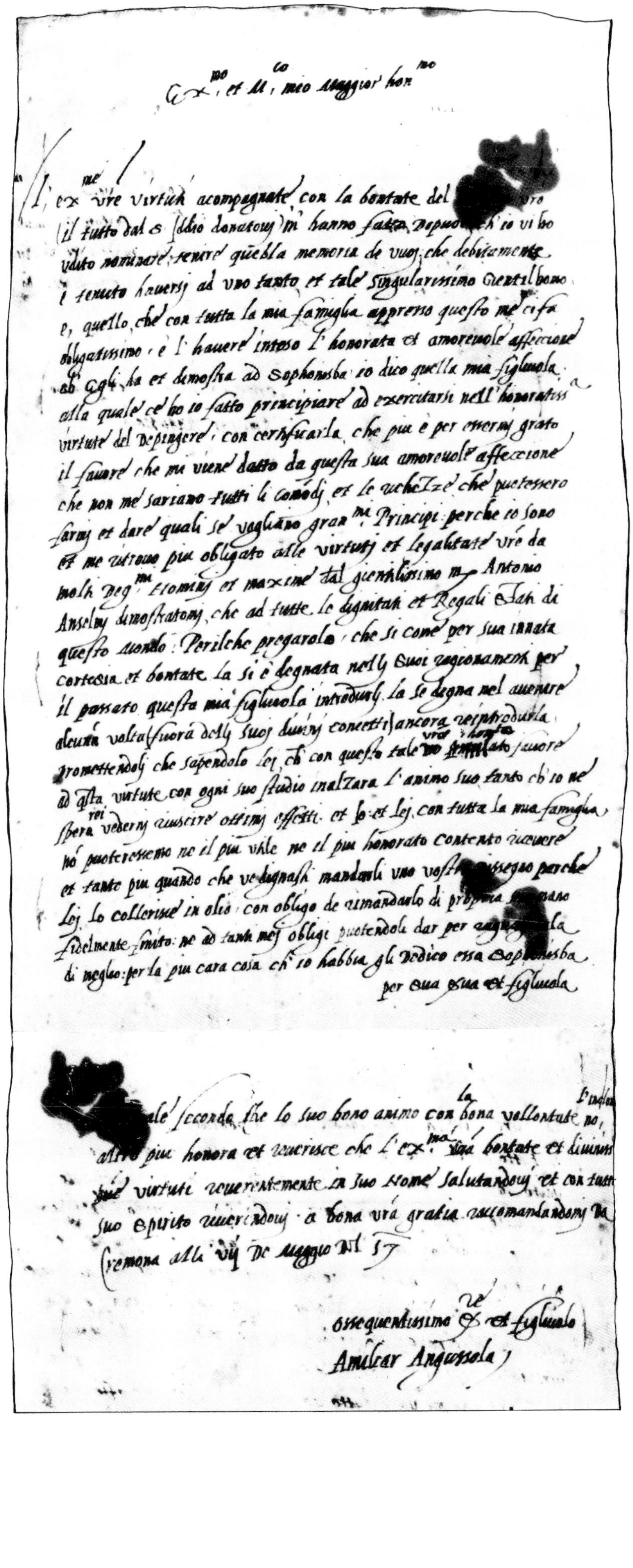

PLATE 38. Amilcare Anguissola's Letter to Michelangelo, 7 May 1557. Medeceo Laurenziana Library, Buonarroti Archives (Casa Buonarroti), Florence.

ing, to live along with my other daughters and son, so that we all could see each other and later enjoy heaven, in which I put all my hope. And with this faith, first for me and then my family, I salute you and send you our greetings. From Cremona, 15 May [15]58.

Your most affectionate friend and servant,
Amilcare Anguissola[17]

It has always been assumed that Anguissola's stay coincided with the dates of these two letters. However, a new chronology now can be established in which, as mentioned earlier, she arrived in Rome sometime about 1554.

Michelangelo was in Rome when Amilcare wrote to him the first time (1557) working for Pope Paul IV (pontificate, 1555–59) on plans for St. Peter's. Amilcare's first letter is stiff with all the usual deference that was not only due the great artist but also in keeping with the style and formality of the period. It also clearly states that Michelangelo had met with Sofonisba ("talked to her and encouraged" her). The second letter (which mentions other correspondence between them) shows warmth and affection and, most important, it indicates that Michelangelo had examined and praised Sofonisba's work. Although neither of Michelangelo's replies have survived, it is obvious that he had helped Sofonisba in some way, as Amilcare refers to the "affection that he had shown her." Further, he says that Michelangelo had "introduced . . . the art of painting" to the aspiring young Cremonese artist. Even if one takes into account the extreme formality of Renaissance writing (and, of course, that she had already studied with Campi and Gatti), there had been contact between Michelangelo and Sofonisba.

Symonds states that "Michelangelo formed no school in the strict sense of the word; yet his influence was not the less felt."[18] This "correspondence between Amilcare Anguissola and Michelangelo has certain further importance in that it presents new evidence of the generous character of the artist. It is already known that he helped a succession of young artists, by sending them drawings, as for example, Sebastiano del Piombo, Benvenuto Cellini, and Antonio Mini. This 'innate courtesy and goodness' extended to Sofonisba is not an exceptional act, but fits in quite well with our conception of the character of Michelangelo."[19] However, it should be noted that painting was customarily a man's domain, and surely Michelangelo would not have bothered keeping in touch with a woman—or helping her—had she not shown promise. Further, Michelangelo was eighty-three in 1558, and "was hardly writing to anyone except his nephew Lionardo, so that writing to Amilcare was irrefutable proof of the affection that he had for the young painter."[20]

It was also during this time that Anguissola's talents became known in wider artistic circles. In a letter written in April 1554 by the painter Francesco Salviati (1510–63) to Bernardino Campi, he praised Anguissola's talents. Salviati also knew Giorgio Vasari, whom he met in 1524; they became lifelong friends and companions. Salviati had returned to Rome in 1548, after a lengthy sojourn in northern Italy, which had begun in 1539.[21] He had studied with Andrea del Sarto in 1529, and by the early 1550s he "was well established as the foremost practicing fresco painter in Rome."[22] In a letter to Campi, Salviati wrote:

40

41

My Magnificent Sir Bernardino,

From the works in front of me which are wonderfully painted by the beautiful Cremonese lady painter, I do understand what a great ability you must have. Moreover, you have acquired renown from your paintings of Milan. From this fame, which we are obliged to confirm, we know that when you were young, you were able to paint your city [Cremona] better than anyone else. Therefore, do not think it surprising that I send you a sketch to show you my affection. With warm regards and remembering you, I let you know that I love you more for your wonderful intellect and your fame than because of our future acquaintance. In the meantime, send my greetings to your brother, and I send you my greetings. From Rome, 28 April 1554.

Francesco Salviati,
painter[23]

That same year, Sofonisba did *Asdrubale Being Bitten by a Crab* (Capodimonte Museum, Naples, see plate 39), a sketch of her sister and three-year-old brother, Asdrubale. The proposed earlier date of her arrival in Rome is based upon both the style and dating of this sketch, which ushers in a change in her art and shows Michelangelo's influence. It is possible that Salviati had seen it, or had a copy of this sketch, as he mentions "the works in front of" him.

PLATE 40. Michelangelo. *Cleopatra*. Sketch. Casa Buonarroti, Florence. Gabinetto Fotografico Soprintendenza Beni Artistici e Storici di Firenze.

PLATE 41. Piero di Cosimo. *Simonetta Vespucci*, c. 1501. Musée Condé, Chantilly/Art Resource.

PLATE 42. Cremonese School. *Cleopatra*, Sixteenth century. Poldi Pezzoli Museum, Milan.

42

The provenance of this sketch goes back to Vasari's *Vite*. According to Vasari, Tommaso Cavalieri (1510–87)[24] who was a close friend of Michelangelo "sent to Duke Cosimo [I] a sketch of Cleopatra from the divine hand of Michelangelo. The other [was done] by Sofonisba's hand, in which a young girl is laughing and a little boy is crying because he put his hand, one finger of which was bitten, into a basket of crabs."[25]

Apparently, this sketch originally was in Michelangelo's possession, probably sent to him by Anguissola as one of the assignments that he had given to her. In 1562, two years before Michelangelo's death, Cavalieri sent this sketch along with Michelangelo's sketch of Cleopatra to Cosimo I (de' Medici, grand duke of Tuscany, 1519–74) in Florence. There is a sketch of Cleopatra in the collection of Casa Buonarroti, in Florence (the house Michelangelo bought but in which he never lived and now a museum for some of his work). In response to Amilcare's request for a sketch, Michelangelo most likely sent Sofonisba this one (see plate 40). The inspiration for this sketch probably came from Piero di Cosimo's *Portrait of Simonetta Vespucci* (Musée Condé, Chantilly, see plate 41), done a half century before, c. 1501.[26] It is possible that Michelangelo's sketch (now kept in the Laurentian Library, Florence) is the very same one sent with Anguissola's to Cosimo. In the letter Cavalieri wrote on 20 January 1562, he says:

I have a drawing done by the hand of a noblewoman of Cremona, named Sofonisba Aguosciosa [viz., Anguissola], today a lady of the Spanish court, I send it to you with this one of Michelangelo [*Cleopatra*] and I believe that it may stand comparison with many other drawings, for it is not simply beautiful, but also exhibits considerable invention. And this is that of the divine Michelangelo who had seen a drawing done by her hand of a smiling girl, said that he would have liked to see a weeping boy, as a subject more difficult to draw. After he wrote to her about it, she sent him this drawing which was a portrait of her brother [Asdrubale], whom she has intentionally shown as weeping. Now, I send them such as they are, and I beg your excellency to consider me as a servant, which, in truth, I am.[27]

Interestingly, a few days later, other copies of these two sketches were sent to Cosimo I:

From Tommaso de Cavalieri, I have received two sketches: one of a head by Michelangelo's hand; and the other, showing a boy crying, by a lady who is now with the Queen of Spain [Elisabeth de Valois]. Until now, he was late in giving them to me, because he wanted to have a friend of his copy the head by Michelangelo, so that he could retain a copy. Moreover, it was difficult for him to be deprived of these sketches because he loved the drawing [of *Cleopatra*] so much, and the other . . . drawing was something quite rare. It would be proper if your Excellency would answer this letter with just a few kind words. I have not received anything [drawings] from the Bishop of Furlì, although I remind him every day. He tells me that, at present, he does not have anything special to give me. He has his hands on some drawings, but, as yet, he does not know the results. I am sending these with our usual procurator, hoping that they are carried to you discreetly and in good condition. From Rome, 24 January 1562.

Your humble servant,
Averardo Serristori[28]

Serristori was Duke Cosimo I's ambassador to the papal court.

Thus, both letters indicate that Anguissola's sketches were guided by Michelangelo, that they also were circulating among the aristocracy, and that he and Sofonisba were in correspondence. Moreover, de Tolnay states that Vasari had "a copy of it in his collection of drawings, the *Libro dei disegni.*"[29] The whereabouts of this sketch were not known until it surfaced again and was found in the collection of Capodimonte's Gabinetto dei Disegni. The museum says that "this was part of Vasari's *Libro dei disegni.*"

Although the sketch has faded considerably,[30] the vibrancy and beauty of the composition are still quite evident and indicate ample improvement in Anguissola's skill. The warmth she felt for little Asdrubale is communicated with vivid realism and tenderness. One of her younger sisters, possibly Minerva, has her hand placed gently over Asdrubale's right shoulder, while in her left hand she holds a basket filled with crabs. Sofonisba has captured Asdrubale's right hand in a jerky, pained manner, just as his right ring finger is being pinched by the crab. This mixture of tension and calm derives from Mannerist principles.

There is an elegance, too, in the sketching of the costumes. The young sister's gown has a boned bodice, which was common even for children's gowns, and full skirt. The dropped sleeves have a scalloped edge just below the shoulders and a full lace cuff. The shirred neckline of the chemise is quite full and is accentuated further by the dropped sleeves. Her hair style is the same fashionable one seen in other portraits that Anguissola painted.

Asdrubale, who appears to be about three years old, is also dressed in the customary miniature version of adult clothing. His chemise has a small collar and full sleeves that are gathered at the cuff and edged with lace. Over it, he wears a doublet with full puffed and slashed sleeves.

Although there is not any document of birth for Asdrubale, the museum has dated the sketch about 1554. If Carlo Bonetti's dating of his birth is correct, then Asdrubale would indeed have been about three years old when his sister sketched him. More importantly, on stylistic grounds, this clearly shows Michelangelo's earlier influence on Anguissola which Bonetti's dating supports. Heretofore, it had been thought to be later in the decade (based on the two letters already quoted that Amilcare wrote to Michelangelo in 1557 and 1558).

This sketch shows an interesting blend of Anguissola's characteristics and Michelangelo's influence. The manner and positioning of the sister's hands, and especially Asdrubale's left hand done in a "square-U," epitomize her work. Typical of Anguissola, too, is the composition that depicts a familial and informal scene for which she became well known, rather than the usual extremely formal setting of sixteenth-century portraits. The triangular arrangement of the two figures—where the eye goes from Asdrubale's pained face, to his hand, and then to his sister's face—is compact and well organized.

Michelangelo's influence is evident in Asdrubale's anguished and tense pose, which contrasts sharply with his sister's calm. These divergent qualities are typical of Mannerism, and Michelangelo explored emotional contrasts extensively in his sketches as he did in his studies of anatomy. Anguissola's understanding of anatomy and perspective are evident here, although not in her other two earlier sketches. She absorbed the lessons of her teacher in Rome; and when she met Michelangelo in person, he surely would have pointed out ways to correct the deficiencies in her anatomical renderings, as had Campi and Gatti. The elongated fingers that she learned from Campi and used in her *Pietà*, now are replaced with solid, anatomically accurate forms—Michelangelo's contribution to Anguissola's growth as an artist. From contemporary sources, it is evident that *Il Divino* helped Anguissola and promoted her artistic development. This sketch clearly shows his influence and a tremendous improvement in her understanding of anatomy and sensitivity to composition.

There is also extant a sixteenth-century oil on wood painting based upon Michelangelo's Cleopatra sketch (Poldi Pezzoli Museum, Milan, see plate 42), that raises some interesting questions. The artist is unknown (according to the museum), the provenance of the painting is sketchy, and it has been heavily restored.[31] Could Anguissola or one of her sisters have painted it? The work definitely shows the influence of Cremonese artists. Did Michelangelo send his sketch to her? Did she in turn use it as a model? Or is this a later copy (perhaps by one of her own sisters) based on Anguissola's original?

As alluded to in Cavalieri's letter, Michelangelo sent his Cleopatra sketch to Anguissola. It is conceivable that she may have sent back an oil painting (mentioned in

Amilcare's letter) of her copied version of the sketch. Then, Michelangelo challenged her to do something more original which led to her own original sketch of Asdrubale. In the unattributed oil painting, the elaborate hair style is done in the tradition of Botticelli and Parmigianino; and the elongation of the neck and the face show a striking similarity to Cremonese art—and Parmigianino's *Madonna of the Long Neck* (see plate 10)—and, in particular, to both *Pietàs* by Campi and Anguissola (see plates 22 and 23). The drooping eyes, which are rolled up (perhaps to illustrate the moment before Cleopatra's death), are not congruent with the large eyes that Anguissola painted so frequently during the 1550s. This may be due in part to the heavy restoration (the date of which is unknown). However, until the painting is x-rayed, it is impossible to distinguish the original work from that of the restorer.

Interestingly, one of Caravaggio's oil paintings, *Boy Being Bitten by a Lizard* (Fondazione Roberto Longhi, Florence, see plate 37), done about 1597, derived its inspiration from Anguissola's sketch of Asdrubale. A second version of the painting is now in the National Gallery, London. So, Anguissola's sketch continued to circulate and to be a source of inspiration in artistic circles half a century after she completed it.

Sometime between 1554 and 1555, Anguissola gave Pope Julius III her *Self-Portrait*. There is a possibility that her *Self-Portrait* in the Uffizi Gallery is the same one given to the pope (see plate 31). It is not known, however, if Anguissola had met or knew the pope before she sent him her *Self-Portrait,* or if he requested it (as a way to find out about her work). It is possible that Anguissola's talents might have come to the pope's attention through the auspices of Michelangelo, since he was working for Julius III at that time. Anguissola is also known to have painted Pope Paul IV, who succeeded Julius (after the very brief pontificate of Marcellus II in 1555). Sacchi mentions seeing it in the mid-nineteenth century in Madrid, but its current whereabouts are not known.

In order for Michelangelo to have given Anguissola artistic assistance, a third party must have introduced them. A mutual friend would have facilitated the formalities, especially since Anguissola was cut off from the usual artistic environment where many of the artists knew each other. Evidence points to the possibility that either Giorgio Vasari or Annibale Caro might have been that intermediary.

Vasari included a discussion of Anguissola in the 1568 edition of his *Vite*. He had known Michelangelo for a long time, but correspondence between them only began in 1550, and he visited Michelangelo whenever he was in Rome. Vasari also knew Amilcare Anguissola. The Cremonese count was anxious to help and promote his artistic daughter in any way he could, and certainly by the mid 1550s her reputation had spread. Vasari writes in his *Vite* that in 1566 he went to visit the illustrious young painter, but by that time she had already been called to Philip's court in Spain, and he had to be content to visit Amilcare's other artistically talented daughters. It is plausible that Vasari's acquaintance with the Anguissola family dated back to the 1550s. He traveled extensively in artistic circles and kept his fingers, as it were, on the pulse of Italian art. Word did not always travel quickly, and even if he did know the family, he may not have known that Anguissola was in Spain when he visited them in 1566.

The other strong contender for the link between Anguissola and Michelangelo is Annibale Caro (1507–66). This noted Italian author—famous for writing more than one thousand letters, *Delle Lettere Famigliare,* with much grace, wit, and imagination—was appointed secretary in 1543 to Pier Luigi Farnese, duke of Parma and Piacenza and son of Pope Paul III, and later to Cardinal Alessandro Farnese from 1548 to 1563. Through his connections, Caro had become friendly with Michelangelo sometime around 1553.[32] Caro also knew Amilcare (and they corresponded with one another) and, naturally, he had heard about Amilcare's talented daughter. In a letter to Amilcare in 1558, Caro wrote that he desired nothing "more than a portrait from you by Sofonisba so that I could keep it together with one by her teacher [Campi]."[3] (See Chapter VI for the entire letter.)

Evidence from this letter suggests that Caro knew Amilcare prior to 1558, as he mentions seeing Amilcare "once again." He also states that he wants to visit the family "more leisurely," indicating at least one prior visit, which may have been quite short. That Caro knew Amilcare in 1558 and, at the same time, Michelangelo, indicates that he could have been instrumental in introducing them earlier.

Michelangelo may have been intrigued by the chance of meeting a woman artist perhaps, in part, because of his close friendship with the poetess Vittoria Colonna, whom he held in very high regard, and with whom he had been in correspondence since 1538.

For Sofonisba, meeting Michelangelo in about 1554 would have been an event filled with tremendous drama and excitement. After all, an introduction to *Il Divino* was one of the most sought after in the civilized world. Surely, that was not lost on Sofonisba who, no doubt, took great care in preparation for their first meeting. Amilcare's letter of 1557 specifically states that Michelangelo (prior to the letter) had talked to her and encouraged her.

The contrast between the aging seventy-nine-year-old Titan—still energetic and visionary—and the twenty-two-year-old aspiring painter must have been striking: he simply dressed (as he was always known to have been); she elegantly attired, as was befitting a nobleman's daughter. Michelangelo probably would have pointed out the difficulties that she would face. She may have been not only persuasive, but, more importantly, clearly a serious and determined artist. Over the next two years, Michelangelo continued to give her sketches to copy, probably pointing out ways to improve the preparation of her canvases and wood panels, the mixing of colors and pigments, and discussing aspects of anatomy and perspective.

Her studies with Michelangelo, although brief and informal, nevertheless had a major impact on Anguissola. Making the long and tiring journey back to Cremona she must have returned to her roots a changed person. Artistically, she had had the advantage of having Michelangelo's substantial guidance. She also had a taste of living in one of Europe's major cities. The new portraits she would paint after her stay in Rome reflected what she had absorbed.

PLATE 44. Sofonisba Anguissola. *Self-Portrait
at the Clavichord*, c. 1555–56. Oil on canvas,
22 1/4 x 18 7/8 in. (56.5 x 48 cm). Museo
Nazionale di Capodimonte, Naples.

V

EARLY PORTRAITS

Sofonisba is rendered eternal . . . by her illustrious fame.
—*Raffaelo Soprani*

By 1555, the year in which Anguissola probably returned to Cremona, her talent was beginning to be recognized by those outside her own circle. Over the next four years, she continued to paint her family and received her first portrait commissions. As a woman, she had taken an important step in overcoming enormous obstacles, the most difficult of which was that she lived in a culture in which men viewed women as weak and inferior. Even their words of praise worked to undercut her significance, because of her gender; and there were implicit biases in their writing, since they were products of a society that saw women as inadequate and capable only of being decorative objects. At best, they saw talented women in a class by themselves, that is, quite separate from other women. Male ambivalence was nothing new. A century before, in the context of discussions of learned women, this attitude abounded. Men were so perplexed that, if a woman achieved her potential, they attributed it either to "a male soul that had been born in one of female sex,"[1] or that learned women "belonged to a third amorphous sex."[2] Anguissola is frequently called a "marvel" by sixteenth- and seventeenth-century sources, just because this outlook so pervaded Renaissance thought. Despite all odds, she excelled in this all-male field, even though no well-known women artists had paved the way for her. She set the precedent.

Anguissola continued to do numerous self-portraits in addition to family or commissioned portraits of the clergy. She was unmarried and continued to sign her portraits "virgo" (an unmarried maiden), which was expected of her as a young noblewoman. By choosing to paint not only her own family but also others leading a spiritual and virtuous life, her own unusual status and motives could not be questioned. In Renaissance society, that was a subtle undercurrent, but present nonetheless. Her self-portraits—thirteen are known—continued to be an important part of her work during this decade. She painted more than any other artist between Dürer (who is recorded to have painted the first self-portrait) and Rembrandt. Two of her self-portraits show interesting artistic changes in her compositions: the first, now at the Kunsthistoriches Museum, Vienna, is signed and dated 1554 (see plate 43); the second, at the Capodimonte Museum, Naples, was done between 1555 and 1556 (see plate 44).

In Anguissola's 1554 *Self-Portrait,* she has chosen the same simple pose she used for her self-portrait sketch in the Uffizi Gallery (see plate 31), where her body is turned three-quarters of the way toward the viewer. Here again, she looks out at the viewer with her piercing, large dark eyes in a half-length portrait. Her gown is simply designed, with a small, standing gathered lace collar showing at the neck. Her sleeve, too, is edged with lace. On a page of the open book she holds is written: "Sofonisba Anguissola virgo se ipsam fecit 1554" (Sofonisba Anguissola, the unmarried maiden painted this herself, 1554).

The other portrait, incorrectly titled *Self-Portrait at the Spinet* (plate 44), is one of two known paintings in which the artist portrays herself at the clavichord (the other one, done in 1561, is in the collection of Earl Spencer, Althorp, England).

This is a more ambitious composition of the youthful Sofonisba. Once again she is turned toward the viewer in a three-quarter pose. Her reddish brown hair is styled a bit differently, with a large, twisted chignon crowning the back of her head. Her black velvet bodice has dark brown sleeves with a small, scalloped fullness at the shoulder. She wears a linen chemise with a ruffled edging in lace at the collar and cuffs. The clavichord is placed on a bright green velvet-covered table with a key nearby. Anguissola's characteristically "square-U"-shaped right hand and fingers are placed on the keyboard. This painting was poorly restored in 1959 and consequently, her left hand is now a chalky white and has completely lost its realism.[3]

There has been frequent confusion over the nomenclature of musical instruments from the sixteenth century, when both the clavichord and spinet were used. The terms have been used interchangeably, when, in fact, they should not have been.[4] This painting should be correctly titled, *Self-Portrait at the Clavichord.*

Adolfo Venturi, writing in 1933, stated that this portrait is in the tradition of Moroni:

> The self-portrait, in the Museum in Naples, shows the young Sofonisba where it calls to better attention her superficial but delicate pictorial qualities. Here, the image is also presented in action with the painter's hands, large, like those large hands of Campi's . . . as they touch the spinet's [*viz.,* clavichord's] keys. The thoughtful face is turned to the viewer. . . . There is something childish, youthful, in the round cheeks, in the delicate features, and the lightness of the hair. The shadows soften the flesh, undoing the antiquated stiffness, and signify a gentleness of spirit. The rough draft of Campi's influence, always superficial and weak, becomes polished in the grand portrait style of G. B. Moroni.[5]

Anguissola, in attempting this more ambitious design, may have taken on not only the polished style of Moroni but also some of his compositional elements. Giovanni Battista Moroni (c. 1525–78) was born in Albino, a small town near Bergamo, and spent most of his artistic life working in and around that city. Although Moroni did numerous mediocre religious paintings for local churches, his fame lies in his skill as a portrait painter, and he was one of the first to paint his sitters in full-length poses.

Moroni has not received the attention or recognition due him. Generally overlooked by scholars, his masterly portraits are, nonetheless, an important part of the evolution of sixteenth-century portraiture, and he is thought to have influenced both Titian and Van Dyck. Despite the compositional complexity he created by doing full-length portraits, he managed to paint them with vibrancy and sensitivity. His work received such acclaim that Titian recommended to the bourgeoisie in Bergamo that Moroni paint their portraits. He did so with superb skill. Whereas Titian's warm Venetian coloring has a predominance of reds, Moroni's palette—like that of his teacher, Moretto da Brescia (c. 1498–1554)—is one of subdued gray tones that reflect his provincial environment.

Moroni's eminence justly originates from his perceptivity and dexterity as a portraitist. Handling his sitters with equal aplomb—whether they were tailor, soldier, aristocrat, or gentlewoman—became his trademark. Each is treated with great feeling, rather than the usual stiff formality. In this approach, Moroni and Anguissola shared common ground, with each portraying their sitters in a new manner but not losing sight of their human qualities and individual characteristics.

As a contemporary of Anguissola, Moroni may have known her (although no documentation remains); she certainly knew his work and may have borrowed ideas from him. Moroni frequently used an architectural column as a backdrop for his sitters—a popular practice during the latter half of the sixteenth century—as can be seen in many of his portraits, including *Portrait of a Man* (National Gallery, London, see plate 45) and *Portrait of a Man* (Prado Museum, Madrid). It is conceivable that Anguissola borrowed this idea after seeing Moroni's full-length portraits, as she used columns in her *Portrait of Massimiliano Stampa* (Walters Art Gallery, Baltimore, see plate 61) and *Don Sebastian of Portugal* (Fundación Casa de Alba, Madrid, see plate 64). The column was also an emblematic device used by the Hapsburg rulers.

Interestingly, a painting that has long been known as Anguissola's work recently has been attributed to Moroni: *A Gentleman With His Two Children* (National Gallery of Ireland, Dublin, see plate 46) formerly had been titled *Amilcare Anguissola and His Children*. In this painting, the father is dressed elegantly in black with just a hint of white ruff and matching collar. The contrast to his two children, dressed in bright colors, is striking. On the left of the painting is a table with a letter on which is written the word "Albino"—Moroni's birthplace. It is now believed that this is a self-portrait of Moroni with his two children. The hands on both children and father are not in Anguissola's style. The face of this gentleman shows no resemblance to that of Amilcare's portrait with Minerva and Asdrubale, which Anguissola painted at the end of the decade (see plate 51).[6] Further, the stiffness of the pose of the two children is not in keeping with Anguissola's sensitive portrayals of young children.

While Anguissola continued to polish her own self-portraits, she also kept up with a series of family portraits during this decade that show her siblings growing up and her parents aging. Discoveries in Cremona, in 1983, have shown that the *Portrait of a Lady* and *Portrait of Asdrubale* (Museo Civico ala Ponzone, Cremona) were originally one single panel.

The bust-length *Portrait of a Lady* is an oil on panel (see plate 47).[7] Her hair is parted down the center with a braided coronet at the back of her head, covered by a jeweled veil—the faded remnants of which can still be seen falling over her shoulders. At her neck, she wears a wide, white linen ruff edged in *punto in aria* lace. The panel has darkened with age, and hence the details of her black, boned bodice have been obscured. There also appear to be remnants of letters—which may be Sofonisba's signature—in the upper left-hand corner.

Although Sofonisba painted her sisters, brother, and father, there has been no known surviving portrait of the artist's mother. (Vasari mentions a portrait of Bianca done by Europa when she was still quite young ["età puerile"] that was sent to Spain while Sofonisba was still there, but its current location is unknown.) This seems quite unusual in that Sofonisba used so many of her other family members as models. The woman does bear a striking resemblance to the Anguissola family, in her eyes, long nose, and shape of her ear. They are reminiscent of Sofonisba's features and coloring in several of her self-portraits. Based upon this and subsequent information discovered about the panel, her identity here is attributed to Bianca Ponzone Anguissola.

The other painting, *Portrait of Asdrubale Anguissola,* shows Sofonisba's brother at about four or five years of age (see plate 48). The coloring of his short-cropped hair is the same rust-brown seen in other members of the family. He wears a small, pleated ruff around his neck and a greenish gray silk chemise. A cape is draped over his left arm, and his right index finger is pointing to the right of the frame.

Closer examination revealed that the dark black-brown background is the same color in both portraits. Asdrubale's portrait shows evidence of retouching and/or restoration; his face has a chalk whitewash.[8] Further, the *Portrait of a Lady* has been cut at the bottom left portion, and a long rectangular wedge has been inserted. Viewed from the back, it is also evident that additional strips of wood have been added to meet the size requirements of the two gilt frames. Despite this, the fit is still inaccurate. Had they been, at one point, one entire panel? On the backs of both panels there are corresponding numbers: 298a and 298b. A search in the old inventories proved that these two numbers correspond to the Ponzone *1842 Inventory Catalogue,* which indicates that these two pictures originally had been one. In 1922, the Ponzone family donated these two works, along with others, to a new museum: the Museo Civico ala Ponzone. The museum is now housed in the Palazzo Affaitati, which was originally the Palazzo ala Ponzone (the family descended from Sofonisba's mother, Bianca, and after whom the museum is named). Therefore, sometime prior to 1922, when the new museum acquired these two portraits, but after the *1842 Inventory* listing, the painting had been cut apart and then placed in separate frames with ill-fitting wedges added. Why this was done is unknown. It is possible that there even might have been other missing parts to what may have been another family group portrait.

Without further documentation, it is difficult to identify a sitter absolutely across three and a half centuries. However, it seems likely that this is another in a series of Sofonisba's family portraits, which included her mother, at whom Asdrubale is pointing. It would make the most sense that a small child (in a closely knit family) would be quite likely to point to his mother. This then would make this the only known portrait of Sofonisba's mother. It also adds to the list of family portraits that Sofonis-

PLATE 43. Sofonisba Anguissola. *Self-Portrait*,
1554. Oil on panel, 6 11/16 x 43/32 in. (17
x 12 cm). Kunsthistoriches Museum, Vienna.

PLATE 45. Giovanni Battista Moroni. *Portrait of a Man*, National Gallery, London.

ba did, including *The Chess Game* and *Portrait of Amilcare, Minerva, and Asdrubale Anguissola* (Nivaagaard Art Collection, Niva, Denmark, see plate 51).

A dating of these two portraits is also possible. If Asdrubale was about five years old—as he appears in this portrait—and he was born in 1551, then these two portraits were done about 1556.

Single portraits were no longer as much of a challenge for Sofonisba as they had been earlier, and the next family painting that she did was a complex and ambitious project. The provenance of *The Chess Game* (Museum Narodowe, Poznan, Poland, see plate 49) dates back to Sofonisba's time. It has sometimes been referred to incorrectly as *The Artist and Her Sisters Playing Chess* or *Three Sisters Playing Chess*. The painting was seen by Vasari who describes it in his *Vite,* saying that it "portrays three of her sisters playing chess and also an old lady of the Anguissola household. It was done with such diligence and quickness that they all seemed truly alive and only lacking in speech,"[9] a phrase frequently used to convey the artist's skill.

Baldinucci also mentions seeing this painting, reiterating Vasari's words that the sisters "truly seemed alive."[10] When Baldinucci saw this painting sometime during the second half of the seventeenth century, it was in the Seneca Room in the Borghese

Palace, Rome.[11] At the turn of the twentieth century, Lulier mentions that "after belonging to Lucien Bonaparte, today [1902] it is in the Gallery Raczinski, Berlin."[12]

The outdoor scene with the three sisters around the chessboard, placed on an Oriental carpet, is set against a pastoral background.[13] Part of a meandering river is seen just behind the backdrop of trees in the center of the canvas. On the opposite side of the river bank, a small town can be seen, and further beyond it is a castle on a hilltop. Could it possibly be Sofonisba's interpretation of an idealized view of Cremona? Although the actual city is situated close to the left bank of the Po River, Cremona's countryside is flat, not hilly. It is possible that she placed the city's famous bell tower, Il Torrazzo, in the painting. In essence, Sofonisba may have incorporated elements of the real city into an otherwise fanciful creation.

This entire background is softly painted in the traditional blues and silver grays of northern Italian painters, giving it a *sfumato* effect (which is also seen in Anguissola's *Pietà* and *Portrait of Amilcare, Minerva, and Asdrubale Anguissola*) that contrasts nicely with the foreground. To achieve this, Sofonisba "probably used a white lead ground, possibly over a chalk layer."[14]

The identities of the three Anguissola sisters portrayed here have never been conclusively established. Although he describes the painting, Vasari never mentions the girls by name, nor does Baldinucci. In the twentieth century, the painting has been mentioned by several scholars but never in terms of Anguissola's technique, style, or the sisters' identities.

PLATE 46. Giovanni Battista Moroni. *A Gentleman with His Two Children*, National Gallery of Ireland, Dublin.

PLATE 48. Sofonisba Anguissola. *Portrait of Asdrubale Anguissola*, c. 1556. Oil on panel, 16 9/16 x 7/16 in. (42 x 31 cm). Museo Civico ala Ponzone, Cremona.

PLATE 47. Sofonisba Anguissola. *Portrait of a Lady* (Bianca Ponzone Anguissola), c. 1556. Oil on panel, 16 1/8 x 12 in. (41 x 33 cm). Museo Civico ala Ponzone, Cremona.

PLATE 49. Sofonisba Anguissola, *The Chess Game*, 1555. Oil on canvas, 27 9/16 x 37 in. (70 x 94 cm). Museum Narodowe, Poznan, Poland.

By process of elimination, Sofonisba and Elena can be excluded. (Elena was already in the convent in Mantua.) This leaves four of the sisters: Lucia, Minerva, Europa, and Anna Maria. Anna Maria can be eliminated, as Vasari describes her in 1566 as a little girl, and none of the sisters in this 1555 group portrait would still be young enough eleven years later. Thus, Lucia, Minerva, and Europa are left. Lucia, as the eldest (who would have then been in her teens), is on the left; Minerva is on the right, and Europa, the youngest, is in the middle.

The portraits of the three sisters have been done with great attention to the costume details. The manufacture of textiles and the magnificent embroidery of sixteenth-century costume usually are not mentioned in the study of portraiture, as most art historians are not familiar with the history or economic and artistic importance of textiles—including dating of paintings via costume styles. Silk velvets and silks were the preferred textiles for the nobility. Women (more often than men) were chosen for their talent in the needlearts. They were considered skilled craftspersons—just as painters were—and were guild members. It was a highly accomplished endeavor, requiring creativity, impeccable manual dexterity, and a sense of composition and color—all necessary gifts for any artist. Embroidery with silk and woolen threads, and silver and gold textile embellishment with jewels and pearls, was a fine art, and it can be considered "painting with a needle."

Most women who were employed by the nobility either worked at home—training from earliest childhood—or were attached to a nobleman's family (and paid through the household accounts). Perhaps if "women's worke" (as it was called in the sixteenth century) had been done in a *bottega,* it would have been valued equally with other art forms produced by men.

Sofonisba, as part of her earliest education, was trained in the needlearts, and she had an artistic eye for its beauty and importance. She incorporated her expertise in the rendering of costume detail into her paintings over the next half a century. *The Chess Game* is one of her earliest examples of the significance she attached to it.

Lucia, on the left, is wearing an elegant gown of what appears to be a rich crimson cut-velvet design with gold. Her sleeves are fitted with turned-back lace cuffs, and a scalloped edging is inserted as a decorative element in the sleeve cap. Over the velvet gown is an overgown in green, which is pulled to the center back, and this gives it an almost "bustle" appearance. Her linen chemise has a high collar edged in pleated lace, and three gold-rope chains are around her neck.[15] Lucia's hair is worn with the usual braided crown, in front of which is a gold, jeweled tiara edged with pearls.

Europa, in the center, wears her hair braided in the same style as her elder sister; and next to her braids she, too, wears a small jeweled-and-pearl tiara. Her chemise is a beautiful gathered linen decorated down the center-front panel with embroidery known as blackwork.[16] Here, the blackwork is done with smocking stitches to gather in the fullness of the chemise. The edges of the ruffled collar and cuffs are also done in blackwork. She is wearing a small, closely fitting carnelian necklace.

Minerva, playing chess on the right, is dressed in somber elegance, befitting an Italian nobleman's daughter. Her black velvet gown is decorated in gold (possibly embroidered) with a high scalloped collar underneath which can be seen the edge of an-

PLATE 50. Lorenzo Lotto. *Family Portrait* (Signore Zuane de la Volta, his wife, and their children), National Gallery, London.

other lace collar—which is part of her chemise worn underneath. Around her neck is a small pearl necklace from which hangs a jeweled pendant. Black scalloped sleeves repeat the pattern of the collar and are fitted to just above the elbow. Underneath are brown-and-gold velvet fitted sleeves edged with a white linen lace. She, too, wears her hair braided with another variation of the pearl and gold hairband, with jewels intertwined into her braids.

Characteristics of Sofonisba's style can be seen in this work. Lucia's left hand is done in a similar "square-U" that Anguissola rendered in her *Self-Portrait at the Clavichord* (see plate 44); and there is an intent gaze in her almond-shaped eyes. All three girls have rosy, youthful complexions done in tremendous contrast to the old woman's face. Simply dressed, as was proper to her position, the servant's face is depicted with great sensitivity, and Sofonisba's technique reflects Michelangelo's influence. A similar elderly face (which, in fact, may be the same person) also can be seen in Sofonisba's *Self-Portrait* in the Earl Spencer Collection, Althorp (see plate 82). The artist must have had a strong bond with this servant since servants, with rare exceptions, were never a part of sixteenth-century portraiture.

Across the bottom of the chessboard is the artist's signature: "SEPHONISBA ANGUSSOLA. VIRGO. AMILCARIS FILIA. EX VERA EFIGIE TRES SUAS SORORES. ET ANCILLAM PINXIT. MDLV" (Sophonisba Anguissola, the maiden daughter of Amilcare, painted this true likeness of her three sisters and a servant in 1555). Here, Sofonisba spells her name with a "ph," harking back to her Carthaginian namesake.

There is a disagreement as to the date. Venturi dates it at 1555[17] and Nicodemi dates it at 1560.[18] However, it appears that the last Roman numeral is a "V," thereby making the date 1555. In that year, Sofonisba was in Rome, although later in the year, she returned to Cremona. In 1560, however, she was already at King Philip's court. Undoubtedly, this was painted before she left for Spain, using both sketches and the physical presence of her sisters.

It is extremely doubtful that this is a self-portrait of the artist, at the left, as has been suggested. While there are facial similarities to Sofonisba's miniature *Self-Portrait* (see plate 33), the other self-portraits do not seem to have exactly the same facial features as this one. The eyes do not have the same large and sometimes "inflamed" quality seen in her self-portraits. Also, she always indicated when she was painting herself, and here she specifically says "three sisters" and not herself. Sofonisba was about twenty-three at the time she painted this, and the girl here, Lucia, is far younger.

With this painting Anguissola broke new artistic ground. The sisters are enjoying themselves and laughing—something never done in sixteenth-century portraiture. Individual and group portraiture was extremely formal. Emotions were absent. A case in point is Lorenzo Lotto's *Family Portrait* (National Gallery, London, see plate 50) of Signore Zuane de la Volta (Lotto's landlord), his wife, and their two children. In Lotto's signed work, there are similarities compositionally to *The Chess Game*: the family is gathered around a table covered with an Oriental rug; the luminous countryside is in the background.

Although Bernard Berenson, in his 1956 monograph on Lotto (1470–?1556), stated that he was "the first Italian painter who was sensitive to the varying states of the human soul"—calling Lotto a "psychological painter"—this family portrait is quite static and devoid of any psychological aspects.[19] Lotto's attempt at portraying the small child in a playful moment, results in a frozen, two-dimensional pose. The little girl, whose awkward hand is in the basket of cherries, is rendered without anatomical accuracy. Any psychological interaction or drama—even of a familial kind—is missing. Sofonisba, on the other hand, included the vivid psychological drama of the game—in which Minerva (on the right) is in check, and her hand is raised, as if to say, "Okay, Lucia, you've won." The playfulness of the children also contrasts sharply with the austerity of the servant looking on. Anguissola added to her composition the dimensions of warmth, vitality, and emotions that, heretofore, had not been attempted by her contemporaries. This painting is lively and informal, a slice of a moment of fun for the Anguissola sisters.

It was almost a century later that the Dutch and Flemish excelled at those daily, intimate moments that had not been depicted before—except by Anguissola. By 1640, the interest in these vignettes had become part of a new vocabulary in art: genre. Anguissola, because she did not have access to the usual avenues of artistic stud-

PLATE 51. Sofonisba Anguissola. *Portrait of Amilcare, Minerva, and
Asdrubale Anguissola*, c. 1557–58. Oil on canvas, 61 13/16 x 48 1/32 in.
(157 x 122 cm). Nivaagaards Malerisamling, Niva, Denmark.

PLATE 52. Sofonisba Anguissola. *Portrait of a Dominican Astronomer*, 1555. Oil on canvas. Formerly Caligaris Collection, Terzo d'Aquileja, current whereabouts unknown.

PLATE 53. Hans Holbein. *The French Ambassadors* (Jean de Denteville and Georges de Selve, Bishop of Lavour), 1533. National Gallery of Art, London.

PLATE 54. Lorenzo Lotto. *The Astronomer,* 1545. Formerly Van Dieman Galleries, New York, current whereabouts unknown.

ies, capitalized on what she did have, her family, and in so doing—as with many other painters who sought solutions to artistic problems—inadvertently pioneered a new style. In essence, she turned what may have been considered a sixteenth-century liability (in painting her family, rather than the accepted standard fare) into an artistic asset.

Anguissola continued on this new path during the latter half of the 1550s, when she painted another family portrait of her father, sister, and brother: *Portrait of Amilcare, Minerva, and Asdrubale Anguissola* (see plate 51*).* Although partially incomplete, it shows her artistic maturation. Vasari mentions seeing this portrait and cites the two children by name.

Amilcare is dressed rather simply in black with matching hose and shoes. Only a slight hint of white collar shows in his otherwise somber attire. Asdrubale is dressed in a rust-colored doublet, short pants (known as upper stocks), and matching hose and shoes. Minerva, on the left, stands in sharp contrast in her elegant blue silk gown. The bodice is heavily embroidered, and the rust and gold right sleeve is vividly painted to accent the gold work. The background drapery is pulled back to reveal another hilly countryside. Again, it is probable that this was painted at the Anguissola home, and the background may be an idealized version of Cremona; or, there may also be another possibility. There are what appear to be Roman ruins in the background. Anguissola surely would have sketched those ruins around Rome as assignments that Michelangelo may have given to her. She may have kept the sketches and then decided to incorporate them into this painting.

PLATE 55. Sofonisba Anguissola. *Portrait of a Dominican Monk*, 1556. Oil on canvas, 22 7/16 x 20 7/8 in. (57 x 53 cm). Pinacoteca Tosio Martinengo, Brescia.

PLATE 56. Sofonisba Anguissola. *Portrait of a Dominican Monk*, close-up showing Anguissola's signature and date.

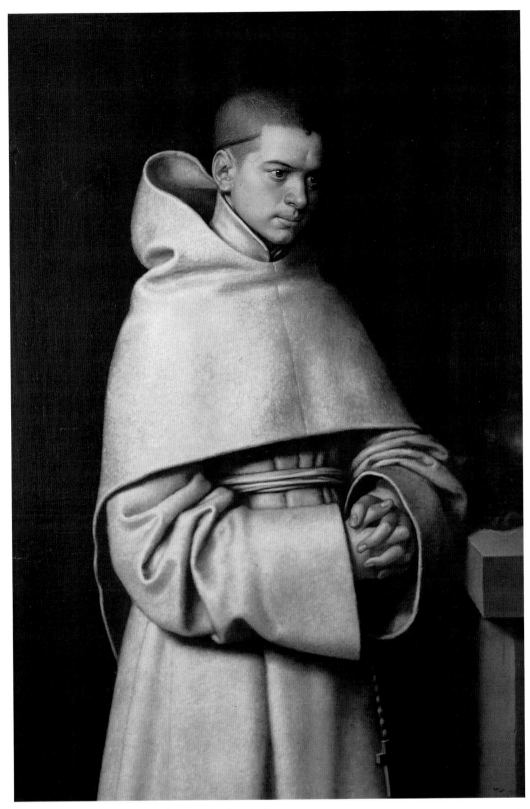

PLATE 57. Sofonisba Anguissola. *Portrait of a Monk,*
c. 1556. Oil on canvas, Private Collection, England.

It is the warmth and sensitivity of this composition that stand out. The aging Amilcare, portrayed here when he was about sixty-two, with his full-face gray beard, is depicted with his arm placed tenderly around his son. The caring and kindness is quite evident in his gentle face. Looking up at his father, Asdrubale has his right hand placed on top of his father's hand. The bond between father and his long-awaited son is portrayed with realism and tenderness. Minerva, looking on approvingly with a slight smile, clasps to her breast (with Sofonisba's typical "square-U" fingers) a small bouquet of flowers.

This painting was probably done c. 1557–58 and is the artist's only known work that is incomplete. Why it was not finished remains a mystery. Perhaps Sofonisba was finishing it at her father's request and became too busy with commissions. If this was done in her spare time, her professional career would have had precedence, and the painting would have remained incomplete when she departed for Spain. Obviously, Amilcare was still proud of his daughter's achievement, as it was on display in the house when Vasari saw it. Sofonisba is also known to have painted another portrait of her father, done earlier, about 1554–55. However, the painting's present location is unknown.

Anguissola also did several commissioned portraits of the clergy during this decade, including *Portrait of a Dominican Astronomer* (1555, formerly Caligaris Collection, Terzo d'Aquileja, current whereabouts unknown, see plate 52), *Portrait of a Dominican Monk* (1556, Pinacoteca Tosio Martinengo, Brescia, see plate 55), and *Portrait of a Monk* (c. 1556, Private Collection, England, see plate 57). In the former, she was following the sixteenth-century tradition of painting a sitter with the accoutrements of his profession, a custom that developed in northern Europe as the emerging bourgeoisie wanted to be memorialized. Hans Holbein's *The French Ambassadors,* 1553 (National Gallery, London, see plate 53), was one of the earliest examples of this new kind of secular painting. It is a tour de force in the artist's rendition of surfaces and accoutrements. Holbein traveled to northern Italy, and so his work was known there. In 1545 Lorenzo Lotto painted *The Astronomer* (formerly Van Dieman Galleries, New York, current whereabouts unknown, see plate 54), and it is possible that Anguissola saw copies of both these works during her studies with Campi, or later in Rome, where sketches might have been circulating.

Anguissola's composition has similarities to Lotto's: both are half-length poses with a globe held in the sitter's left hand, and both are portrayed behind a table spread with astronomical paraphernalia. Whereas, Lotto's portrait is somber, Anguissola has painted the bearded Dominican monk with a smile, again, something not usually done by sixteenth-century painters. He looks content in his chosen profession, with the solitude of prayer during the day—the crucifix is his constant reminder—and the tranquility of his research and the stars at night. She has captured him lost in his astronomical calculations, but in an instant when, momentarily, he has looked up. Has he, perhaps, just discovered something? Interestingly, Anguissola signed this work on the sheet of calculations and therefore had to turn the painting upside down to do so.

The other Dominican monk (possibly named Ippolito Chizzola) was painted the following year. Anguissola signed it in the lower right corner: "Sofonisba Anguissola virgo coram Amilcaris patre pinxit, MDLVI" (Sofonisba Anguissola, the maiden daughter of Amilcare, painted this in 1556, see plates 55, 56). It is conceivable that these two Dominican monks commissioned the portraits at the suggestion of Sofonisba's sister, Elena, who also belonged to the Dominican order. Although Elena was cloistered in the convent at San Vincenzo in Mantua, it is possible that word of Sofonisba reached other monasteries; or, these two monks may have been living at San Vincenzo.

During this time, Anguissola also painted *Portrait of a Monk* (Private Collection, England, see plate 57). Here she has portrayed another monk in three-quarter-length pose. Hands clasped—and rendered in a manner similar to that used in *Portrait of a Nun* (Portrait of Elena Anguissola, plate 30)—head slightly bowed, he appears deep in prayer. As with the artist's *Portrait of a Dominican Astronomer* (see plate 52), she has rendered this monk (whose identity is unknown) in a very sensitive fashion.

Vasari also mentions that Anguissola painted several other portraits of the clergy (but he does not go into detail), including a portrait of the archdeacon of a church in Piacenza, who also owned one of Anguissola's self-portraits. Although many of her paintings have disappeared, it is apparent from contemporary records that Anguissola was kept busy with numerous commissions.

By 1557, Anguissola's life must have fallen into some kind of routine in which she spent time living at home (and setting an artistic example for her four younger sisters) and also participating in family affairs. Periodically, however, she would travel to Piacenza, Mantua, or Milan when commissioned to do a portrait. It must have caused much gossip among the local nobility when a young noblewoman, dressed in fashionable brocades and silk embroidery, arrived with her chaperone and boxes of paint and canvas to do a portrait. When she was home, Amilcare probably gave her a spare room in the house as a permanent studio where she could continue to sketch and spend time teaching her younger sisters. Amilcare also continued to promote his daughter by publicizing her talents to the Cremonese nobility. Soprani states that "many Cremonese gentlemen wished to have her do their portraits."[20]

Lucia, the third Anguissola daughter, also showed a keen desire to paint, and so Sofonisba taught her. There was no longer any need to send Lucia to study with a master since her sister's talents were already acknowledged. Very little is known about Lucia's life. Again, no birth record remains, although her death (in her twenties) has been traditionally dated to 1565. The cause of her death, so young in life, is not known, but life expectancy during the sixteenth century was only about thirty. Early deaths were common both from the plague (which swept through Europe periodically) and other illnesses, including smallpox, malaria, typhus, tuberculosis, pleurisy, and typhoid, for which there were no cures.

Few of Lucia's paintings are known, but it is possible to identify some of them based upon stylistic grounds. As a student of Sofonisba, Lucia naturally assimilated her sister's techniques and style. Lucia also painted fingers with a "square-U." However, whereas Sofonisba's fingers are painted in a slender, delicate, and sometimes more angular manner, Lucia's are more pudgy, less angular.

Two of Lucia's paintings are signed and therefore can be used as benchmarks to distinguish her works from unsigned paintings by Anna Maria and Europa (Minerva devoted her time to writing). In the twentieth century, the few art historians who

PLATE 61. Sofonisba Anguissola. *Portrait of Massimiliano Stampa*,
third marchese of Soncino, 1557. Oil on canvas, 53 7/8 x 28 1/8 in.
(136.8 x 71.5 cm). Walters Art Gallery, Baltimore.

PLATE 64. Sofonisba Anguissola. *Portrait of Don Sebastian of Portugal*, 1572. Oil on canvas, 13/16 x 3/16 in. (2.08 x 1.05 cm). Fundación Casa de Alba, Madrid.

PLATE 58. Lucia Anguissola. *Dr. Pietro Maria*,
early 1560s. Prado Museum, Madrid.

have examined some Anguissola works have frequently attributed paintings first to
one sister and then to another. Unfortunately, the paintings are scattered throughout
Europe, making side-by-side identification and comparison impossible. Lucia signed
both the sensitive portrait of *Dr. Pietro Maria* (Prado Museum, Madrid, see plate 58)
and an oil-on-wood *Self-Portrait* (Civico Museo d'Arte Antica, Castello Sforzesco,
Milan, see plate 59). Another "signed" inscription, on the back of Lucia's *Self-Portrait*,
in the Borghese Gallery, Rome (see plate 60), is not written in a sixteenth-century
hand and the writing has been tampered with.

Vasari mentions seeing the portrait of *Dr. Pietro Maria* when he visited the Anguissola household in 1566, and by 1686 this work was part of the Spanish royal collection. Although no documents remain, it has been thought that this painting was of
Sofonisba's maternal grandfather (Bianca Ponzone's father). However, that does not
accord with the fact that Bianca's father was Count Ponzino Ponzone, and not Dr.
Pietro Maria. Why would the noble family name of Ponzone have been omitted, if
this is a portrait of the grandfather? The face, with its faint smile, is sensitively painted, and, as with many of Sofonisba's works, great attention has been paid to all the
costume details (now quite vivid since the painting was cleaned in 1976).

In Lucia's *Self-Portrait* she portrays herself seated and holding a book in her left
hand. Her right hand clasps the bodice of her gown. It is the Anguissola face, but here
the "square-U" fingers are thick, as they are in *Dr. Pietro Maria*. Based upon costume
details, this half-length signed self-portrait was probably done about 1557, when Lu-

98

cia was in her late teens or early twenties; *Dr. Pietro Maria* probably was executed in the early 1560s.

Another *Self-Portrait* (Borghese Gallery, Rome, see plate 60) with a very similar half-length pose, in which Lucia holds a gold necklace in her stocky left hand, shows a more mature face. This, too, was probably done in the early 1560s. The fingers in this painting are strikingly similar to those in the other two aforementioned portraits. Both self-portraits show a pronounced dimple in the chin (which is also noticeable in Lucia's portrait in *The Chess Game)*. This painting has been attributed to Sofonisba as her own self-portrait, but based upon the stylistic and compositional similarities to Lucia's two other signed works, it is here attributed to her.

Lucia's whereabouts in the 1550s are not documented—although she may have and is also noticeable in Lucia's portrait in *The Chess Game)*. This painting has been attributed to Sofonisba as her own self-portrait, but based upon the stylistic and compositional similarities to Lucia's two other signed works, it is here attributed to her. On some occasions, however, she may have accompanied Sofonisba when she traveled from Cremona on a commission, and such trips would have been part of Lucia's apprenticeship.

In 1557, about the same time that Sofonisba painted *Portrait of Amilcare, Minerva and Asdrubale Anguissola* (see plate 51), she was commissioned to do the full-length *Portrait of Massimiliano Stampa*, third marchese of Soncino (Walters Art Gallery, Balti-

PLATE 59. Lucia Anguissola. *Self-Portrait*, c. 1557. Civico Museo d'Arte Antica, Castello Sforzesco, Milan.

PLATE 60. Lucia Anguissola. *Self-Portrait*, early 1560s. Borghese Gallery, Rome.

PLATE 63. Sofonisba Anguissola. *Portrait of Three Children*. Oil on panel, 33 1/16 x 42 1/8 in. (84 x 107 cm). Lord Metheun Collection, Corsham Court, Wiltshire, England.

PLATE 65. Sofonisba Anguissola. *Portrait of an Old Man*, c. 1558–1565. Oil on canvas, 35 x 29 in. (88.9 x 73.6 cm). Burghley House, Stamford, Lincolnshire.

more, see plate 61).[21] Another version of this painting also exists at the Musée St. Denis, Reims (once attributed to Moroni).

Until recent conservation of the painting, it was believed that the subject might have been Asdrubale, who was almost the same age as the young marchese. The large Anguissola eyes also lent verisimilitude to his being Asdrubale. Discovery of an inscription on the back of the original canvas, however, now has established the marchese as the sitter: "Max. Sta. Mar. Son. III Aet. An.VIIII 1557" (Massimiliano Stampa, third marchese of Soncino, age nine, 1557). It is believed that the sitter's mother, Isabella Rangoni, commissioned the portrait shortly after the death of her husband, Ermete, the second marchese of Soncino, in 1557. Massimiliano, at nine, was invested as the third marchese on 22 July 1557.[22] The portrait may have been done to commemorate this event.

The somberness of the painting—muted colors, black costume, and a sleeping dog—are further evidence of the recent death of Massimiliano's father. The dog was also part of the Stampa heraldic arms. In his 1941 article, Charles de Tolnay thought this portrait was of Asdrubale and noted that the curled up, sleeping dog was similar to Albrecht Dürer's 1514 engraving *Melencolia I* (Patrick and Beatrice Haggerty Museum of Art, Marquette University, Milwaukee, see plate 62).

Massimiliano bears a striking resemblance to the boy in *Portrait of Three Children* (Lord Methuen Collection, Corsham Court, Wiltshire, England, see plate 63), who had been thought to be either Asdrubale with two of his sisters, or one of the Gaddi children (as this triple portrait came from the Gaddi Gallery in Florence). Sofonisba

PLATE 62. Albrecht Dürer. *Melencolia I*, 1514.
Patrick and Beatrice Haggerty Museum of
Art, Marquette University, Milwaukee, gift
of Mrs. Otto H. Falk.

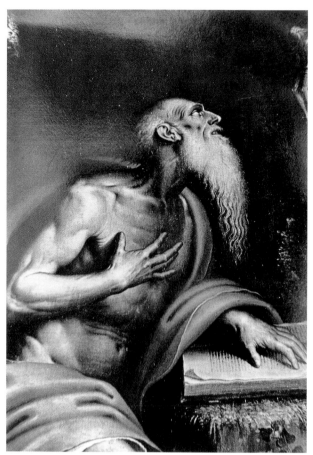

PLATE 66. Bernardino Campi. *Saint Jerome*,
1666. San Sigismondo, Cremona.

usually did not sign her name on the back of her canvases, where this newly discovered inscription regarding Massimiliano's identity was found.

The young marchese Massimiliano was wont—as had been his father—to spend a great deal of time at the family's palazzo in Milan (rather than in Soncino, which is in the province of Cremona). Still under his mother's care, he may have met Sofonisba Anguissola while she was in Milan, or through mutual aristocratic connections in Cremona. In any event, she would use this same pose—down to the positioning of the left hand—when she painted Don Sebastian, king of Portugal, in 1572 (see plate 64 and also the discussion in Chapter VIII).

Anguissola's use of "pictorial techniques was in the best tradition of sixteenth-century Venetian painters," according to Frank Redelius, an expert on Renaissance painting techniques.

> [Anguissola used] an umber-tinted transparent prime coat laid over an oil-based ground of white lead. Her choice of a moderately rough woven canvas and the well-scraped-on ground and prime coats lent (by preservation yet, nourishment of the weave) optical advantages to her paints and coloring. . . . Sofonisba's use of contrasting qualities of paint, that is, thick against thin, transparent against opaque, as well as ordi-

nary light and dark, enhanced the spatial effect of the subject within the pictorial atmosphere. This play between paint qualities is readily evidenced by the rather solid rendering of her transparentizing pictorial vehicle allowing, thereby, the umber-tinted transparent coat to show through.[23]

Redelius goes on to say that "any Venetian master would praise the effect of *sfumato* found in the rendering of soft contours, features, and silky hair of the sleeping dog. It must be noted, however, that Sofonisba did not employ as many glazes . . . as did many Venetians. . . . Nevertheless, she shows us through her masterful rendering of . . . clothing and accessories that she was well aware of how those glazes were used."[24]

Even though Anguissola no longer took art lessons from her first teacher, whom by now she had far surpassed, she continued to keep in touch with Campi and his wife. There is a sensitively done painting by Anguissola, known as *Portrait of an Old Man* (Burghley House, Stamford, Lincolnshire, England, see plate 65), that shows Anguissola's continuing connection to Campi.

This elderly gentleman, wearing a black cut-velvet robe with fur trim at the collar and cuffs, is seated facing the viewer. Through his long gray beard, one can detect a faint smile. His right hand is resting on the arm of the chair, while his left—showing Anguissola's typical "square-U"—is resting on an open book which is placed on a table draped with an Oriental rug. His hat rests to the left of the book.

The date of the painting most probably falls between 1558 and 1565, and most likely was done before Anguissola left for Spain. An interesting comparison can be made with this portrait and *Saint Jerome* (San Sigismondo, Cremona, see plate 66) done by Campi. Both Saint Jerome and the old man (whose identity is unknown) have their left hands placed on open books in a very similar fashion. Whether Anguissola's work came before Campi's, or his influenced hers is not known. In either case, one inspired the other's composition, and it is possible that the artists exchanged sketches with each another.

Campi's reputation had grown and his commissions often took him to Milan. On one of these trips, his illustrious student's capabilities may have been discussed. It is possible that through Campi's—or Amilcare's—contacts with the nobility Anguissola was invited to Milan. Her trip there was to be pivotal in her long career.

PLATE 70. Unknown Artist. *Sofonisba
Anguissola*, 1558. Bronze commemorative
medal. Diameter 3 3/8 in. (8.5 cm). Department of Coins and Medals, British Museum.

JOURNEY TO MILAN

In everyone's opinion, Sofonisba was the most valiant of all who painted.

—*Filippo Baldinucci*

ometime in 1558, Anguissola went to Milan. It is approximately seventy-five miles from Cremona to Milan, but the distance probably would have been greater on the winding, unpaved dirt roads, and the coach journey must have been arduous. Traveling by coach, perhaps with her sister Lucia, a chaperone, one or two servants, and oak chests known as *cassoni* (which were often used to store bridal linens and were elaborately carved and painted) filled with embroidered silk and velvet gowns, it presumably took the group more than a tiring week to arrive in Milan.

In Annibale Caro's letter to Amilcare, written at the end of the year, he laments having missed Sofonisba, for whom he had made a special trip to the Anguissola household.

> To Amilcare Anguissola in Cremona
>
> Passing through Cremona, I came solely to visit your house. However, I was not content in this visit alone just for friendship and conversation, but also to see all of its marvels. Consequently, before I leave Lombardy, I shall endeavor, at least once again, to see you and enjoy more leisurely the merits and virtues of your daughters, especially Lady Sofonisba. So far as I am concerned, this would gratify me, because I regard your esteem more than anyone else's. If you would be so kind and courteous, there is nothing I desire more than a portrait from you [by Sofonsiba] so, in the future, I would be able to show two marvelous works together: one by Sofonisba and the other by her teacher [Campi]. And this confirmation is what I hope to receive in your answer. Thanking you again for the kind consideration you have shown me. From Parma, this 23rd December 1558.[1]

Although Sofonisba's exact whereabouts at this time are not known, it is probable that she was already in Milan. It is conceivable that she went at Campi's request. He may have had more work than he could manage himself and, therefore, may have recommended her to some of his Milanese patrons.[2]

The political situation between Spain and France was to affect the next twenty years of Anguissola's life, and it coalesced in Milan; the two key figures were King Philip II of Spain and the duke of Alba. The duchy of Milan had been ruled by the Sforza family for generations, but when Francesco Sforza (b. 1495) died in 1535 without an heir, the duchy was incorporated into the imperial dominions of Charles V. Subsequently, Charles's son, Prince Philip, was created duke of Milan in 1554 (upon his second marriage, to England's Queen Mary).

Italy's political upheavals required Charles (with strong persuasion from Philip) to appoint Charles's most trusted general, Fernando Alvarez de Toledo, third duke of Alba, as commander-in-chief of all Spanish forces in Italy. His position also included total civil powers. In 1555, the duke of Alba was appointed viceroy of Naples and captain-general of Milan. At the same time, the Neapolitan Cardinal Pietro Carafa had just been elected pope, taking the name Paul IV. The pope was opposed to Spanish rule in Naples and wanted to free Italy from the Spanish Hapsburgs, whom he considered barbarians. Alba's threatening presence only sparked more hostility from the pope and his allies.

Charles's health had been deteriorating rapidly and, in 1556, weakened by gout and excessive eating, and prematurely aged, the emperor abdicated in favor of his son. Philip was created king of Spain and the Netherlands on 16 January 1556; the balance of the Holy Roman Empire went to Charles's brother, Ferdinand I.

Father and son were very different, and so Philip's long rule took quite another direction politically. Charles was born in Ghent, Flanders, traveled considerably, but remained a Northerner at heart; whereas Philip, born in Valladolid (a few miles from Castle Simancas, where the great Hapsburg archives were housed), was totally Spanish in his outlook, and viewed anyone who was not a Spaniard with suspicion. For many years, Philip's closest advisor was Alba.

The duke of Alba, born in the Spanish province of Avila in 1507, played a pivotal role in sixteenth-century Spanish and European history (see plate 67). The duke was a strange amalgam of diplomat and soldier (and he reveled in plans for fortifications). Although he received an aristocratic and exemplary education, it was not the customary background of a military leader; but it proved to be an invaluable tool in his many diplomatic missions for Philip. He was an unusual military leader, as he could speak and write several languages—Latin, French, and Italian—and was well versed in court etiquette, something that would hold him in good stead when Philip married Mary Tudor. Traveling to England in 1554, Alba played a large part in arranging the marriage, and he was one of the few Spaniards that the English respected. When Philip married his third wife, Elisabeth de Valois, Alba was Philip's proxy at the wedding in Paris in 1559. It was great credit to Alba that he was equally able to manage his vast troops—which often numbered more than thirty-eight thousand, without any common language and having questionable loyalties—as well as the intricacies of international politics.

Alba was a complex man, "authoritarian . . . and adept at intrigue."[3] He was ambitious, but more for the glory of the crown than for personal aggrandizement. Although he did gain significantly by serving Charles and Philip, he frequently would pay the imperial troops out of his own pocket when the king was in arrears. The king

PLATE 67. Alonso Sánchez Coello.
Portrait of Fernando Alvarez de Toledo,
third duke of Alba, 1567. Duke of Alba
Collection, Monterrey Palace,
Salamanca.

had the better part of the bargain. Excessively reserved, yet with a quick temper and
a sharp tongue nonetheless, Alba adhered to a strong personal code, and when many
"men of his age and class were either avowed lechers or the continual victims of scur-
rilous innuendo,"[4] the duke was a man who "was a model of fidelity" and had "truly
exceptional piety."[5]

In 1548, Charles V appointed Alba *mayordomo mayor,* which made him responsible for supervising court rituals, appointments, and discipline. Alba traveled with
Philip when he left for Italy that year in order to inspect the king's imperial dominions. It is conceivable that Alba was in Cremona when Philip stopped there, and he
may have met the Anguissola family at that time.

As part of the military responsibilities imposed on him by Philip, Alba was also
sent to Milan in 1555, leading his troops in skirmishes against the French; in 1556 he
was in Naples and Rome (threatening war with the pope). Due to the duke's peripatetic existence on Philip's behalf, Alba found himself in Milan at the same time that
Anguissola was there.

When she arrived in Milan, she may have stayed with the branch of her family

PLATE 68. Sofonisba Anguissola. *Self-Portrait*,
1558. Oil on panel, diameter 5 1/8" (13 cm).
Fondation Custodia, Collection F. Lugt,
Institut Néerlandais, Paris.

living there. Her reputation must have preceded her, and the family must have looked on their cousin with a mixture of skepticism and awe. However, pride must have superceded all other feelings when the duke of Alba commissioned her to do his portrait sometime in 1558.

Anguissola must have requested several sittings from the duke over the few months necessary for the portrait's completion, as mentioned by Nicodemi, De Soresina Vidoni, Zaist, and Lancetti. Inevitably, conversation must have ensued between them about her studies in Cremona, perhaps even the politics of Spanish rule in Milan—she even may have mentioned the completed *Portrait of Massimiliano Stampa*, the third marchese of Soncino (see plate 61). Anguissola no doubt talked about seeing Philip nine years before in Cremona, when the young prince was touring his territories. She also may have remembered meeting the duke—an imposing figure—at a banquet arranged for Philip by one of the Cremonese nobles. The duke, as Philip's *mayordomo*, was in charge of arranging Spanish participation in these festivities and seeing to it that the proper protocol was followed. Tactful, when the need arose, and fluent in Italian, he also may have made a signficant impression on the teenage noblewoman.

In 1988, a search of the current duke of Alba's archives, Palacio Liria in Madrid, did not turn up his ancestor's portrait, although several sixteenth-century portraits of Alba are still in the family's possession, including one by Alonso Sánchez Coello (see plate 67). On 24 December 1563, at Alba's request, one Sebastian Cuarteron, in the duke's employ, brought back twelve Italian paintings to the ducal residence in Madrid,[6] and although the paintings were not listed individually, it is very likely that Anguissola's portrait of the third duke was part of this collection. The location of the duke's portrait by Anguissola is currently unknown. Clearly he was pleased with her work because he commissioned her to do at least three more paintings, which are listed in the Fundación Casa de Alba archives. These, too, are lost.[7]

According to Baldinucci, after the duke's portrait was completed, Alba wrote to Philip in Spain, as he was impressed with this talented painter-noblewoman.[8] Philip then requested her presence at his court in Madrid. There also may have been another reason for the duke's suggestion that this unusual painter come to court.

It was during this same time that Anguissola did a *Self-Portrait,* known as the Ashburnham medallion (Fondation Custodia, Collection F. Lugt, Institut Néerlandais, Paris, see plate 68), which she signed and dated 1558. The bust-length portrait shows a somber but youthful—she was twenty-six—woman who may have painted this oval at the suggestion of the duke of Alba, so that he could send her portrait either to King Philip II or the king's bride-to-be, Elisabeth de Valois. Comparison of this small self-portrait, the one at Boston, and the Brera (Milan) show great consistency in the shape of Anguissola's face, right ear, and eyes—note the slight droop of the left eyelid.

Plans were underway at this time for Philip to marry a third time, as Queen Mary Tudor had recently died. When Philip left Spain in 1554 to travel to London to marry his cousin (Mary's mother, Catherine of Aragon—Henry VIII's first wife—was Charles V's aunt), he was reported to have said, "This is not a pleasure party that we go to, but a crusade."[9] England, under Mary's half-brother, Edward VI, had had a brief

PLATE 69. François Clouet. *Mary Stuart, Queen of Scots.* Sketch. Bibliothèque Nationale, Paris.

interlude with Protestantism. With Mary's accession, both she and Philip were anxious to bring the country back to Catholicism. Charles was also quite concerned, and wrote to Alba, saying, "Duke, for the love of God, see to it that my son behaves in the right manner; for otherwise, I tell you, I would rather never have taken this matter in hand at all."[10] Philip, at twenty-seven, was eleven years younger than his dour bride, who was a religious fanatic. The marriage lasted four years, with Philip visiting Mary twice. She was devoted to her young husband—then heir to the Spanish throne—but he did not share her feelings. He kept this tactfully to himself and always treated Mary with "the utmost courtesy and consideration, but that was all there was to it; so far as he was concerned, love never entered into the relationship at all."[11] Philip spent most of his time in Spain away from Mary, tending to his own political problems.

At the end of 1558, Philip lost both his wife and father within two months: Charles died in September and Mary on 17 November in the midst of peace negotiations between France and Spain (after the Battle of San Quentin and the capture of Calais by the French). The duke of Alba was one of the most important of the Spanish delegates appointed by Philip to explore a peace settlement.

After six months of difficult bargaining, a peace treaty was signed at Cateau-

Cambrésis in March 1559, with Alba dealing "almost single-handedly with the English ambassadors."[12] It was sealed by the ratification of a double marriage: Margaret, sister of France's King Henry II, was to marry the duke of Savoy; and Philip was to marry Elisabeth de Valois, daughter of Henry II and Catherine de' Medici (although originally it had been suggested that Don Carlos, Philip's fourteen-year-old son, marry Elisabeth). This treaty marked the end of conflict between France and the Hapsburg empire that had dated back to 1494, and peace was kept until the end of the century.

After the conclusion of the treaty, Alba went to Paris, where he stayed until August, partly to serve as a diplomatic hostage (to ensure that all prisoners were repatriated and fortresses were given back to their rightful owners) and also to arrange for Philip's marriage to Elisabeth and act as the king's proxy at the ceremony itself. Preparations were already under way when Alba arrived there. The agreement was signed on 21 June and the next day the proxy wedding took place amid great pomp and grandeur on the steps of the Cathedral of Nôtre Dame.

Princess Elisabeth, at thirteen a frail beauty resplendent in a myriad of jewels, was accompanied by her parents. The bride's train was held by the young Mary Stuart—Mary, Queen of Scots (see plate 69)—who was Elisabeth's closest childhood playmate (until 1553 they shared the same palace room) and confidante. At this proxy marriage, Alba stood in for Philip, wearing cloth of gold (instead of his usual somber black), until Elisabeth went to Spain several months later. Since "the young bride had not reached puberty, it was decided that she should not depart for the Spanish court until the autumn."[13]

Eight days later, amidst the wedding festivities and tournaments, tragedy struck the royal house of Valois: when Henry II was jousting in his daughter's honor, his opponent's lance pierced through his visor, mortally wounding him. Vesalius, the great Renaissance anatomist and physician, was called in immediately by Alba; but nothing could be done, and the king died on 10 July. The wedding celebration turned to funeral arrangements.

Gloom hung over the French court as Henry's sickly fifteen-year-old son became the new king, Francis II, along with his new sixteen-year-old bride, Mary Stuart. They just had been married two months before at Nôtre Dame on 24 April. Mary, who already was queen of Scotland, now also became queen of France. Francis was crowned on 18 September, and his sister (now Philip's new queen), Elisabeth, left for Spain on 25 November. It was a tearful leave-taking. Elisabeth, her mother, and Mary Queen of Scots were all overcome with grief upon Elisabeth's departure.

Queen Catherine finally permitted her child to depart, with grief so extreme that even the Spanish ambassador was moved by it. Mary, herself, was especially distraught at the prospect of the departure of her friend: she entrusted Elisabeth with a touching letter to King Philip from his new sister-in-law, saying that she could hardly bear to part with Elisabeth, were it not for the fact that she knew Elisabeth would be happy and content in her new life. Nevertheless, for Mary herself the loss would be irreparable. She ended the letter by begging the Spanish king to receive it 'as from the person who loves her [Elisabeth] the most in the world, and who wishes always to be —*Vôtre bien bonne soeur Marie.*'[14]

Over the next few months, Elisabeth's large entourage slowly made its way south to Guadalajara. Probably more than one hundred people—including ladies-in-waiting, dressmakers, embroiderers, cooks, servants, priests, and stable boys—accompanied the new queen and dozens of her *cassoni* filled with her household goods and personal possessions.

When Alba left Paris in August, he was acutely aware of how distraught the young queen was. Despite her new status, sheltered from political realities at the elegant and opulent French court, she was still a child. Still grieving for her father and now torn away from her mother and best friend, she was going to an unknown country to marry a thirty-two-year-old stranger as a pawn in the political marriage game.

Perhaps realizing that the queen needed a new friend, Alba may have thought of Sofonisba. Both would be strangers at court (and this might create an immediate bond), and the queen would need a court painter. What better choice than an aristocratic lady who could also share with the queen a love of art, elegant clothes, and music? Alba, already impressed with Sofonisba's qualities as a painter, shrewdly saw her other assets as well.

Sofonisba must have received this request to go to Spain with mixed feelings. It was a great honor to be invited to the court of the most powerful ruler in Europe. However, Spain was considerably further away than Rome or Milan. There may also have been financial considerations: although Sofonisba was earning money (and given jewels and expensive pieces of fabric, which were considered important mediums of exchange), all of it may have been going to Amilcare.

As an unmarried lady of twenty-seven, technically she still was in her father's care. This, then, required Amilcare to give his permission for his daughter to leave Italy. It also is possible that Sofonisba's sojourn to Spain under royal patronage would transfer financial responsibility to the king, thereby easing somewhat Amilcare's own financial concerns (with six unmarried daughters).

The Anguissola household must have been abuzz with excitement at the honor that the king was bestowing on Sofonisba and, therefore, on the family. In due course, Amilcare came to Milan to discuss this important decision with Sofonisba, and then he wrote to King Philip. His letters were discovered in 1988 in the Hapsburg archives at Castle Simancas and are printed here in their entirety for first time.

Sacred Royal Catholic Majesty

The duke of Sessa and Count Broccardo have asked me on your behalf to allow Sofonisba, my eldest child, to enter the services of her Serene Highness the Queen, your wife. As your devoted and obedient subject, I willingly have obeyed. However, at the same time, it was a great sorrow to me and my family, because of her virtues and dear behavior, to see this my beloved daughter go so far away. Yet, when I think of giving her in service to the most powerful Catholic and Christian King in the world, whose house is famed as a religious monastery, I am much consoled. I thank God to have allowed me the opportunity to serve you. I regret that my old age [65] and the responsibility of my other daughters are preventing me from coming with my daughter to pay you homage, as a good subject would wish to do. Wishing not be tedious to Your Majesty, I end this, kissing Your Majesty's feet and hands, praying together with my family to God for the growing happiness of your kingdom. From Milan, 6 September 1559.

Your humble, faithful servant and vassal,

Amilcare Anguissola[15]

Philip answered (although the letter has not been found), and Amilcare, back in Cremona, promptly responded:

Sacred Royal Catholic Majesty

A few days ago, the duke of Sessa and Count Broccardo told me of Your Majesty's wishes to have Sofonisba, my dearest daughter, serve her Most Serene Highness, our Queen. My paternal sorrow still is great because she is going so far away from me and my other daughters. Until now, in this my old age, I have been enjoying her rare virtues and company, which she acquired through her own efforts and study, as well as my religious diligence. Nevertheless, as a faithful subject, which I am, of both the late emperor [Charles V] and Your Majesty, I willingly give her with much affection to enter the Queen's service, being certain that she could not be placed in better service, than that of the well-known fame of Your Serene Highness which surpasses any other Christian prince or king. Owing to your outstanding qualities, I am greatly consoled so that this, in part, diminishes the sorrow which my family and I feel due to the departure of my dearest daughter. By this time, I would think that she should not be too far from Your Majesty who will know from her virtuous works the talent she has been given by God. I humbly supplicate Your Majesty to forgive my boldness in writing this letter and the other one, which will be delivered devotedly by Sofonisba to Your Royal Majesty. With humility, I kiss your honorable feet and virtuous hands, praying to God to give you a long and happy life.

From Cremona, 17 November 1559.

Your faithful subject and humble vassal,

Amilcare Anguissola[16]

According to Amilcare's letter, Sofonisba would be arriving shortly in Madrid. Elisabeth de Valois, having left Paris on 25 November for Guadalajara, would arrive in Spain soon after Sofonisba. Alba's timing for the queen's future companion could not have been better.

Venturi writes that, before she left Milan, Anguissola completed one other commission, a portrait of the duke of Sessa, Consalvo Ferdinando di Cordova, governor of Milan form 1558 to 1560 and again from 1563 to 1564. Pleased with the results, "he gave her four pieces of material embroidered in gold before she left for Spain."[17] The location of this portrait is not known.

It was approximately at this time that a commemorative medal was struck in Sofonisba's honor. The bronze medal, cast in two parts without a reverse, was discovered by this author in storage in the Department of Medals at the British Museum in 1953 (see plate 70). It has never been mentioned in any of the literature on Anguissola.

Medals had their origins in ancient Rome. Whereas coins were used as a monetary exchange, the medal or medallion did not have any fixed value. It was used for decorative and artistic purposes—usually to honor the military exploits of a ruler. By the Renaissance, they had developed into a distinct art form and were used as com-

113

memorative mementos to express the importance of a person's *virtù*.[18] Benvenuto Cellini (1500–71) and Leone Leoni (1505–90) were considered the two greatest exponents of this art form. Leoni also had a long career working at the Papal Mint in Milan from 1550 to 1590, and his son, Pompeo, worked for Philip at the Escorial.

Women's status at mid-century had not changed. In 1558, John Knox, the extremist Protestant evangelist, had published his *First Blast of the Trumpet Against the Monstrous Regiment of Women* (published against Philip's wife, Mary Tudor), wherein he wrote that women were "weak, frail, impatient, feeble and foolish creatures."[19] Further, he wrote, no women should hold any position of power, as it was "the subversion of good order, of all equity and justice."[20] Despite his four marriages, Philip also had a reputation for not liking women. Yet there must have been something sufficiently compelling for the most august ruler of the day to invite Anguissola to his court. That was more than ample reason for a bronze commemorative medal to be cast in Anguissola's honor.

This medal is unsigned, but it is conceivable that Leoni, who was working in Milan at the time, might have cast it.[21] Anguissola is portrayed in bronze with her face in profile, while the bodice of her gown is done in three-quarter view. She is wearing a gown similar to the one she wore in many of her early self-portraits. The total diameter of the medal is three and three-eighths inches, but the design itself is two and five-eighths inches. A Latin inscription around the edge says, "Sophonisba Angussola Amilcaris, Fil[ia]" (Sophonisba Anguissola, daughter of Amilcare).

Did Alba commission it? Did Amilcare commission it to commemorate the honor King Philip had bestowed upon his daughter? Even taking into account Amilcare's embellished letters to the king, it is obvious that he was very attached to his children—it is evident in the gentle facial expression portrayed in Sofonisba's unfinished painting with Minerva and Asdrubale. It definitely was not in keeping with the usual formal distance between parents and children in a sixteenth-century aristocratic family. Amilcare may have been shrewd, as has sometimes been said, but kindness and gentleness appear to have been the predominant aspects of his character. Whatever his motives may have been in promoting his daughter, it would have been fitting for Amilcare to commemorate the success of his daughter and honor of his family with a medal.

According to Amilcare's letter to Philip of 17 November, Sofonisba would be arriving in Spain shortly. On 26 August a document was drawn up through the Spanish Chancery arranging for a "payment of 1500 scudi to allow Sofonisba Anguissola to travel to Madrid."[22] After some weeks of packing oak chests filled with art supplies and gowns, she probably left Milan sometime in late September or early October, depending on the weather. By comparison, her other trips to Rome and Milan had been quite short. This would be a long and arduous one completed in several stages: Milan to Genoa; Genoa to Barcelona by ship; Barcelona to Madrid. Generally, long trips were done in the spring or summer when the dirt roads were dry. Fall or winter travel was extremely difficult due to the hazards of the weather when coach wheels could get stuck in the mud. If during any part of the journey the weather was inclement, the coaches—already loaded down with many *cassoni*—could slow down to less than ten miles per day. That Sofonisba did not wait until the warmer weather suggests some urgency. Her presence was needed to ease the trauma of the queen's arrival.

The first part of the journey, by coach from Milan to Genoa, was approximately eighty-five miles. Baldinucci (writing in the seventeenth century) states that Sofonisba was "accompanied by two gentlemen, two ladies, and a staff of six servants."[23] There was no mention of any of her sisters accompanying her. Depending upon the weather, it could have taken anywhere from one to two and a half weeks to arrive in Genoa. It was one of the great Italian seaports of the day and an important center of commerce. The "Genoese were the principal bankers of southern Europe and controlled the Spanish trade by controlling the monetary and credit system."[24] For Sofonisba, there was another interest in traveling to Genoa, as it was a major center for lace-making. Before embarking on her four-hundred-mile journey to Barcelona, she probably took time to purchase new lace to be starched into matching ruffs and cuff trimmings to decorate her linen chemises. Her interest probably was both personal and professional: she certainly would have wanted to see any new designs that could be incorporated into future portraits. When she was ready to leave, Sofonisba probably carried with her letters of safe passage from the duke and King Philip, which was customary for long trips. She was now embarking on a journey that would change her life.

PLATE 82. Sofonisba Anguissola. *Self-Portrait*,
1561. Oil on canvas, 32 11/16 x 25 5/8 in.
(83 x 65 cm). Earl Spencer Collection, Althorp.

JOURNEY TO SPAIN

The queen spends a great deal of time painting in which she takes great pleasure. Within a year, she will be as good a master as the one from whom she learned [Sofonisba] who is the best in the world.

—Madame de Vineux,
letter to Queen Catherine de' Medici

The long voyage across the Ligurian Sea to Barcelona must have been taxing for Anguissola and her entourage. The cabin in which she stayed was quite small—they were usually built without much headroom—with space for one or two beds, a *cassone*, small table, and chairs. She probably stayed below with her servant for a good portion of the trip and had her meals brought to her. The captain most likely discouraged her from wandering around: it was unsafe and improper for a woman to appear above deck. After they disembarked in Barcelona, there was still another three hundred twenty-five miles to travel to Madrid.

In the meantime, Philip's new wife, now known by her Spanish name, Isabel, was journeying south from Paris with her extensive retinue. While she was traveling through the snowdrifts of the Pyrenees to meet Philip, the king was making his way north to meet her in Guadalajara. The city belonged to the house of Mendoza, and Cardinal Mendoza (1508–66, Don Francisco, Cardinal Mendoza y Bobadilla, cardinal archbishop of Burgos) was one of the ranking noblemen at Philip's court. The king sent frequent dispatches, via his couriers, on each leg of Isabel's journey to make sure that his new bride was well treated and that court protocol was followed to his exacting specifications. On 31 January 1560, the young queen arrived in the bitter cold at the Mendoza palace and met her husband.

Catherine de' Medici had trained her docile and obedient daughter to do whatever was necessary for the benefit of France. Isabel, who had an excellent memory, had been drilled in all the somber intricacies of Spanish court etiquette. She was already being hailed as "Isabella of the Peace," a "princess perfect in everything."[1] Young, elegantly attired in the latest French gowns—which contrasted sharply with the perennial, solemn black of the Spanish court—she had been practicing her Spanish so that she and her husband would be able to converse with each other. When they first met, Philip (who, at thirty-two, was eighteen years older than his bride) greeted Isabel by saying, "What are you looking at? To see if I have any gray hairs?"[2] Her reply was a warm smile, and the ice was broken.

At the wedding, Cardinal Mendoza read the marriage service; and Philip, instead of his usual custom of wearing black, was attired in a suit of white silk—a color reserved for special occasions—embroidered with gold threads. The duke of Alba and the king's son, Don Carlos, were also in attendance. After the service, there were lavish festivities.

It has been thought that Anguissola met the king and queen in Madrid ("after several days rest," according to Baldinucci, she "was introduced to the queen"[3]), but Carl Justi, citing a sixteenth-century source, states that Anguissola was at the wedding party:

> This Frenchwoman [Isabel], the only one of his wives whom Philip is said to have loved, occasionally brought a freer, happier touch to life at court. On her wedding night, when the king had ordered the dancing of a galliard, and no one was bold enough to begin the dancing, Ferrante Gonzaga went over to Sofonisba [asking her gallantly to be his partner], and began the dance with her.[4]

The extravagant wedding preparations also included an unusual gift from the house of Mendoza. In the dead of winter, the Mendoza family had arranged to have a "grove of trees in full leaf and flower transplanted from a great distance."[5]

A few days later, the court traveled to Toledo. The new queen became ill (of an unknown ailment), and it was sufficiently serious to require a courier to be sent to France to inform Queen Catherine. She was a doting, over-protective, overbearing mother who kept up a prodigious international correspondence. When her favorite child was ill, she hung on every bit of news. Typical of her letters is the following:

To My Son, the Catholic King

Sire, my son, I received a letter from you last night by which I heard of the illness of the Queen, my daughter. And even though you are doing your best to assure me of her recovery, for which I cannot thank you affectionately enough, I am also aware of the honor you are conferring upon her by the care that you are taking for her health. In spite of all assurance that has been given to me, I cannot help but wanting more news, and it is because of this that I am sending you this [letter] by messenger to know that she is continuing to recuperate. After so much loss and unhappiness that I have had for the past year and a half, I am always in fear of seeing another [death], because she is the dearest thing that I have left to me. It is for this reason, Sire my son, that I implore you to do all that you can for her health, so that it would please you to give her back her health that you and I desire for her. I do not want to be so unhappy as to see more misfortune for you. I hope she would have the grace to live for you, to be agreeable and serve you, and to continue the friendship which exists between you as it will please God to keep her in this world.

Your good and affectionate mother,
Catherine[6]

After Isabel's recovery, the court arrived in Madrid on 6 February 1560. It was customary for rulers and their large staffs to travel frequently from one palace to another largely to make the royal presence felt throughout their realms, but also for the more mundane reason that the building had to be cleaned out, as there was no efficient sanitation system. These trips, euphemistically called "progresses," were not to Philip's liking, and this peripatetic existence was one of the reasons for the building of the Escorial, the king's greatest architectural monument and a place where he could stay on a more permanent basis.

Philip ruled over a court noted for its somberness and tedious adherence to court minutiae. The gloom that hung over his court was, in great part, a visual one. Whereas the French and Italian nobility wore costumes of vibrant hues—rust, gold, and burgundy—the accepted dress for a Spanish courtier was black. Philip's own personality added to the oppressiveness. He was a man thoroughly Hispanocentric, despite his brief travels to see his Hapsburg dominions and his brief marital stay in England. Dogmatic, secretive, and formal—he disliked familiarity, except with a few members of his family—the king involved himself in the smallest details of governing. With his vast empire (which also included the riches of the Americas), this methodical approach almost ground the government to a halt, although on occasion such cautiousness did work to Philip's political advantage. By 1560, "Philip's methods and character were well matured, and he began the regular routine of government which continued unbroken for almost the next forty years; he endeavored to rule the world from his desk, and although he never spared himself the task was beyond him, as it would have been beyond any man."[7]

Taciturn and withdrawn, Philip was not comfortable with women. His marriages (especially to Mary Tudor, which was a total failure) were political alliances, not affairs of the heart. That changed somewhat when he married Isabel. By the time the newlyweds had reached Madrid, court gossip had it that the king was a changed man, and they "noticed how much more gladly and sincerely he paid [Isabel] those same little attentions which he had forced so painfully on Mary Tudor."[8] With the arrival of the new queen, there was a noticeable difference at Philip's somber court. As much as the king was capable, he had grown to love Isabel and called her "the light of my eyes."[9]

She delighted in music and had been raised surrounded by some of the century's most beautiful art, to which she had been exposed throughout her childhood when the French court moved from one opulent palace to another: Fontainebleau, St. Germain, Blois, and Chambord. She had been painted frequently by François Clouet (c. 1516–72), who gave "an attractive impression of her lively face, full but slanting eyes, dimpled chin and large faun-like ears: she [had] an air not so much of beauty as enjoyment of life. . . . In girlhood she was a sweet-natured child . . . and also, according to the French chronicler Brantôme [Pierre de Bourdeilles, 1535–1614], was fond of poetry, music . . . and learning."[10]

How happy Isabel must have been to discover that Philip had brought an Italian noblewoman—a painter, no less—to the Spanish court. Their first meeting must have been formal, as required by court etiquette. Sofonisba would have undoubtedly curtsied and extended her condolences to the queen on the recent death of her father. It is quite probable that they shared one of the Romance languages in common, and so a translator was not needed. Thus, a bond must have formed immediately. They shared a love of art and they both played the clavichord. Amidst the austerity of the Spanish court, Sofonisba must have been a delightful relief to Isabel. Sofonisba, in turn, was no doubt overjoyed that the queen, despite her royal status, shared her interests.

From the beginning, the queen was interested in practicing sketching and painting. Cooped up during the cold winter months of 1560, the queen "renewed her enjoyment of art, and she brought from Paris the highest quality colored chalk pencils with her."[11] She asked Sofonisba to give her lessons. They spent countless hours together drawing, and it became a favorite topic of court gossip. In a letter dated 18 February 1561, Girolano Negri wrote to Duke Guglielmo Gonzaga, "The queen, who shows much ingenuity, has begun to paint, and Sofonisba, who is a great favorite of hers, says that she draws in naturalistic way in a fashion in which it appears that she knows well the person whom she is painting."[12] The queen, at that time, had just recuperated from a serious bout of smallpox and would have been happy to resume painting lessons.

Not only did Sofonisba give her lessons, but she also painted the queen and other members of the royal family, including Philip's sister (Juana), Don Carlos (his son), and the king himself. Federico Sacchi, writing in 1872, noted that Sofonisba painted at least three portraits of Queen Isabel (one lost in a seventeenth-century fire), and says further (citing a sixteenth-century source) that during her stay in Spain "Sofonisba painted many portraits in Toledo."[13] There were serious palace fires in 1604 and 1734 at the Alcázar and Palacio del Pardo (the king's hunting lodge near Madrid); five hundred paintings were destroyed in the 1734 fire, among them a number of Sofonisba's works.

Baldinucci mentions that "as partial payment for a portrait Anguissola did of the king, he assigned her a pension of 200 scudi which was available from the city of Milan."[14] On 1 July 1561, King Philip ordered her to be paid, and the senate of Milan arranged for her to receive this money from taxes on Cremonese wine. The money originally had been paid to Isabella Sforza, and upon her death reverted back to the Milanese treasury to which taxes from Cremona were sent.[15] Although the money was supposed to be paid to Anguissola, it was sent erratically from Cremonese customs. In 1563, Anguissola requested that the delayed payments (twelve hundred imperial lire) be sent to her.[16]

For centuries, historians have not delved into Anguissola's Spanish period. When she is mentioned in Spain, she is dismissed abruptly as merely the queen's lady in-waiting. Equally overlooked, yet important, was her highly unusual status at court. Formally, she was attached to the queen's household, which was separate and independent of King Philip's to which Alonso Sánchez Coello, (a Spanish contemporary of Anguissola and the king's painter) was attached. Indeed, it is in the archives at Castle Simancas—where Anguissola is not listed in any of the indices—that the queen's household accounts are found and documents relating to Anguissola were discovered by this author.

Anguissola was invited to Spain to be Isabel's court painter; however, her status as a noblewoman had precedence over that position, as artists did not rank very high in sixteenth-century society. Therefore, she was given the official title of lady-in-waiting (*dama*) to the queen, a position that could encompass both her noble status and also her responsibilities as court painter. Historians have ignored her perhaps because her title did not indicate her artistic duties. Lafuente-Ferrari, in his book on the Prado Museum, said "she was not a professional" (*que no fue propriamente un professional*).[17] Bonetti was not sure if she went to Spain as a "painter, or in the queen's service."[18] Baldinucci, although acknowledging her important paintings, demeaned her status and contributions by calling her a "young girl" (*una fanciulla*) when she was twenty-seven and at Philip's court. Even the queen's controller, Luis Sigonei, responsible for her majesty's household accounts, did not know how to list Anguissola. Sometimes she is listed along with the queen's French ladies-in-waiting (as was done in 1565, where she is listed as French); sometimes she is listed separately.

The queen's household, numbering in the hundreds, was in reality a small city, complete with all the layers of Spain's extremely stratified society: from the lowest stable boys and servants (both kitchen and household), tapestry makers, embroideresses, seamstresses, jewelers, doctors, musicians, *mayordomo,* and confessor, to the nobility. Court documents list fourteen Spanish and six foreign ladies-in-waiting.

On 24 September 1560, Anguissola was paid "wages"*(gages)* of 21,980 maravedis.[19] The following year, the queen's household accounts list payment of more than nine thousand reales to Anguissola and also a payment to her servant, Cesar Brunel, who was paid forty-six-and-a-half reales.[20] Even after the queen's death in 1568, Anguissola continued to be paid from the queen's household accounts. Frequently, a court painter might be paid in jewels in addition to money. In Anguissola's case, she was paid in expensive pieces of fabric as well. Sixteenth-century textiles—silks, brocades, and silk velvets embroidered with pure gold and silver threads—were so lavishly made that often they were considered as good as money.

Anguissola's attention to costume detail was both artistic and fashion-oriented. She and the queen loved the beautiful Italian textiles that were imported into Spain. Together, they planned the designs of new gowns, looking at many bolts of fabric, and shopping for material. When the queen was too busy, she entrusted Anguissola to choose fabric for royal gowns at the market in Madrid (when Bernardin Viscarreto, the proprietor of the fabric shop, did not bring samples to court for the queen's approval). Discovered in Castle Simancas, the queen's household account lists the following:

> Bernardin Viscarreto will give Sofonisba Anguissola 300 escudos of silk cloth or whatever merchandise she may want which the queen . . . orders to be given to her in exchange for a piece of silver fabric with blue silk that her Majesty took, to be given to the Lady Sofonisba in payment for the said piece of silver cloth. This order of 300 ducats in merchandise was given to her [Sofonisba]. Madrid, 21 July 1561.
>
> Bernardin Viscarreto[21]

In the fall of 1561, Anguissola was in correspondence with Pope Pius IV (1499–1565, pontificate, 1559–65, Giannangelo de' Medici, but he was not related to the Florentine Medici):

PLATE 71. Sofonisba Anguissola. *Portrait of Queen Isabel de Valois*, c. 1561. Oil on canvas, 17 3/4 x 14 1/2 in. (45 x 37 cm). Pinacoteca de Brera, Milan.

Holy Father,

I have learned from your Nuncio [Alonso Crivello] that you desire a portrait of my royal mistress by my hand. I consider it a singular favor to be allowed to serve your Holiness, and I asked Her Majesty's permission, which was readily granted, seeing the paternal affection which your Holiness displays to her. I have taken the opportunity of sending it by this knight. It will be a great pleasure to me if I have gratified you Holiness's wish, but I must add that, if the brush could represent the beauties of the queen's soul to your eyes, they would be marvelous. However, I have used the utmost diligence to present what art can show, to tell your Holiness the truth. And so I humbly kiss your most holy feet. Madrid, 16 September 1561.

Your Holiness's most humble servant,
Sofonisba Anguissola[22]

Two weeks after Anguissola wrote this letter, Claude de Vauperge, Madame de Vineux, in a letter to Catherine de' Medici, wrote that Sofonisba "has just done a painting of the queen . . . which resembles her more than the one I had already seen. I think, madame, that another one will be comissioned for you and sent to you. I strongly desire this for the pleasure you will receive from it."[23]

Vasari goes on to say that the pope, upon receiving the queen's portrait, sent her gifts[24] and the following letter:

PLATE 72. François Clouet. *Portrait of Elisabeth de Valois*, c. 1558–59. Toledo Museum of Art, Toledo, Ohio.

Pius Papa IV. Dilecto in Christo filia.

We have received the portrait of our dear daughter, the Queen of Spain, which you have sent. It has given us the utmost satisfaction both for the person represented, whom we love like a father for the piety and good qualities of her mind, and because it is well and diligently executed by your hand. We thank you and assure you that we shall treasure it among our choicest possessions, and commend your marvelous talent which is the least among your numerous qualities. And so we send you our benediction. May God save you. Rome 15 October 1561.[25]

The queen's portrait had not been documented in over four hundred years. In 1988, this author discovered a portrait of Queen Isabel in the Pinacoteca di Brera, Milan, which may well be the one Anguissola did for the pope (see plate 71). The portrait was in storage at the museum and was erroneously listed as a seventeeth-century Flemish *Portrait of a Woman*,[26] but clearly the costume is neither seventeenth-century nor Flemish. Further, the queen's face is immediately recognizable.

In the oil on canvas, bust-length portrait of the queen, her cheeks are pink with a soft brownish peach outline around her face, reminiscent in coloring of many of Anguissola's self-portraits. Her face is portrayed with great warmth, sensitivity, and just the slightest suggestion of a smile. However, the bust-length portrait does lack Anguissola's recognizable "square-U" hands.

123

PLATE 73. Sofonisba Anguissola. *Portrait of Queen Isabel de Valois,* 1561. Oil on canvas, 26 3/4 x 21 1/4 in. (68 x 54 cm). Kunsthistoriches Museum, Vienna.

There is careful attention to the smallest detail of the gold embroidery on the bodice of the queen's gown and on the jeweled collar (called a *carcanet*). The intricacies of the lace ruff are done with the paint applied thickly in a raised manner (known as *impasto)* to give the illusion of depth. Based upon the youthfulness of the queen's face (she was about fifteen or sixteen) and the details of her gown (including the small ruff which was popular at the time), as well as comparison with other known portraits of Isabel, this portrait was probably done about 1561, when Anguissola was in correspondence with the pope. It is here attributed to Anguissola, and the Brera supports this attribution.

Anguissola's painting appears to be based upon an earlier portrait of the queen (Toledo Museum of Art, Toledo, Ohio, see plate 72) by François Clouet probably done just before her departure for Spain and perhaps commissioned by Catherine de' Medici. There are some variations between the two portraits. The Toledo rendition is slightly longer (hence there are more details in the bodice and sleeves); and Isabel is not wearing any earrings. The Brera portrait concentrates on the queen's face, and here she wears a gold earring. Her jeweled headdress is different in each portrait. The bodice of Isabel's gown is exactly the same in both portraits: apparently the queen brought this gown to Spain. Isabel had an extensive wardrobe, and it would not have been in keeping with her station to wear one gown too often. However, she would have wanted to be painted in the latest fashion just before she left Paris, and then show it off in Spain. Even in the sixteenth century, the French were leaders in fashion. The

124

PLATE 74. Sofonisba Anguissola. *Portrait of Queen Isabel de Valois*, 1563–65. Oil on panel, 46 7/8 x 33 1/16 in. (119 x 84 cm). Prado Museum, Madrid.

Brera portrait shows a slightly more mature face—the queen would have been a year or two older—and thus supports this dating of about 1561.

Several weeks after Anguissola received the pope's letter, she "answered a letter from Bernardino Campi in which he asked her to send him a portrait of the king done by her own hand."[27] The reply, which follows, shows the warmth and esteem in which she still held her teacher:

> My Very Magnificent Signore Bernardino,
>
> A few days ago, I had a letter from you which was very dear to let me know about your health and that of your wife, whom I love like a sister. I have written [other letters] to you but have never received any answer, except this one which was given to me by a gentleman of the Secchi family. About the portrait of the king that you requested, I cannot help you as I would like, because I do not have any portrait of His Majesty. At the present time, I am busy doing a portrait of her Serene Highness, the King's sister [Juana], for the Pope. Just a few days ago, I sent him [the pope] the portrait of our Serene Highness, the Queen. Therefore, my dearest teacher, Signore Bernardino, you see how busy I am painting. The Queen wants a great part of my time in order for me to paint her portrait, and she does not have enough patience for me to paint [others], so that she is not deprived of my working for her. Despite this problem, I would like to mention, as I have on other occasions, that I will not do any less than my ability in this portrait. And with this, I recommend myself to you and kiss your hand and that of your dearest wife, whom I love, and your mother, Signora Barbara, your sister, Signora Francesca, and your father, Signor Pietro.
>
> From Madrid, 21 October 1561.[28]

The location of Anguissola's portrait of Juana, the king's sister, is not known. There are, however, two other significant portraits of Isabel by Anguissola, one in the Kunsthistoriches Museum, Vienna, and the other in the Prado Museum, Madrid. Anguissola's half-length portrait of the queen (erroneously called Isabel Clara Eugenia, the queen's daughter, who had not yet been born) in Vienna is signed and dated 1561 (see plate 73). Unfortunately, the painting is in extremely poor condition, and it is hard to distinguish what is later restoration from original work.

The Prado three-quarter-length portrait of Queen Isabel (see plate 74) is currently attributed to Alonso Sánchez Coello, and in the past to his disciple, Pantoja de la Cruz. In fact, Pantoja was only ten when this portrait of Isabel was painted, and his work is associated more with the reign of Philip III.[29]

Coello was born in 1531/32 at Benifairó del Valls, near Valencia, but he was of Portuguese extraction. He was educated first in Portugal at his grandfather's home (after whom he was named); and he also may have studied for a brief time in Italy. By 1550, he was living in Madrid and later that year went to study with Antonio Moro in Flanders.

Moro, also known as Anthonius Mor van Dashorst (c. 1516–c. 1575/77), was a court painter for Philip and also the founder of a school of "cold objective portraiture that produced aristocratic and distinguished effects by the use of greys."[30] His background color was a somber gray with a tinge of green.

After he had done an apprenticeship under the well-known Utrecht artist Jan

PLATE 75. Antonio Moro. *Portrait of Queen Mary Tudor*. Prado Museum, Madrid.

van Scorel, Moro traveled briefly to Rome in about 1547. The exact date is not known, and it is possible that the trip to Italy may have been made earlier. Later in 1547, it is thought that Moro was in Antwerp, where he became a master of the guild. In 1548, he is recorded as having been paid for work commissioned by Philip of Spain. Later that year, Moro was working in Brussels for Antoine Perrenot de Granville, bishop of Arras, where he saw numerous portraits by Titian. However, unlike Titian, Moro's works "are linear, strongly modelled, and very life-like, showing a Nordic miniaturist's delight in precision and detail of skin, drapery, and jewels."[31] It was through Moro's connection with Granville that the painter came to Philip's attention. Moro's court portraits are an important historical documentary of the Hapsburg family and illustrative of the accepted angular and sometimes elongated distortions of anatomy and perspective—known as "Northern realism"—that were incorporated into portraiture and became the accepted "accurate" norm.

Moro is well known for his austere portrait of Philip's second wife, *Portrait of Queen Mary Tudor* (Prado Museum, Madrid, see plate 75). While Coello was studying with Moro, he also spent time copying some of Titian's works. From Moro, Coello learned precision in representation, and from Titian he incorporated Venetian gold tones, generous workmanship, and the use of light on a canvas.[32] When Moro came under suspicion for having Protestant sympathies in Catholic Spain and abruptly left the country in 1561 (most probably to escape the tortures of the Inquisition, although he was in good standing with the king), Coello succeeded him at Philip's court.

PLATE 76. Sofonisba Anguissola/ (?) Alonso Sánchez Coello.
Portrait of King Philip II, c. 1570. Oil on canvas, 72 1/2 x 41 in.
(184.15 x 104.14 cm). National Gallery, London.

By 1555, when Anguissola was in Rome, Coello was working for Philip in Castile. The king enjoyed watching Coello paint and treated him well. Coello later married Louisa Reynaltes in either 1560 or 1561 in Valladolid (Philip's birthplace), and they had seven children—Philip was godfather to two of them. Coello's daughter, Isabel (1564–1612, and most likely named after the queen), studied with her father and became a painter. Very little is known about her life or her works, some of which were collaborative projects with her father, whom she helped in his studio. It seems conceivable that Anguissola's example at court paved the way for Isabel's talent to bear artistic fruit.[33]

There has not been any biography written on Coello, and many of his works are still confused with those of Anguissola and Pantoja. To complicate matters further, King Philip III "ordered Pantoja [de la Cruz] to restore some [of the paintings destroyed in the 1604 fire] and to paint thirty-five new ones, most of them after the mutilated versions by Sánchez Coello."[34]

In 1915, a portrait of the king was attributed by C. J. Holmes to Anguissola.[35] The full-length painting (in storage at the National Gallery, London, see plate 76) shows the king sporting a graying beard and moustache and elegantly dressed in gilt-edged steel armor with a burgundy ribbon around his neck from which hangs a pendant of the Order of the Golden Fleece (the king's order of knights). Underneath his armor, he wears a small white ruff at the neck and wrists. His left hand rests on a tall ostrich-plumed helmet placed on a table covered with a burgundy-colored cloth. The king holds a baton in his right hand. He also wears short slops (breeches or short pants, sometimes made in two parts) and white silk hose. The background of the painting is a very dark brown. This pose may have been copied from an earlier portrait of Philip done by Titian about 1549.

Prior to 1915, this portrait of the king had been attributed to Alonso Sánchez Coello. Holmes dated this painting c. 1570 and attributed it to Anguissola, in part because of the shape of the king's ear, saying that it was "clearly not Spanish, but Italian, and at first view . . . [of] the coarse canvas, and perhaps some memory of Titian in the pose and in the key of rich crimson, white and black, it seemed reasonable to connect it with some painter from the Venetian territory . . . and [its] North Italian regions."[36]

In 1969 Sir Roy Strong, a noted English Renaissance art historian, wrote that Holmes's attribution was incorrect, and stated that "one would incline back to believe that the picture was basically Spanish . . . and definitely connected with the full-length Coello at Berlin."[37]

In fact, this portrait of King Philip shows elements of both Spanish and Italian portraiture. The coloring is Italian (Coello's backgrounds at times were dark greenish gray), while the austerity and awkward pose of the king's left hand are more in line with Spanish painting. The shape of the king's hands and fingers are not characteristic of Anguissola, but resemble both those on a signed and dated (1577) portrait by Coello, of the king's six-year-old son, Don Fernando (Monasterio de las Descalzas Reales, Madrid, see plate 77) and another full-length portrait of the king, also by Coello in the Prado Museum. However, the coloring of the king's head is more in keeping with Anguissola's. It seems clear from the historical record that Coello was employed by the court as a copyist for some of Anguissola's works. In 1564, he was

PLATE 77. Alonso Sánchez Coello. *Portrait of Don Fernando*, 1577. Monasterio de las Descalzas Reales, Madrid.

paid to complete a portrait of Queen Isabel of which Anguissola had painted the head; and in 1568, he painted six copies of Anguissola's original portrait of the king's son, Don Carlos.[38] It is evident that Anguissola's work—especially the realism and facial expression—was valued and esteemed by the Spanish royal family, but if a work was needed quickly, assistants helped out with parts of the background. This collaboration was in keeping with sixteenth-century workshop tradition where the "master" painted key elements—facial features and/or the body—while assitants did the background. It is, then, possible that this portrait of King Philip, which has both Spanish and Italian elements, was a collaborative effort of Coello and Anguissola.

The issue of collaborative paintings and/or assistants also raises the question of whether Anguissola had a regular assistant. She did not have a workshop, as did Coello. So, it seems likely that—in addition to all her other responsibilities at court—she did much of the preparatory work of stretching and priming her own canvases, tasks that would normally be assigned to an assistant. It is conceivable that Isabel Sánchez Coello may have assisted Anguissola in the 1570s in addition to helping her father in his workshop.

This confusion between Coello's, Pantoja's, and Anguissola's works is still present in two recent international exhibitions: the 1988 *Armada* exhibit (Prado Museum, Madrid, and the National Maritime Museum, Greenwich) and the 1990 *Alonso Sánchez Coello and Portraiture at the Court of Philip II* exhibit (Prado Museum, Madrid). Both included in their catalogues a portrait of Philip II done about 1575 (Prado

PLATE 79. Alonso Sánchez Coello. *Portrait of Queen Anne of Austria*, c. 1575. Prado Museum, Madrid.

PLATE 78. Alonso Sánchez Coello. *Portrait of King Philip II*, c. 1575. Prado Museum, Madrid.

PLATE 80. Pantoja de la Cruz. *Portrait of Isabella Clara Eugenia*, c. 1599. Alte Pinakothek, Munich.

Museum, Madrid, see plate 78) that they incorrectly and inexplicably attribute to Anguissola. Based on the shape of Philip's rounded hands and facial coloring (neither of which is mentioned in these catalogues), this attribution seems quite unlikely. The companion portrait to Philip's, a painting of Anne of Austria (c. 1575; Prado Museum, Madrid, see plate 79), is also given to Anguissola in these catalogues. Although it would be a happy coincidence if two more portraits by Anguissola had been found again, the style of the queen's pudgy, round hands and her facial coloring make this attribution insupportable.

On the other hand, *Portrait of Queen Isabel de Valois* in the Prado, although listed in 1988 by the museum as the work of Coello and in the 1990 Coello exhibition catalogue as Pantoja's copy of Anguissola's work, is most arguably by Anguissola (see plate 74). This is a fairly detailed painting both in costume and background. Painted against a light-to-darker olive green-gray (with slight tinges of yellow background), the queen is set against a gold and rust-colored velvet tapestry with fringe, which goes the length of the canvas on the right. Her right hand is placed on a wooden chair decorated with an orange-red and gold tapestry edged with an interwoven fringe.

Over her curly brown hair, Queen Isabel is wearing a small velvet cap, which has a small brim trimmed with pearls. It is also decorated with a series of slanted, alternating rows of three and four pearls finished with sapphires, rubies, and feathers. Un-

PLATE 81. Sofonisba Anguissola. *Portrait of Don Carlos*,
c. 1560. Oil on canvas, 42 15/16 x 34 3/16 in.
(109 x 95 cm). Prado Museum, Madrid.

derneath, she wears a jeweled *coif* (a piece of linen or lace that follows the shape of the head and is worn underneath a hat) with a jeweled brooch from which is dangling a pear-shaped pearl. In her left ear, the hoop of a gold earring is visible, but the rest of it is obscured by a large lace ruff, edged in gold.

Isabel's fitted bodice and bell-shaped farthingale are black, but they are set off by an undersleeve of red and gold. The *carcanet* matches the jeweled girdle with alternating settings of gold with sapphires and four pearls. The queen also wears a double-strand pearl necklace. The jewels down the center front of the bodice match the alternating rubies and sapphires going diagonally from the shoulder to the waist.

The sleeve cap has the customary padded "roll," and there are three sleeves: a black velvet outer sleeve, opening at the elbow and decorated with *puntas*[39] (jeweled points, traditionally seen only in Spanish costume) made of red satin bows and red and gold vermeille; and a red satin undersleeve slashed to show a third undersleeve of white linen or silk. It is in this decorative costume detail that Isabel showed her French fashion flair. The Spanish court may have required black, but the queen—as a product of Renaissance Paris—added dashes of vibrant color to mitigate its austerity.

Based upon the style of the costume, the painting was done about 1563–65, after Anguissola completed the portrait now in the Pinacoteca di Brera in which the queen appears younger. Anguissola was at the height of her artistic powers when she painted this. All the attention to costume detail was Anguissola's trademark, in addition to the "square-U" positioning of the queen's left hand and left index finger, and the light brown coloring that outlines her face. Coello, who became Philip's court painter in 1571, did not paint hands in this manner. In fact, portraits done by Coello after Anguissola left Spain indicate that she influenced him, as some of his works show an awkward attempt to copy her "square-U" delineation. Pantoja's works—even his copies—show that his understanding of anatomy was weak. The hands and fingers have an unwieldy, almost geometric, angular shape (as exemplified in his portrait of Isabella Clara Eugenia, 1599, Alte Pinakothek, Munich, see plate 80). The flesh-tone coloring of the queen's hands and face are also Anguissola's and show a warmth, a vibrancy that Pantoja was incapable of duplicating. It is possible that this painting of the queen is the same one that was listed in the *1564 Inventory* from the Pardo Palace (and now kept in the Prado Museum), which lists a portrait of the queen by Anguissola.

There is also a portrait in the Prado of the king's son, Don Carlos, attributed by the museum to Coello (and ironically the cover portrait for the 1990 Coello catalogue), which in fact, also appears to be by Anguissola (see plate 81). The three-quarter-length portrait, according to the Prado catalogue, may have been cut off at the knees sometime during the last century.[40]

Set against a dark olive gray background—a color frequently used by many mid-century artists—the prince wears a black velvet cap, tilted to the viewer's left. Around the brim is a gold braid alternating with jewels and ostrich feathers, one white, the other yellow. His hair is cropped short. His eyes are grayish green. Both little fingers on his left and right hands have a distinct "square-U" shape, and are almost identical in shape to those of the *Portrait of Knight* (Accademia Carrara, Bergamo, see plate 104). His complexion is painted in Anguissola's tones, rather than the sallow ones associated with Coello. The painting has been cleaned recently, and through the window (in the upper left-hand corner) one can now see a scene filled with allegorical allusions: Jupiter and an eagle flying through the sky, the eagle holding a column—a Hapsburg emblem—in its talons. Here the column may have referred to his position as heir to the throne and the continuing power of the Hapsburg family.

The velvet doublet that Don Carlos wears has a high collar with a small ruff edged in gold with a matching pair of cuffs. The small buttonholes are embroidered. He is wearing matching rust-colored slops with a satin fabric showing through the wide velvet strips. The black velvet cape discreetly hides the prince's spinal scoliosis; it is edged at the bottom with a band of red velvet, which has a tiny horizontal stripe of reddish gold. It is lined with lynx fur. Baldinucci specifically mentions a painting by Anguissola that fits the description of this portrait, saying that Don Carlos was "dressed in a suit of lynx fur, for which Anguissola received a diamond worth 1,500 scudi."[41]

Don Carlos (1546–68) was one of those tragic historical figures about whom much has been written, but whose real personality and life lie buried. His mother (Philip's first wife, Mary of Portugal) died a few days after he was born. He was placed under the care of his aunt, Juana (Philip's sister), during his formative years, "and she seems to have had regard for her nephew's bodily health at the expense of the formation of his character."[42] Being heir apparent to the Spanish throne would have grave consequences later in his brief life.

Philip did not see his son very much; the boy grew up obstinate, with a streak of cruelty and a vicious temper. In 1561, perhaps shortly after Anguissola painted this portrait, Philip sent him to the University of Alcalá. In the following year, he fell down a flight of stairs and fractured his skull. He probably suffered brain damage because his behavior became even more aberrant after the accident.

In January 1568 Philip had his son placed under house arrest, in a locked room, on the pretext that Don Carlos's prior request to leave Spain for Germany might create a civil war in the Low Countries, with the Catholic heir apparent siding with the Protestants. On 24 July 1568, at twenty-three, Don Carlos died under mysterious circumstances. Philip "was ultimately a party to his son's death,"[43] although all the details may never be known.

Although Isabel became Don Carlos's new stepmother in 1561, she may have been more like a sister because they were the same age, both having been born in 1546 (she on April 13, he on July 8). She was gentle and kind in a way that he had never known growing up with his Aunt Juana. He had his own apartments in the palace, but he spent much time with the queen. She was very pleased with the portraits that Anguissola had painted and most likely as a result, the prince sat for Anguissola's sympathetic portrait, which was done prior to 1562, when he had his accident.

The Spanish court was constantly on the move. It wearied Philip, who began thinking in terms of a more permanent royal residence. Sometime around 1560, Philip decided that he would keep a promise to build a mausoleum for his father (who was buried at Yuste) and his descendants. The building would also proclaim his devotion to Catholicism on a grand scale. After winning the Battle of St. Quentin on St. Lawrence's Day (10 August 1557), the king vowed that he would erect a building in the shape of the gridiron on which St. Lawrence had been martyred. The king also wanted to incorporate some other aspects into the building, including elements of the ancient Temple of Solomon which was arousing much interest at this time.

In 1561, Madrid became the official Spanish capital, and on 23 April 1563, the first gray granite stone was laid for the monastery of the Escorial, about thirty miles outside of Madrid. Escorial literally means "slag heap," named for the gray granite stones, quarried in Spain, that were used in its construction. San Lorenzo el Real de El Escorial, its full name, was part monastery and church, part palace, college, and library. It was an architectural tribute to King Philip.

The architect chosen for the project was Juan Bautista de Toledo, a Spaniard who had worked as an assistant to Michelangelo at St. Peter's from 1546 to 1548. Toledo died in 1567 before much of the building had been started, and the task of completion finally fell to Juan de Herrera (1530–97), who had been a courtier in Philip's entourage in 1548 when the latter traveled to Italy. "The new architect fortunately soon proved to be the equal of his predecessor"[44] and won Philip's confidence. For the first time in Spain's history, the royal family would have a fixed abode. The complex was completed in 1584. The record time in which it was completed indicates Philip's total commitment—especially financial—to this project. Philip wrote to Herrera, saying that he wanted a building with "simplicity of form, severity in the whole, nobility without arrogance, majesty without ostentation."[45] The austerity of this enormous complex matched that of the king. Yet, there is no doubt that Philip's Italian travels had an enormous impact on his artistic tastes, and he sought to incorporate his own concept of Italian architectural design into the Escorial.

Philip withdrew to become involved in all the details of running Spain as well as planning (both architecturally and artistically) this monumental architectural compound. Anguissola was at court throughout all the stages of planning and most of the construction.

Although the king originally invited Anguissola to his court as the queen's painter and companion, his initial skepticism at having a woman court painter, more noble companion than painter, surely changed (as it had after Titian painted his first portrait of Philip) when he saw the caliber of her work. A shrewd judge of the arts, he commissioned more court portraits than are now extant. Artists became an important part of portraying "functional and political"[46] portraits of the king and queen.

> The wide spread of the state portrait during the sixteenth century . . . is explained by its functions. Not only did it represent rulers, where in public buildings their portraits were needed, but it aided foreign princes and princesses in the choice of a spouse, gave advance notice to one already selected, or was dispatched to the far-flung dynastic relatives with whom such courtesies were customarily exchanged.[47]

Anguissola was a vital key both in doing royal portraits to be kept for personal enjoyment at Philip's palaces as well as in the dissemination of Italian portraiture at court along with Titian, who had been painting the Hapsburgs since the days of Charles V, a great admirer of his work. Titian, however, never lived at court. "He was far too busy at home, in fact, overwhelmed by commissions."[48] Charles placed Titian

PLATE 83. Sofonisba Anguissola. *Self-Portrait*,
c. 1561. Oil on canvas 14 3/16 x 11 7/16 in.
(36 x 29 cm). Pinacoteca di Brera, Milan.

on a lifetime pension, "but the artist received not a penny until 1558, subsequent to the emperor's death."[49] Philip then ordered Titian be paid two thousand scudi.

> A detailed study of Renaissance patronage of artists in relation to the recompense received from the great families would certainly yield astonishing results. Titian himself has often been accused of avarice, without consideration of the fact that popes and rulers did not always pay artists or architects or even their mercenary troops. The soldiers, in consequence, normally sacked the cities through which they marched. The Hapsburgs, unable to pay their debts, were in a state of constant bankruptcy. . . . Nevertheless, that situation did not convince them of any need to limit their expenditures.[50]

Anguissola was fortunate to have a position at court that took care of her living expenses, paid her amply in gold, textiles, and jewels. It was a far better lot than even that of Michelangelo, who, despite his own financial problems, refused payment for his work on the Sistine Chapel, saying that he could not take money for working for the glory of God. He struggled all his life and was in debt frequently because the popes and Medici family were always in arrears to him.

At Philip's request, Spanish court portraiture in the 1560s was formal. If Anguissola's paintings during this time do not show the same warmth and informality as those of her family portraits, it was because she was adhering to the king's wishes and was also in a severe and ceremonious environment. Then, too, royalty was perceived in the sixteenth century in somewhat godlike terms: living icons who, in all their majestic splendor, did not show emotions. Nonetheless, there are still exquisite costume details and subtleties to be seen in Anguissola's portraits: a faint smile or sympathetic portrayal of a disturbed personality. It was a tribute both to Anguissola's artistic gifts and her personality that she remained at the Spanish Court for twenty years.

In 1561, Anguissola found time to paint a self-portrait (Earl Spencer Collection, Althorp, see plate 82). It is still possible to discern the somewhat obliterated signature and date. This was the second portrait that she did seated at the clavichord, and Sir William Stirling-Maxwell (writing in his 1891 book, *Annals of the Artists of Spain*) called it "no mean gem amongst the treasures of the galleries . . . at Althorp."[51] Her aged servant, off to the left of the canvas, (who must have had a strong bond with Sofonisba) is portrayed with warmth and sensitivity, as she was in *The Chess Game*.

Anguissola's large, luminous eyes stare out hauntingly at the viewer. In many of her self-portraits, her eyes are pink, puffy, and sometimes without eyelashes. This may indicate the presence, even at this date, of the ophthalmic problems that Van Dyck would describe after visiting Anguissola when she was in her nineties. Ophthalmologist Milton Lincoff has looked at numerous enlargements of Anguissola's self-portraits and said that the way she painted her eyes shows great anatomical accuracy. According to Dr. Lincoff, Anguissola possibly was suffering from blepharitis, an inflammation of the eyelids, in her teens and twenties. It could have been due to granulated eyelids, which in severe cases can cause eyelashes to fall out, or possibly some kind of allergy. Despite what appear to be large eyes, they are still "within the normal range of eye size."[52]

The bulging of the eye closest to the viewer seen in many of her self-portraits (including those at Boston and Paris) is due to the distortion of having viewed herself in a mirror. It is quite conspicuous in the beautiful bust-length *Self-Portrait* (Pinacoteca di Brera, Milan, see plate 83) which also dates from this time. Anguissola painted herself turned in a three-quarter pose toward the viewer. Her complexion has a soft peach tone and her left eye appears pink and inflamed. Her hair is worn in its usual fashion and is decorated with jewels interspersed in a braided crown.

The bodice of Anguissola's black velvet gown is embellished with silver "purl" embroidery, and a double strand gold necklace is visible. The V-shaped neckline of her raised collar is wired invisibly and is trimmed with what appears to be white fur (possibly ermine). The chemise she wears underneath her bodice is richly embroidered, and the two tassels are tied at her neck. The painting is known to have been signed: "[S]ophonisba [Angu]issola [Am]ilcaris filia [?]MLXI" (Sofonisba, daughter of Amilcare…[illegible]…1561). However, none of this is now visible. Since Sofonisba found time in her busy schedule to paint two self-portraits in the same year, it is likely that they were done either as gifts or possibly as commissions (to spread the word of her talent to other European courts).

Anguissola's court routine was a busy one: painting and playing music with the queen—who ordered a new clavichord sent from Paris in 1564—and teaching her royal pupil, as well as the regular court functions that she was required to attend as the queen's lady-in-waiting. She found time, however, to write to her family, sending the letters via the regular couriers going to Milan.

Sometime in 1565, Sofonisba must have received news that her sister Lucia had died, although no document has been found. All the sisters were close, and the death of one so young must have been a blow to Sofonisba. Death at an early age was a frequent occurrence in the sixteenth century. Queen Isabel would have understood the loss and consoled her friend, and it is most likely that she would have allowed Sofonisba time away from the court rituals.

In May, plans were underway for the court to travel to Bayonne. Catherine de' Medici had planned a conference between Philip and herself to discuss the problems that both Catholic leaders feared from the rising tide of Protestantism. The king did not go himself and sent Alba as his representative. The duke of Alba was also put in charge of the arrangements and traveled there ahead of the court. The conference also gave Catherine an opportunity to embrace her daughter, whom she had not seen in almost six years. Isabel also could visit with her brother, now King Charles IX (1551–74), at a reception planned in his honor. The spring weather made traveling easier for both the long French and Spanish caravans.

From 1564 to 1566, Catherine and her son went on a royal progress throughout France, so that the fourteen-year-old king could see his own estates and the country over which he ruled. His sickly brother, Francis II, had died at sixteen, in 1560, leaving his wife, Mary, Queen of Scots, a young widow. Charles became king at nine, in name, if not in deed. Catherine de' Medici was regent for her son from 1560 to 1563, and after that continued to wield a great deal of power.

In Bayonne, Isabel, her mother, and her brother would be together for festivities and feasting. It was a happy time when they met on 14 June. Sofonisba, along with the other ladies-in-waiting, had new gowns made for the special occasion. After the muted colors of the Spanish court, the queen, her French ladies-in-waiting, and

Sofonisba must have been delighted to see the new fashions. The French court, ever on the move, was elaborate and elegant. Catherine's heritage, both her Florentine Medici background and her marriage to Henry II, enabled her to draw to the French court the best from both worlds.

On 28 June, during the festivities in Bayonne, there was an evening performance of Giangiorgio Trissino's (1478–1550) play "Sophonisba" given for the court. The tragedy, which was based on the Carthaginian heroine's life during the Punic Wars, had originally been written by Trissino between 1514 and 1515, but it was not actually performed until 1556. It was then adapted into a comedy by Mellin de St. Gelais for the French court. It seems quite probable that this performance was planned, in part, because of Sofonisba's presence in the queen's retinue.

Nothing was accomplished politically at the conference, but courtesies were observed, and everything went smoothly thanks to the efforts of the duke of Alba. Isabel had an opportunity to see her family: it was the last time she would do so.

The following year, on 12 August 1566, Queen Isabel gave birth to her first child. The royal couple had been married for seven years, and Philip hid his dismay when the queen gave birth to a girl. Their daughter, Isabella Clara Eugenia, was to become her father's favorite child and, as an adult, a capable administrator of the Netherlands. The queen was quite ill after her daughter's birth, and the Spanish doctors bled her, only aggravating her already weakened condition. Miraculously, she survived.

On 25 August, the child was baptized in the church of Valsaín Palace (known as "The Wood in Segovia" in the northern Sierra de Guadarrama). The cardinal of Rossano, Juan Bautista Catteneo (the nuncio of Pope Pius IV), presided over the ceremonies, and the infanta was named after her grandmother, the Empress Isabella (wife of Charles V). Don Juan of Austria (1547–78, Philip's illegitimate half brother), and Philip's sister, Juana, acted as godparents. Philip was not present but, for some unknown reason, watched secretly from behind one of the windows of the chapel. Sofonisba was present at the baptism and later was made the child's governess. A bond was to develop between the painter and the infanta that lasted into the next century.

In September there was an outbreak of the plague at Valsaín. Philip had left for Madrid at the end of August and came down with a high fever, but recovered. Among those who were still at Valsaín were the queen, her retinue, the infanta and her new household, and the duke of Alba. The duke also came down with a serious fever; but by October he, too, was well again.

Queen Isabel gave birth to a second daughter fourteen months later, on 10 October 1567. Four days later, the queen was ill with a fever, and for a while her life hung in the balance. On 19 October the new infanta was baptized Catalina (after her maternal grandmother) Micaela. The queen convalesced in Madrid after the infanta's birth but had periodic bouts of ill health which lasted until her death the following year.

In February 1568, the queen's health improved somewhat, and she resumed her usual round of music and court games with her ladies-in-waiting. By May, she left Madrid for Aranjuez; and the next month Sofonisba painted a portrait of Queen Isabel to send to her mother in France. Unfortunately, the location of this last painting of the queen is unknown.

On 1 July the queen had a serious migraine attack that lasted several days. Don Carlos had been found dead (on 24 June), and the queen had been close to him before he was placed under house arrest. She was distressed about his death, and perhaps that triggered her migraine in her weakened state. From then on, her health slowly deteriorated. On 16 September 1568, Isabel had a severe attack of nephritis.[53] The duchess of Alba, who had precedence over all the other ladies at court, wrote to Catherine de' Medici, giving her all the details of the queen's illness. The pain in the queen's side persisted, and the doctors applied ointments, but the renal complications grew worse. For five days she seemed better, and then she received a letter from her mother saying that Charles IX was critically ill. Isabel read the letter about her brother's illness and "spent the day crying."[54]

By the beginning of October, the queen was dying. She was lucid and put her affairs into order, adding a codicil to her will, which she had drawn up on 27 June 1566 (prior to Isabella Clara Eugenia's birth). Sofonisba was mentioned in the will: the queen left her three thousand ducats and a piece of brocade. She stayed with the queen throughout the long illness. The final blow came when the queen had a miscarriage on 3 October and died at noon. She was twenty-three.

Queen Isabel was much beloved by everyone, and the court went into deep mourning. The king, who had always controlled his emotions, wept; no courtier had ever seen him so upset.

> No matter how well-born or privileged, wives risked death in childbirth. A study of the . . . aristocracy from 1588–1641 estimated that a wife's chances of dying early were double those of her husband. About twenty-five percent of the wives who died before the age of fifty died in childbirth from its complications. The history of the royal houses of Europe . . . are filled with the deaths of princesses and queens in childbirth. . . . Everything about childbirth assumed such importance because a wife's inability to produce children, especially a son, had serious consequences for a . . . royal dynasty.[55]

Within the span of a few months Philip had lost both his son and third wife. It left the Hapsburg dynasty without a male heir.

Isabel had left two infants to the care of others. Philip had withdrawn to pray and become even more of a recluse. In England, Mary, Queen of Scots, now a prisoner of Elizabeth I, was the last person to receive the news of her childhood friend's death. She wrote to King Philip saying, "in the midst of all my own adversities, I have received another blow . . . the death of the Queen, your wife, my good sister . . . who was so good and virtuous."[56]

Over the next few months, the queen's household slowly dispersed; the French ladies-in-waiting and staff returned to Paris. Sofonisba stayed in Madrid, apparently at the king's request. Documents show that she was still being paid in 1569. She had grown attached to the Infanta Isabella Clara Eugenia, now her closest link to the queen. Without family or children of her own, the little two-year-old infanta must have been a comfort to the thirty-five-year-old painter.

PLATE 91. Sofonisba Anguissola. *Portrait of Husband and Wife*, c. 1570–71. Oil on canvas, 28 5/16 x 25 5/8 in. (72 x 65 cm). Galleria Doria Pamphili, Rome.

THE 1570s IN SPAIN

The king gave her in marriage to a noble and rich
Sicilian cavalier named Don Fabrizio de Moncada.

—*Filippo Baldinucci*

Now that King Philip was a widower for a third time, he began to look again for a wife to give him a much-needed male heir. In 1570 Philip chose his niece, Anne of Austria (1549–80), to fill that role. Her father, Emperor Maximilian II (1527–76), had married Philip's eldest sister, Maria (1528–1603). The king was forty-two and the new queen, twenty-one. The wedding took place in Segovia on 12 November 1570.

Queen Anne "was a plain girl with a good complexion, gentle, kind, dull, and as devout as Philip himself. She cared for gaiety no more than he; she was prepared to love him as an uncle as well as a husband; she grew fond of Isabel's two little girls; she took naturally to the formal, rigid, tiring etiquette of this most ceremonious of all courts, and she was of such a piously retiring temperament that the French ambassador [Pierre de Séguesson, seigneur de Longlée] reported: 'She never leaves her rooms, and her court is like a nunnery.'"[1]

To celebrate their marriage, the king and queen had their portraits done. Sánchez Coello was commissioned to paint Philip (Glasgow Museums and Art Galleries, Glasgow, see plate 84) in a three-quarter-length pose.[2] The king is wearing a black splintered suit of armor with gold damascene work and a gold-link chain through which is threaded a maroon silk scarf. A gold pendant of the Order of the Golden Fleece is hanging from the chain. He wears a white lace ruff at the collar and wrists; this portrait shows Philip with a receding hairline, his moustache and neatly trimmed beard turning gray. The background has a column to the left (that is devoid of any dimensionality) and is painted in Coello's usual olive gray tones.

The queen's portrait (Glasgow Museums and Art Galleries, Glasgow, see plate 85) is almost the same size as that of the king. She is dressed in what was probably a black velvet gown with elbow-length bell-shaped sleeves decorated at the edge with "purl" embroidery done in silver with a pair of gold and silver *puntas* tied with a silver satin bow. Another matching *punta* can be seen just below her left hand (and al-

PLATE 85. Sofonisba Anguissola. *Portrait of Queen Anne of Austria*, c. 1570. Oil on canvas, 42 7/8 x 36 5/16 in. (109.5 x 93 cm). The Stirling Maxwell Collection, Pollok House, Glasgow Museums and Art Galleries, Glasgow.

PLATE 84. Alonso Sánchez Coello. *Portrait of King Philip II*, c. 1570. The Stirling Maxwell Collection, Pollok House, Glasgow Museums and Art Galleries, Glasgow.

though only partially visible, would have have continued down the center front of her gown). Underneath these sleeves, she wears a second set of tightly fitted sleeves in white satin alternating with gold bands of embroidery and finished at the wrist with lace ruffs. The bodice of her gown is decorated with the same silver "purl" embroidery seen trimming the sleeves.

Queen Anne wears two rings on her left fingers; and her right hand is covered with a brown leather glove and holds its mate. Her right hand is resting on the back of a rust-colored velvet chair. She also wears a gold jeweled *carcanet* around her neck, pearl and gold buttons down the center front of the bodice, and a matching gold girdle. Her pale blonde hair, parted down the center, is topped with a black velvet hat rimmed with gold, jewels, white pearls, and two white ostrich plumes set off elegantly by a jeweled brooch and pear-shaped pearl.

Although this portrait is attributed to Sánchez Coello, there are numerous stylistic indications that this is, in fact, a work by Anguissola, and it is here attributed to her. Indicative of Anguissola's techniques are the soft peach coloring (with pale brown outlines) of the queen's face and hand and the "square-U" of her left hand. Hands painted by Coello are usually more rounded (as seen in plate 84), his coloring more sallow.

The king may have wanted both portraits done fairly soon after the wedding took place, and to expedite matters, Coello was commissioned to do the king's and Anguissola did the queen's. Sánchez Canton specifically mentions a "portrait of Queen Anne of Austria done in 1570"[3] but erroneously attributes it to Antonio Moro who had already fled Spain.

145

PLATE 86. Alonso Sánchez Coello. *Portrait of the Infantas Isabella Clara Eugenia and Catalina Micaela*, c. 1571. Prado Museum, Madrid.

The new queen lived only another ten years and had five children (four of whom died in childhood). In 1578, she bore a son, who would become the future Philip III. While Queen Anne and Sofonisba did not share the same bond as the latter had with Queen Isabel, both loved Queen's Isabel's two children.

Sánchez Coello painted the two infantas (Prado Museum, Madrid, see plate 86), about 1571, when Isabella Clara Eugenia was about five and Catalina Micaela was about three years old. The double portrait of the sisters shows the rigid costumes that even small children were required to wear. Both girls wear matching greenish olive velvet gowns with tightly boned bodices and bell-shaped farthingales. The high ruff collars are edged with *point de Venise* lace. The long, V-shaped bodices each have a peplum girdled with jewels interspersed with two gray-and-white pearls alternating with rubies and sapphires. Each sister wears a long strand of pearls wrapped around the back of the neck and then pulled through the pearls.

At the top of the shoulders, the sleeve caps are padded. The full-length undersleeves of grayish white satin are decorated with an orange scroll design. In her right hand, Isabella Clara Eugenia is holding an orange-gold handkerchief with tassels, and she hands Catalina Micaela a wreath of flowers. The dark olive gray background is simply done, showing only a part of a table on which some flowers—painted with a lack of realism—are placed.

PLATE 87. Sofonisba Anguissola. *Portrait of the Infantas Isabella Clara Eugenia and Catalina Micaela*, c. 1569–70. Oil on canvas, 52 9/16 x 57 1/16 in. (133.5 x 145 cm). Royal Collection, © Her Majesty Queen Elizabeth II, Buckingham Palace, London.

Coello's portraits "reflect the reserve, austerity, sobriety, and strict etiquette of the Spanish court."[4] Adhering to these rules of Spanish court portraiture (and following in Moro's artistic footsteps), he stresses form and precision—even in the limning of the king's children. His portraits are devoid of emotional content. Anguissola's remaining court portraits, although following the prescribed Spanish formula, generally do incorporate these emotional subtleties (enhanced by her exquisite use of color): the soft coloring in her faces always conveys warmth, and as the sitters look out at the viewer, one can detect real persons behind the courtly façade.

The somberness of the two small sisters' portraits further testifies to the extreme formality of Philip's court. Yet the king is known to have let down his formal, "public demeanor, the control of emotion and gesture, the outward calm the Spanish call *sosiego*"[5] when he spent time with his children. He was attached to all his progeny and shared with them his love of flowers, gardens, and nature. When he had to travel, he often sent them gifts and coloring books.[6]

Philip was closest to Isabella Clara Eugenia (more so than to Catalina Micaela or his son), and as Baldinucci states, the king made Anguissola governess "in charge of the infanta."[7] It is possible that while Coello was painting this double portrait of the infantas, Anguissola was there reminding the children of the importance of standing still and looking regal, heads—bedecked with pearl tiaras—held high. As a bond had formed early on, it is conceivable that Isabella Clara Eugenia may have been permitted to watch when Anguissola painted other members of the court, and so the infanta would have been inclined to listen to her grown-up friend. Anguissola also may have remembered the attachment that she had had for her old servant

PLATE 89. Alonso Sánchez Coello. *Portrait of the Infanta Isabella Clara Eugenia*, c. 1588. The Metropolitan Museum of Art, Bequest of Collis P. Huntington 1900. (25.110.21) New York.

(seen in a Uffizi sketch, *The Chess Game,* and the *Self-Portrait* at Althorp); now the cycle had come full circle, and Anguissola was the adult.

A second, less well-known double protrait of the infantas is in Her Majesty Queen Elizabeth II's Royal Collection (Buckingham Palace, London, see plate 87). This painting, dated 1569-70, was done when the two sisters were younger: Isabella Clara Eugenia appears to be about four years old and Catalina Micaela about two. This painting has been attributed to the workshop of Sánchez Coello, but based upon stylistic grounds, it is here given to Anguissola.

Both paintings are quite interesting for comparison. Coello's Prado portrait of the infantas is obviously based upon the one done when the children were younger: the sisters are placed in the same positions, Isabella Clara Eugenia on the left and Catalina Micaela on the right. Although they are still quite young, Coello has rendered them in Spanish royal fashion: miniature icons, stiff and formal. Neither child looks at the viewer; nor do they even look at one another, even though Isabella is handing the wreath to Catalina.

However, in the 1569 painting the style is markedly different. Here, both children look directly at the viewer. Their faces are limned in a warm manner: softer skin coloring—in Anguissola's tones with a pale brown outline—that wonderful glow of "peach fuzz" skin that small children have. They do not have the appearance of icons; they are real children. Catalina appears to be holding back a smile, as she holds the spaniel's paw. Here, too, the props are alive: Isabella is holding a parrot, and a small spaniel is curled up on the red velvet chest. What better way to bring these royal children to life than to have their pets—perhaps gifts from Philip—incorporated into the painting? It would have been something that Anguissola would have thought of in order to put the children at ease. Further, in her *Portrait of Massimiliano Stampa,* she had already placed a curled up dog at the boy's feet in memory of the recent death of his father. So, the dog in the infantas' double 1570 portrait would also be in memory of Anguissola's dead royal mistress—the children's mother—Queen Isabel. Another allusion to Queen Isabel is seen in the floral crown with three gold fleur de lys—the symbol of France—adorning Isabella's hair. Anguissola also was Isabella's governess, and had formed a close bond with both the children. Perhaps she even told the children about her *Portrait of Massimiliano Stampa,* thereby capturing their attention. It is conceivable, too, that Isabel Sánchez Coello—who was two years older than Infanta Isabella—may have been present at these portrait sittings.

The children's faces have been captured warmly, and there is an appealing compositional harmony to the painting, something at which Anguissola was most adept. There is also the noticeable "square-U" of Catalina's right fingers, which is quite similar to the way Anguissola did her brother Asdrubale's fingers in her sketch of him at Capodimonte in Naples.

It was the realism of the two infantas' faces that had priority during these royal sittings. Anguissola would have been most aware of the limited attention span of the children. Then the costume details—which have been rendered impeccably—could have been done later when the artist could mix her colors in a more leisurely fashion when the gowns could be brought to her. All the exquisite fashion details have been done meticulously: from the beautifully starched linen ruffs, the matching jeweled *carcanets* (with double sets of pearls, rubies, and sapphires), to the embroidered "S" shapes done with pearls and gold embroidery (seen on both the gold silk sleeves and down the center front and hem of the farthingales), to the inclusion of the tuck lines visible above the hems of the two brown velvet gowns—additions to be let down for the growing infantas.

Sánchez Coello also would paint both sisters as adults: Catalina Micaela, in a portrait done about the time of her marriage c. 1585 (Prado Museum, Madrid, see plate 88), and Isabella Clara Eugenia later in 1588 (The Metropolitan Museum of Art, New York, see plate 89). The painting, a bit larger than half-length, shows the infanta in all her regal splendor: with an elaborate starched and wired collar; tightly boned bodice; slashed undersleeves; and a myriad of jewels. There is no hint of emotion. Coello was accurate in his costume detail, but any suggestion of humanity—the person behind the royal mask—is missing. This was Spanish court portraiture at its impersonal, but precise, best. However, Anguissola's remaining portraits from Philip's court show that, ever so imperceptibly, she broke through the icy façade and gave those who sat for her their regal poses but with warmth.

According to Zaist, sometime before Philip's marriage to Anne of Austria, he and Anguissola had a discussion about marriage and children. The subject might even have been brought up before Queen Isabel's death (as the queen had willed her brocade for a bed); but now, Philip took an additional interest in Anguissola's future welfare since he knew how close the two had been. In 1570, Anguissola was thirty-eight, but technically still a ward of the king, as she was unmarried. Anguissola told the king that if she married she would be "inclined to marry an Italian."[8] The clos-

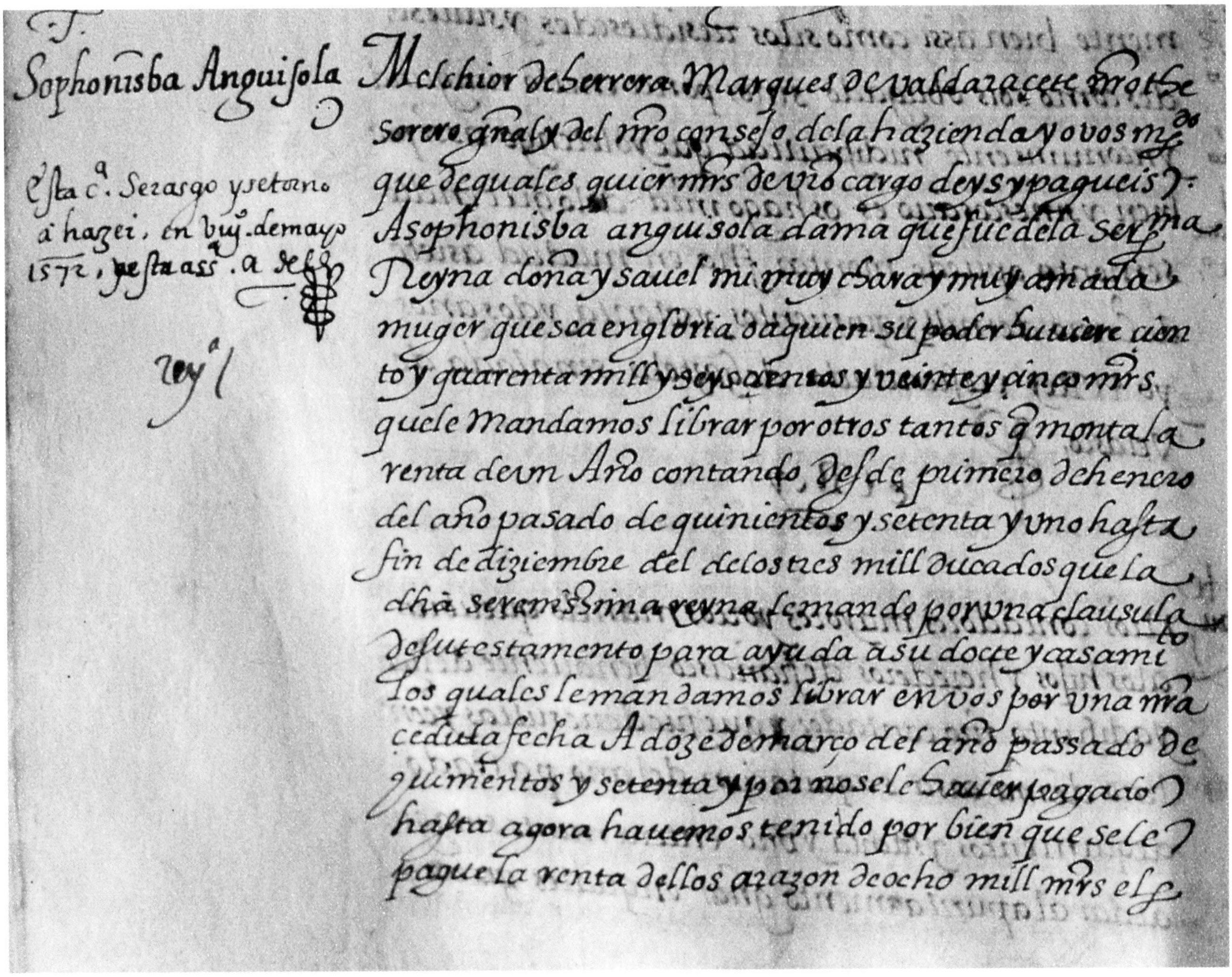

PLATE 90. Sofonisba Anguissola's Dowry document (one of four) drawn up on 8 May 1572. Madrid, Archivo Historico Nacional. Consejo, Camara de Castilla, Lib. 252. fol. 107.

est that Philip could come—since it was his responsibility to choose her husband—was a Sicilian, Don Fabrizio de Moncada, son of Francesco I (d. 1566), prince of Paternò and viceroy of Sicily.[9]

The Moncada family had a noble Spanish lineage that went back to the eleventh century. Over the centuries, they "earned an honored place in the history of Catalonia . . . and it included lords . . . archdeacons of the See of Barcelona, and a queen in the kingdom of Aragon."[10] By the Renaissance, the family also had a number of "distinguished barons"[11] at the Spanish court. In *Don Quixote,* Cervantes listed the Moncadas as part of Spain's venerated nobility.[12]

Philip had to arrange for Anguissola's dowry, since she was his ward. Four documents were discovered by this author in 1988 relating to her dowry. In 1569, the king, following a clause in Queen Isabel's will, gave Sofonisba "1,500 maravedis for her dowry and marriage."[13] Then, on 12 March 1571, a second dowry document was drawn up. In the margin of this decree, a handwritten note states that this one supersedes two other documents drawn up on 1 January 1571, and 8 May 1572.[14] It is published here for the first time (see plate 90).

Whereas we hold in high esteem the fine manner in which you, Sofonisba Anguissola, served the most serene Queen Doña Isabel, my very dear and beloved wife (may she rest in glory), and were a lady of her private service, and in satisfaction and reward of your residence, cares of your office, and such related matters which you held on the staff of her household and for which she bequeathed for you in her will and for whatever responsibility and obligation in which the forementioned most serene Queen and we may be to you. For this cause, we have had and now do have consideration to grant you with this document 3,000 ducados which are worth 125,000 maravedis, as capital benefice to your dowry and marriage, which comes to, above and beyond others, a sum of 250,000 maravedis which we have ordered in your name through our account to Melchior de Heirera, our general treasurer, on the date of this document, in fulfillment of the two sums of 375,000 maravedis. Therefore, by this document we promise and assure you, the aforementioned Sofonisba Anguissola, that once it had been made clear to us by faith and sufficient testimony that you have married and taken all vows according to Holy Mother Church, and for whose effect are promised to you the aforementioned 3,000 ducados, we will have them delivered to you so that the payment may be made to you openly and in due form. I desire from you still another favor: residence in any of our royal estates in Castile or in some place equivalent. Should I die before your marriage or taking of vows, which in any of these cases may cause stoppage of payment, so that you may be certain and assured of all stipulated above, I order you to present this document, signed by our hand and countersigned by our secretary below. Dated in Madrid, 6 August 1569.

The King[15]

Sofonisba's marriage to Don Fabrizio probably took place at court sometime in 1570 or 1571. The wedding would have been an elaborate affair, possibly at the Escorial with the king and queen in attendance, as well as Don Fabrizio's parents. Sofonisba would have been happy to have the king's royal favor—even to have the generous offer of one of his royal residences. The Moncada family also would have been pleased that Fabrizio had made such an important match with an Italian noblewoman whose dowry was sizeable.

In commemoration of her marriage to Don Fabrizio, Sofonisba painted a wedding portrait. There is a *Portrait of a Husband and Wife* (Doria Pamphili, Rome, see plate 91) which for many years was attributed to Sofonisba (and had been misnamed *Titian and His Wife*). In 1983, the museum took that attribution from her and it became an anonymous Italian sixteenth-century work.

This half-length oil on canvas double portrait is most appealing in its vivid warmth. A bearded nobleman is gently placing his left hand on his lady's arm (as Sofonisba had portrayed Amilcare with Asdrubale in her triple portrait at Niva). She is elegantly dressed in a velvet gown, with pearls at her neck and a soft silk-gauze chemise beaded with pearls and a slightly raised collar edged with pearls. She holds a piece of fruit in her right hand—with a slight hint of the "square-U" shape. Is the fruit a wishful sign to be a fruitful wife?

However, the most noticeable feature of this portrait is the striking similarity of her face, which is an older—by ten years—version of Sofonisba's *Self-Portrait* at Althorp (see plate 82): the same face with a slightly dimpled chin; same shape of the

PLATE 92. Anna Maria Anguissola. *Holy Family with Saint Francis*, Museo Civico ala Ponzone, Cremona.

left ear; and tiny curls at her hairline—all softly colored. This vividly sympathetic double family portrait is here reattributed to Sofonisba—again indicative of the tenderness of which she was capable when not working on court commissions.

The year of her wedding proved to be a busy one for Sofonisba, possibly with a great deal of travel to her husband's properties, since newlywed brides traditionally were shown their husband's estates. Following a clause in her dowry, they even may have resided at one of Philip's estates. It is conceivable that they also would have made a trip to Palermo and Paternò. If she and her husband traveled to Sicily, they probably went via Italy—with stops in Cremona and Mantua—and word probably spread that the illustrious painter was back home again.

Traveling south through Italy, the couple would have stopped to visit Sofonisba's family, whom she had not seen in twelve years. It must have been a joyful reunion with her parents and sisters. She visited Europa (who had married in 1568) and her new brother-in-law, Carlo Schinchinelli. They now had a son, Antonio Galeazzo,[16] and so, for the first time, Sofonisba was an aunt, and she must have been delighted to see her young nephew.

Sometime during this decade, Sofonisba's youngest sister, Anna Maria, married Jacopo Sommi, a nobleman from Cremona. The exact date of their marriage is not known, nor have any dowry documents been found. Baldinucci states that Anna Maria was still living in 1585.[17] If Amilcare knew that Sofonisba was returning to

93

94

PLATE 93. Sofonisba Anguissola. *Portrait of Margarita Gonzaga*, 1571. Oil on panel tondo, diameter 5 1/2 in. (14 cm). Captain Patrick Drury-Lowe Collection, Locko Park, Derbyshire.

PLATE 94. Sofonisba Anguissola. *Portrait of Margarita Gonzaga,* 1571. *Verso*.

PLATE 95. Sofonisba Anguissola. *Doña María Manrique de Lara y Pernstein and One of Her Daughters*, c. 1574. Oil on canvas, 53 1/8 x 39 3/4 in. (135 x 101 cm). Central Gallery of Bohemia, Prague.

95

Maria was still living in 1585.[17] If Amilcare knew that Sofonisba was returning to Cremona, it is possible that Anna Maria's wedding festivities could have coincided with her visit.

Sofonisba taught Anna Maria, who was a gifted painter in her own right. Baldinucci mentions that Anna Maria sent Sofonisba a portrait of their mother, Bianca.[18] Another painting by her, *Holy Family with Saint John* still hangs in Cremona's Church of Sant'Agata, and a third painting, the *Holy Family with Saint Francis* (Museo Civico ala Ponzone, Cremona, see plate 93), is also known, which she signed "Annae Mariae Amilcharis Anguissola Filiae."

Anna Maria's work differs from Sofonisba's in several ways. She does not use her sister's "square-U" finger positioning (nor do any of the other sisters, although Lucia's *Self-Portrait* [see plate 60] in the Borghese attempts it, but the hands and fingers are done in a plumper manner). Anna Maria's figures, while somewhat elongated, are more solidly painted. The few known works by her concentrate on religious themes.

From Cremona the Moncadas would have traveled the short distance to Mantua. While there, Sofonisba may have visited her sister Elena at San Vincenzo's Convent of the Holy Virgins. Mantua was also the home of the Gonzaga family—Sofonisba had danced with Ferrante Gonzaga at King Philip and Queen Isabel's wedding in 1560. So, Sofonisba's visit would have had a dual purpose: to see her sister and to do several commissioned portraits of the Gonzagas.

Writing in the nineteenth century, Federico Sacchi mentions seeing four double portraits of some of the dukes and duchesses of Mantua done by Anguissola, including one of Guglielmo (1538–86), duke of Monferrato, and his wife, Eleanor (1534–94, daughter of Emperor Ferdinand I, who was the younger brother of Charles V); they were married in 1561. The current whereabouts of these paintings are not known. Anguissola is also known to have painted a tondo portrait of Margarita Gonzaga (Captain Patrick Drury-Lowe Collection, Locko Park, Derbyshire, see plates 93, 94) in 1571. In their 1976 catalogue, Harris and Nochlin state that it was impossible for Anguissola to have painted this tondo of Margarita. However, since their catalogue did not include any new archival research on Anguissola which placed her in Mantua,[19] it seems likely that Anguissola did paint Margarita's portrait at the same time she did her parents' portraits (in Mantua). This small and beautiful tondo shows many characteristics of Anguissola's hand. The child's face is painted in pale peach tones with a soft brown outline around her face, and there is meticulous attention to the smallest costume details.

Decorating her chestnut brown hair with copper glints are a jeweled tiara and three tiny white satin bows. Her ruff is painted with a slight *impasto* to give dimension to the lace, and a dot of white paint on the tiny button below brings out the shine of the gold. The jeweled *carcanet*, with alternating bands of rubies and pearls, and the gold embroidery have been limned with great precision. Around the top of the tondo (which is only five and one half inches in diameter) is the inscription "Margarita Gonzaga ANNORVM VI XIIII MAII MDLXXI" (Margarita Gonzaga, Age 6, 14 May 1571). Of interest as well is the reverse of the tondo where a circular, swirling pattern of gold leaves decorates the surface. This careful attention to the verso suggests that the portrait was placed so that both sides could be viewed.

So it appears that Anguissola was in Mantua; and Baldinucci states that she left Spain with Don Fabrizio and went to Palermo,[20] most probably via Cremona and Mantua.

The Gonzaga family probably first learned of Anguissola's talents through their Hapsburg connection—Eleanor Gonzaga was related to Philip—as well as through Campi (who knew Giulio Romano, the architect of the Gonzaga's Palazzo del Tè).

By the following year, Sofonisba and Don Fabrizio were back at Philip's court. The king wanted her there, and the Infanta Isabella, who had grown attached to this noble lady painter, may have missed her a great deal. Philip's sister, Juana of Portugal (1535–78), whom the king had made regent in 1554 when he left Spain to marry Mary Tudor in England, also may have urged the king to have Sofonisba back at court, as she wanted the artist to paint a portrait of Don Sebastian of Portugal, her son.

Don Sebastian (1554–78) was heir to the Portuguese throne and became king as an infant. His father, Don Juan of Portugal, died before Sebastian was born. The boy had "a natural disposition [that was] generous, truthful, and sincere; he was neither suspicious or cruel; and he would have nothing to do that smacked of double dealing."[21] Yet like his cousin, Don Carlos, Sebastian also was arrogant, sullen, "haughty in the extreme, and generally unyielding . . . [but] he had the outlook of a crusader born four centuries too late."[22] In fact, in 1573, the year after Anguissola painted his portrait, Don Sebastian, King Philip, and the duke of Alba met in Guadalupe, Spain, to discuss a crusade in North Africa against the Moors. Philip was reluctant to mount and pay for such an expedition, but in 1578 he finally agreed. Sebastian was killed in the ill-fated Battle of Alcázar-al-Kebir in the same year.

Juana knew Anguissola well—they were also contemporaries; Juana was born three years after Anguissola, in 1535—and had had the artist paint her portrait several years earlier, as mentioned in Anguissola's 1561 letter to Campi. It is likely that at Juana's suggestion, Don Sebastian had Anguissola paint his portrait (Fundación Casa de Alba, see plate 64), which was discovered in 1988 still listed as done by an anonymous sixteenth-century artist.[23] Based upon stylistic details, it is here attributed to Anguissola, an attribution supported by the current duke of Alba.

The oil on canvas full-length portrait has an inscription above the king's head: "Sebastianus Primus Rex Portugaliae Agens 18 Anos" (Sebastian I, king of Portugal, age eighteen). Thus, the portrait can be dated 1572. The king stands in front of a column—a Hapsburg emblem—on the left side of the canvas, and there is a window in the upper left. He is wearing a suit of black splintered armor decorated with gold damascene work. Underneath his high metal collar, he wears a white ruff, with matching pleated ones at the wrists. His reddish hair is worn short without the usual addition of a plumed hat. His rust-colored velvet slops are made in two parts: the outer wide bands, which are decorated in gold thread, and underneath a pair of breeches edged in gold.

Anguissola has captured, in his somber face, the same jutting Hapsburg chin that is so evident in portraits of King Philip. As uncle and nephew, the king and Sebastian bear a strong resemblance to one another. More important, Anguissola already had used this exact pose successfully in 1557, when she painted Massimiliano

PLATE 96. Sofonisba Anguissola. *Portrait of a Lady*. 27 x 21 3/8 in. (68.58 x 54.29 cm). Hermitage, St. Petersburg.

Stampa, third marchese of Soncino. (see plate 61) Some of the details are different: a dog in one, a window in the other. However, both paintings use a column on the left as an architectural foil; both subjects are holding gloves and have a similar stance (but leaning on opposite feet); and most significantly, Anguissola's trademark "square-U" is almost identical in the shape and positioning of each man's left hand.

Another painting from this period, *Doña María Manrique de Lara y Pernstein and One of Her Daughters,* c. 1574 (Central Gallery of Bohemia, Prague, see plate 95), was recently attributed without substantiation to Georges van der Straeten, who was at Philip's court from 1560 to 1568 and worked for Queen Isabel. The painting is neither signed nor dated.[24]

María Maximiliana Manrique de Lara was a contemporary of Anguissola, having been born about 1535. She was the daughter of García Manrique de Lara, commander of the fortress at Piacenza, and his wife, Isabel de Briceño. María married Vrastislaw de Pernstein and had nineteen children. Doña María is listed in 1567 along with Anguissola as a lady-in-waiting to Queen Isabel.

Although this is a court portrait, maternal warmth is immediately striking: Doña María stands, while her three- or four-year-old daughter is seated. Custom and court formality required the opposite. The child tenderly holds her mother's thumb, while her mother's right arm is placed lovingly next to her daughter's head. The child is dressed in a white satin gown decorated with gold, jewels, and embroidery. Her lace sleeves and ruff are meticulously limned to enhance their delicacy. She wears a white coif decorated with gold-thread embroidery. Her left hand rests outstretched on the arm of the chair and quite obvious are the positioning of her left thumb and index finger: done in Anguissola's typical "square-U" fashion. Her soft complexion is delicately outlined in Anguissola's pale peach brown tones. Doña María looks directly at the viewer, while the child's smiling gaze is elsewhere.

Anguissola was the only sixteenth-century court painter to capture familial warmth—even when adhering to Spanish formality. It is quite evident in this work, just as it was in Anguissola's portrait of her father, who placed his arm tenderly around Asdrubale (see plate 51). Based on these stylistic grounds, this work is here attributed Anguissola.

During this decade, Anguissola also painted *Portrait of a Lady* (Hermitage, St. Petersburg, see plate 96). The half-length profile of an unknown noble lady shows the magnificent costume details that Anguissola had achieved. This lady is dressed in a gown, probably made of black velvet, and the entire bodice is covered with intricate raised gold-work embroidery. This embroidery technique was done by hammering solid gold into a thin layer and then cutting it into thin strips to be worked into the embroidery. Before being couched down (tacking stitches invisibly to hold the gold strips in place), a cotton stuffing was placed underneath the gold strips to give it a raised effect. The raised collar is covered with another popular type of metal embroidery known as "purl," in which gold wire was twisted around a core (sometimes silk), and then the core was removed, leaving hollow spirals. The effect of pure gold or silver embroidery done against a black velvet or silk ground is quite striking.

Whereas most sixteenth-century Spanish costume was monochromatic, the tedium of one basic color was offset by superb embroidery done in colored silk threads and gold and silver metals. The Spanish were known all over Europe for their magnificent embroidery. Staggering amounts were paid from every royal or noble household account to embroideresses and suppliers for this handwork. Over the eight years that Queen Isabel lived in Spain, for example, her household accounts list vast amounts paid for brocades, silks, and velvets, all heavily embroidered and covered with a fortune in jewels. At her death, Isabel left hundreds of gowns and jeweled embroidered accessories, including vast quantities of handmade lace ruffs.[25] Catherine de' Medici gave one Federico Cinciolo, a Venetian who wrote a popular book on needlework, "exclusive rights to manufacture the enormous starched lace ruffs which she made fashionable in France."[26] Every lady was expected to be proficient at sewing and embroidery, and time was regularly devoted at court to needlework, as well as discussions of designs to be done by professionals. Unfortunately, most of these magnificent artists were women who worked anonymously at home, rather than in a workshop environment where artists frequently signed their works.

Federico Sacchi mentions seeing this portrait in the Hermitage in the nineteenth century, but then it was titled *Portrait of a Princess*. He wrote that Anguissola's painting had "great strength of color and exquisite detail . . . [and] elegance in its design."[27] The gown worn by this unknown lady (whom Sacchi could not identify) shows the elaborately detailed fashion that was part of daily life at court. Even her undersleeve, done with raised gold work and silver embroidery, has been lavished with the same exacting artistry that is seen on the outer sleeves.

Anguissola also painted with great care the details of the strands of her braided hairdo, the shimmering pearls set into her chignon, the vase, and the petals of the flowers (a carnation and two roses). Interesting, too, is the softness of the lady's pale peach skin, something seen in other court portraits that Anguissola painted, including the *Infantas Isabella Clara Eugenia and Catalina Micaela* (1569) and *Queen Anne of Austria*. This muted coloring gives a warmth to the sitter's face which contrasts well with the exacting skill shown in the embroidered gown. Across the centuries, it gives this lady—even in profile—great realism. Anguissola has captured her musing and daydreaming, as she placed these flowers in the vase.

This painting also shows another interesting aspect of Anguissola's work: the incorporation of a still life into a portrait, something rarely done in the sixteenth century. The genre of still-life flower painting did not become popular until the next century, when the discerning eyes of Dutch and Flemish artists—many of whom were interested in botany, including Maria Sibylla Merian, Maria van Oosterwyck, and Rachel Ruysch—helped make this form a marketable type of art. Yet, in Anguissola's painting, done fifty years earlier, these three flowers are rendered with meticulously accurate botanical detail. Even Sánchez Coello, who paid careful attention to the costume details in his double *Portrait of the Infantas Isabella Clara Eugenia and Catalina Micaela,* did not have an eye for botanical accuracy. On comparing the flowers in Coello's portrait and Anguissola's bouquet of flowers in her portrait, one thing is quite clear: Coello's wreath of flowers, although somewhat lifelike, have a flat, two-dimensional, static quality; those by Anguissola have a beautiful botanical accuracy, something that had not been painted so beautifully since Dürer's works.

PLATE 97. Luis de Morales. *Madonna and Child*. National Gallery, London.

The St. Petersburg *Portrait of a Lady* has not figured in the scholarly literature (the only mention is by Federico Sacchi), and most likely this is because of its location in Russia. It shows that Anguissola, although restricted in the range of emotions that could be included in court portraiture, instead paid careful attention both to fashion details (which a courtly lady would know so well) and to the sitter's human qualities. She also incorporated the beauty of botanical realism—something Sánchez Coello did not do.

Much of Spanish art (especially from northern Spain) of the late Middle Ages and Renaissance was influenced by French and Flemish artists. It was not until the reigns of Charles V and Philip II that the Italians played a more prominent role in the dissemination of the Renaissance to Spain. There was a temperamental and geographic undercurrent in art. Northern climates are cold, people reserved; Italy is warmer, its people outgoing. It was in this warmer climate, too, that during the Renaissance artists began representing a broader range of human emotions and artistic concerns that slowly worked their way north. The sixteenth-century Spanish aristocracy was extremely formal and reserved, and that, combined with the Flemish influence and the tradition of portraying rulers as icons, resulted in careful delineation of details (costumes, furniture, architectural backdrops), but it was a realism without warmth or any outward display of emotion.

Anguissola, raised in the warmth and beauty of the Italian countryside, and the

161

traditions of Michelangelo and Titian, found subtle ways—yet, obviously permissible and pleasing to King Philip—to circumvent the traditional formula for Spanish court portraiture. Philip is known to have given Titian great artistic freedom, which was unusual because, most often, Philip would put in writing the exact details he wanted incorporated into the paintings he commissioned. It is highly likely that the king's discerning eye noticed Anguissola's subtleties in her court portraits. His partiality to Italian artists may have accounted for the acceptance of Anguissola's style—especially as Titian had paved the way.

Philip wanted the best not only for the construction of the Escorial but also for its decoration. He realized that, artistically, it could best be found in Italy, as most Spanish art was still Gothic and out of the mainstream of Renaissance art. During Anguissola's stay at court, there were two well-known artists painting in Spain. Luis de Morales (active mid-century, died 1586) was asked to do a "trial piece for the Escorial"[28] but Philip rejected it. Subsequently, Morales moved out to the provinces, primarily painting altarpieces for many churches. He was familiar with da Vinci's *sfumato* technique; and Morales's *Madonna and Child* (National Gallery, London, see plate 97) has the large eyes that were characteristic of Anguissola's self-portraits as well as her later religious works. Whether he knew her work is not known.

El Greco also was commissioned to paint for the Escorial. His *Martyrdom of the Theban Legion* also met with the king's disfavor and he, too, retired from life in Madrid to live out his days painting in Toledo. So Sánchez Coello was the only Spanish artist who was consistently attached to the king's household and received royal patronage for court portraits.

Philip's 1548–49 trip to Italy, which also included extensive travels to Germany and the Low Countries, made a lasting impression on him. His artistic tastes became international. He had relished the splendor of north Italian cities and their magnificent architecture which, in his view, surpassed his own native city of Valladolid and certainly the provincialism of Madrid. Philip was to become the first ruler in Spain who would systematically, resolutely, and consistently influence his country's art. However, when it came to choosing many of the artists, he turned to the Italians. Pompeo Leoni, whom the king met on his Italian voyage, was commissioned to do realistic bronze statues of Charles V and Philip. Other Italian artists whom he hired included Luca Cambiaso, Federico Zuccaro, and Bartolomeo Carducci.

> To trace the influence of the great Italian masters upon the art and architecture of the Iberian peninsula is in no way to belittle Spanish genius, which always possesses an individual character of its own, tending to the expression of interior feeling and mystical yearning. That Spanish artists should have looked to Italy for inspiration was inevitable, for the Renaissance, in its strict sense, was an Italian achievement, and was recognized as such throughout Europe. The history of sixteenth-century Spanish painting must be seen in the same context, and the variegated qualities of Italian Renaissance painting, ranging from the subtleties of Leonardo . . . to the Venetian splendor of Titian . . . elicited a correspondingly varied response from their Spanish contemporaries.[29]

Art historian Federico Zeri has called Anguissola's art "chameleon-like, with so many changes that it is hard to know what her style is."[30] Zeri's comments, however, are based on the general historical confusion about which Anguissola sister painted what, as well as a lack of any archival research or detailed study of Anguissola's own artistic maturation. She evolved from the awkward student copying the attenuated figures of her teachers, Campi and Gatti, then to absorbing additional Mannerist principles directly from her informal but important studies with Michelangelo, its greatest master. All these influences were combined into her own style which she developed at the Spanish court, where she had to make artistic concessions dictated by the king, who loved Italian art—and patronized it lavishly—but saw it through austere Spanish eyes. Anguissola adapted to these court requirements (a formality of pose and exacting costume details) but also brought her own Italian heritage, insight, and brighter, more vibrant coloring into her court portraits during her lengthy stay in Spain. That Titian had paved the way for a variation in accepted Spanish court portraiture inevitably facilitated what Anguissola could do in her own portraits for the king and his court.

In 1573, the Spanish royal family finally was able to take up residence frequently during the year at the Escorial, even though work would continue on it for another eleven years. During the heat of the summer (when there was fear of contracting malaria), the court continued to stay at other palaces, but at least Philip would no longer have to travel so extensively from one castle to another up and down the breadth and length of Spain. The Spartan exterior of the Escorial was matched by Philip's own quarters. The room in which he worked and carried on much of the business of state was starkly simple, with the barest of essentials, but, in keeping with his devout nature, had many "pictures of saints so that he could meditate on their virtues and sufferings and be inspired by their example."[31]

> This belief in the power of an image to instruct as well as to delight was evident in the decoration of the other rooms. The king's great audience chamber was filled with nearly seventy maps. . . . The antechamber, also used as a dining or banqueting room, was decorated with views, flora and fauna from the Spanish colonies. The sheer number of paintings of a theme, or even the detailed enumeration of saints within the monastery, also attest to the king's passion for collecting.[32]

Philip was one of Spain's greatest patrons and collectors: sculpture, maps, religious relics and paintings, books, and portraits—all were part of his avid interest in the arts. His particular fascination with Italian art came both from his father's love of Titian's works and from his own early trip to Italy, when he would have realized for the first time how provincial Spanish art was. The king also was deeply religious—by 1598, he had collected an unbelievable seven thousand five hundred relics—and his art collection included numerous religious paintings, which were the "bulk of his purchases after 1562."[33] Even his collecting works by Hieronymous Bosch and other Flemish so-called "primitives" cannot be thought of as very unusual when looked at in context of his forty years of purchasing art. His great-grandmother, Queen Isabella, and his father both collected Flemish masters; and his devoutly observant Catholicism, steeped in sixteenth-century mysticism and literal belief in the Bible, would have found expression in Bosch's allegories. The king's rejection of both Luis de Morales's and El Greco's works for the Escorial in favor of Italian artists reveals his strong ties to Italian art.

While Philip continued to collect relics, books (by the thousands), and paintings on religious themes, he still had need of court portraits to make the might of Spain visible in all parts of the known world. Philip kept Coello at court and attached to his own household, and he continued to balance the austerity of Spanish portraiture with Italian exuberance, via Anguissola, whom he kept on at court until the end of the decade. Yet, inevitably, questions remain. The problems of definitive cataloguing and attribution of some of Anguissola's works and Coello's later works—because of the copying of portraits, collaborative efforts, and overpainting by Pantoja de la Cruz after the 1604 palace fire, the loss of many of her works, and lack of cleaning or x-ray on most of those extant—remain unsolved.[34]

Philip had frequent bouts of illness and had been suffering from gout since 1557. He had a moveable chair that was especially designed for his gout-swollen limbs, so he could continue to work, if need be, when he was in pain. Often, he worked late into the night. Despite the sobriety of his own living quarters, the rest of the court did not lack in "splendor or laughter. The king's rooms might be no bigger than a monk's cell, but the rest of the palace was grand and colorful. Although the Escorial was both monastery and palace, the courtiers did not live like monks; they whiled away the time there, as elsewhere, hunting, gambling, reading, talking, working at their government or courtly posts and, above all, struggling for positions or powers."[35]

Sofonisba's routine at court was disrupted considerably when she received word that Amilcare Anguissola died at seventy-nine in July 1573.[36] Asdrubale, then twenty-two, became the head of the family and looked after his mother, Bianca, whom he named as attorney in a document date 27 August[37] drawn up to settle the family estate. Following the usual long delays in receiving mail, Sofonisba probably did not hear about her father's death for a month or two. She must have been devastated. Amilcare had nurtured her talent, supported her in a most unusual fashion for the time, inculcated in her a pride in her namesake and in ancient heritage, and always strove to advertise her capabilities. Early on, he was her staunchest advocate. Now that Amilcare was gone, Asdrubale would carry on the family name.

As Amilcare's firstborn, Sofonisba must have felt the lack of not having an heir; but it may have been a blessing in disguise, as the mortality rate in childbirth was staggering. There have not been any documents found concerning any children that Sofonisba and Fabrizio might have had (although the chance of her having children after her forties would have been slim). However, there is a puzzling entry in the 1825 edition of the *Genealogy of the Noble Families of Genoa,* which lists a son, of Sofonisba and Fabrizio, Giuliano, who died before Sofonisba.[38] The existence of a child has never been documented anywhere else.[39]

The year 1578 proved to be a transitional one for both the king and Anguissola. Philip's sister, Juana, died, and her son, Don Sebastian, was killed in battle. Philip withdrew to pray. Even when gout made moving difficult, he was always able to view the sanctity and peace of the interior of the Escorial's church, as there was a special opening in this room from which he could watch church services.

Sometime during 1578, with the king's permission, Sofonisba and Don Fabrizio traveled back to Palermo. Before she left Spain, she painted her favorite infanta,

PLATE 98. Sofonisba Anguissola. *Portrait of the Infanta Isabella Clara Eugenia*, c. 1578. Oil on canvas, 45 5/8 x 40 1/8 in. (116 x 102 cm). Prado Museum, Madrid.

Isabella Clara Eugenia, who by then was by twelve years old. *Portrait of the Infanta Isabella Clara Eugenia* (Prado Museum, Madrid, see plate 98), has been attributed to Coello, but again, there are characteristics of this painting that indicate Sofonisba's hand. If Isabella Clara Eugenia knew that Sofonisba was leaving Spain, she certainly would have insisted upon a portrait being done by her favorite painter and governess. The tie between the two women was strong enough that in 1599 the infanta would go out of her way to have Sofonisba paint her wedding portrait.

In this three-quarter-length portrait, the infanta has been painted in a composition very similar to the portrait of her mother (also in the Prado, see plate 74) painted by Sofonisba many years before. Daughter and mother looked a great deal alike and, by using the same pose, Sofonisba may have been paying homage to the dead queen. Sofonisba already had used the same composition twice for portraits of Massimiliano Stampa and Don Sebastian.

The background is an olive-black with perhaps a hint of a window (obscured by centuries of accumulated dirt). The infanta has her right hand—painted in a "square-U"—resting casually and informally on the top of a wooden chair, the back of which is covered with a rust-colored velvet with tassels. She is wearing a velvet hat, tilted to the right (as her mother's had been), with a tiny brim covered with white pearls. Attached to it is a gold pin and several feathers. Underneath it, she wears a coif of jewels and pearls. Her light brown hair is curly, as was her mother's.

The tightly boned bodice of satin brocade with gold has a high collar with a *carcanet* around it and, underneath it, a ruff made of *point de Venise* lace. There are jewels girdling her waist and matching jewels—of gold with alternating sets of two pearls and square-cut sapphires—that go down the center front of the gown as well as diagonally from each shoulder to the waist.

The top of each sleeve has a padded roll; the sleeves and train have matching striped fabric of white and gray with gold embroidery. At the wrists of her fitted sleeves, Isabella is wearing two small lace ruffs. In her left hand, she holds a silk handkerchief edged with *point de Venise* lace. On her left index finger is another sapphire ring, and a cabochon ruby ring is worn on her little finger. This ruby ring is quite similar to the one worn by Queen Isabel in Sofonisba's portrait of her. It would appealing to think that it is the same one, and that the infanta had inherited it, since Queen Isabel's substantial collection of jewelry was divided at her death between her two daughters. On her right index finger, she wears another gold ring.

Sofonisba's characteristic soft brownish peach tones outline the infanta's face and hands. She looks out at the viewer with somewhat drooping eyelids. The portrait memorializes a young princess whom Sofonisba had grown to love and also harkens back to the pose in which she had painted Queen Isabel. It was a fitting farewell present to the young princess.

After Don Fabrizio and Sofonisba left Spain, they traveled south through Italy on their way to Palermo. It was probably during this time (1578) that they stopped in Rome and Sofonisba painted *Portrait of Giorgio Giulio Clovio* (Zeri Collection, Mentana, see plate 14). Clovio was sometimes called *Il Macedone* because it was thought that he was born in Macedonia, when in fact he was born in Croatia (his real name was Clovitch). He was a well-known illuminator, miniaturist, and painter. In 1527, during the sack of Rome, he was taken prisoner but managed to escape.

From there, he traveled to Mantua and entered the priesthood. Subsequently, Pope Paul III called him to Rome. There, he worked for the pope from 1534 to 1549. He also had as his patrons the Grand Duke Cosimo I de' Medici and Pope Julius III (pontificate, 1550–55). Clovio may have known about Anguissola's work while she was studying with Michelangelo, whom he knew when both were in Rome working for Pope Julius. Clovio also knew El Greco, who also painted his portrait (Capodimonte, Naples). The portrait that Anguissola did of Clovio dates from 1578, the last year of his life.

Here, Anguissola portrays Clovio in a half-length pose seated in a chair with his hands placed on a table covered with a green tablecloth. In his left hand he may be holding a miniature of his student, Lavina Teerlinc.

When the portrait was completed, Sofonisba and her husband left for Palermo. Proof of her visit here lies in a document discovered in 1988 dated 2 September, 1578, in which Asdrubale Anguissola petitioned Cremona's *comune* in order to travel to Palermo to visit his sister.[40] Asdrubale was a *decurione,* one of the members of Cremona's governing body,[41] and probably did not have any problem securing permission to travel. The document, drawn up by the *comune* on Asdrubale's behalf, reads as follows:

> Very Magnificent Gentlemen
> This faithful compatriot, Asdrubale Anguissola, wanted to visit Sicily and perhaps other parts of the world. He felt that he had to justify that the illustrious Signore Amilcare Anguissola and the noble Lady Bianca Ponzone were legitimately married and from this legitimate marriage came the illustrious Sofonisba and the said Asdrubale Anguissola, legitimate children . . . of Amilcare (who died in 1573). It was public knowledge from everyone who knew the family that the children were legitimate. . . . Asdrubale is asking the Council to recognize this information, so that he can obtain the document he needs. 2 September 1578.[42]

This document confirms much of the oral tradition that was common knowledge in Cremona regarding the Anguissola family. Since most people in the sixteenth century still could not read or write, the oral tradition of recalling who people were and what they did was extremely important in keeping history alive (and this then would include the emphasis placed on Asdrubale's legitimacy). How long Asdrubale remained in Sicily is not known. However, because of the long trip and winter months approaching, most probably he stayed with Sofonisba and Don Fabrizio for a few months.

Sometime after Asdrubale's return to Cremona, Don Fabrizio died. Tenoghi (writing in 1836) states that "after not too many years [of marriage], a violent disease claimed her beloved companion."[43] The plague decimated Europe with regularity. It is possible that early in 1579 it claimed Don Fabrizio's life.

Zaist mentions that King Philip then asked Anguissola to return to Spain. Now a widow, she must have wanted to return to Cremona to be with her mother, sisters, and brother. It even is conceivable that Asdrubale was still in Palermo at the time of Don Fabrizio's death. Anguissola had been traveling extensively and, at forty-seven, she may have wanted to feel more settled than she could have been at the Spanish court. So, in 1579, she left Palermo and embarked on her journey back home.

PLATE 105. Sofonisba Anguissola. *Holy Family*, 1559. Oil on canvas, 14 7/16 x 12 9/16 in. (36.7 x 31.9 cm). Accademia Carrara, Bergamo.

IX
THE RETURN OF AN ILLUSTRIOUS DAUGHTER

Manet avita virtus (Virtue lasts for life)
—*Lomellini family motto*

Until now, almost nothing has been known about Anguissola's life after Don Fabrizio's death. Several historical sources tell conflicting stories, but none of them are archivally documented. Some thought that she took a ship from Spain to Italy while others thought that she took a Genoese ship from Palermo and planned to sail for Naples. From there she is thought to have traveled by coach to Cremona. In fact, Anguissola sailed from Palermo (probably with a brief stop in Naples) to Livorno (Leghorn). Whatever her original plans were, they changed on board, as the ship's captain, Orazio Lomellino, fell in love with her. As Lancetti wrote:

> She wanted to return to her native land [instead of returning to serve King Philip]. So, she embarked on a Genoese ship commanded by the nobleman, Orazio Lomellino, and during the voyage he fell in love with his celebrated passenger. Love blossomed, their personalities pleased each other, the occasion was right, and she agreed to a second marriage. Not sterile ["istrile"] as her first had been, Sofonisba's pure heart was won over.[1]

This sixteenth-century shipboard romance has captivated other writers as well. Zaist, writing in a similar vein, called Orazio a "captain of renown," going on to say that "when they arrived in Genoa, they celebrated the solemn rites of marriage."[2] However, some twentieth-century writers have not waxed so lyrical and have viewed the marriage more cynically. Germaine Greer, writing in 1979, states:

> Life for an unattached foreign woman in the Spanish court cannot have been easy. Although all authorities repeat that she bore herself with irreproachable dignity and reserve, she might well have quailed at the thought of going back to drudgery and dependence upon royal whim. Her long employment at the Spanish court may have been less a matter of choice than commentators usually suppose. Marrying Lomellino may have been less an indication of how 'buoyant' she was in her private life than how keen a sense of self-preservation she had.[3]

Greer's term "drudgery," however, is too harsh. Philip is known to have been very generous and kind to his court painters, and Anguissola was among that favored group. Perhaps the truth lies closer to its being a sixteenth-century romance, rather than an arranged marriage. It seems to have been a happy one, and it lasted more than forty years. Orazio was grief-stricken at her death.

As documents have been discovered (published here for the first time) that clarify Anguissola's whereabouts in 1579 and 1580, a new chronology now can be established. In December 1579, she was in Pisa and wrote the following letter:

> To His Serene Highness and Patron
> The Grand Duke of Tuscany
>
> It has been a few days since I left Sicily, in order to go to my home in Cremona. Because I was troubled by the sea journey, and this long trip, I decided to lodge myself at the monastery of Santo Mazzeo. I disembarked at Livorno where I took the land road to Pisa. I had a few of my personal things sent to me here.
>
> I am asking your Highness, if it could be ordered that I do not have to pay customs duty on these said things, as they have been in my possession, and I have made use of them. Having been in your Highness's service for a long time, I do not have any doubts that you will oblige me in this, and I will be forever obliged to your Highness.
>
> With this, I pray to our Lord that he bless and keep your Highness well for many happy years to come. From Pisa, 18 December 1579.
>
> In affectionate service,
> Sofonisba de Moncada et Anguissola[4]

As a new widow, Sofonisba was still signing herself "Moncada et Anguissola." The letter shows that she must have been exhausted from grief over her husband's death and a long sea voyage—by "troubled" she may have meant seasick. Her need for rest in a monastery would not have been unusual in her circumstances. There were numerous monasteries and convents all over Italy that had (and still have today) rooms for weary travelers. It was customary for a traveler—even in the sixteenth century—going from one independent state to another to pay duty on valuables. It is noteworthy, however, to see that she signed the letter in a most informal manner, indicating that she knew the duke.

The grand duke answered, and Anguissola promptly replied (in a combination of Sicilian and Spanish) to him:

> To the Grand Duke of Tuscany
>
> I received a letter from your Serene Highness with which I felt great consolation in these my times of troubles. I appreciate with what kindness your Serene Highness favors me with his remembrance of me for which I am so much obliged. I assure your Highness that even without the consideration that your wishes come first, not only in matters about which I had not been properly informed, but also in matters which could be to my advantage. Had the wishes of your Highness, of whom I am a faithful servant, been known to me, I would have submitted all my actions to the wishes of your Highness. But in so far as marriages are made first in heaven and then on earth, the letter from your Serene Highness arrived late, so that I was not able to show my

most affectionate service to your Highness, whom I beg to pardon. From now on, I pray you would favor me by keeping me as one of your subjects. From Pisa, 27 December 1579.

Your obligated servant,
Sofonisba Anguissola[5]

While waiting for the duke's reply, Sofonisba apparently decided to pay the duty on her belongings. Then he answered her, but, again, his reply has not been found. Still upset "in these [her] times of troubles," and, with the utmost courtesy and tact, she tried to resolve a bureaucratic problem. This time, she signed her letter simply with her maiden name.

Her allusion to marriage now makes sense, as Orazio was courting her. Probably a few days later (although not dated), she sent a third letter to the grand duke. Most likely, it was sent to him at his request so that it could be formally filed with the customs office, and, thereby, she would be exempt.

To Your Serene Highness

Sofonisba Anguissola in the service of your Serene Highness, being in Pisa, arrived from Sicily with the galley of the Republic of Genoa [Orazio's ship], and brought some of her own silver and clothing, and a few other personal objects which have been inspected at the Customs House, having been compelled to pay the duty. As Lady-in-Waiting to his most Catholic Majesty and the Queen of Spain, I ask most graciously to be exempted from this said customs duty. I will consider this a sign of your great kindness and courtesy. I pray God to give your Serene Highness every happiness.

Your servant,
Sofonisba Anguissola[6]

Some time after this letter was written, probably the first week in January 1580, Sofonisba and Orazio were married. King Philip was notified, and he "granted Sofonisba an income of 400 scudi on her marriage."[7] Whatever other personal reasons she may have had for this alliance, it seems likely that she was tired of a peripatetic existence and wanted to settle down to a quieter life. Certainly, she had been happy at court while Queen Isabel was alive and had continued as lady-in-waiting to Queen Anne of Austria (as mentioned in her last letter). However, it appears from her first letter to the grand duke of Tuscany that she had been working for him—as she calls him her "patron"—after her marriage to Don Fabrizio. None of these commissions has been found, and even Sacchi (who, in the last century, had an extensive list of her works) does not mention any for the duke.

Francesco I de' Medici (1541–87), son of Cosimo and Eleanor of Toledo, was the second grand duke of Tuscany. Cosimo I had been created an hereditary duke on 28 February 1537 (see plate 99). It was Cosimo who ordered Vasari to build the Uffizi (today the majestic museum) facing the Arno River; and also under this duke's orders, the port of Livorno was constructed. Approximately thirty years later, Pope Pius V elevated Cosimo to the status of grand duke of Tuscany. It was to this very same Cosimo that Tommaso Cavalieri wrote in 1562 sending him sketches by Michelangelo and Sofonisba.

PLATE 99. Bronzino. *Portrait of
Grand Duke Cosimo [I] de' Medici.*
Private collection, on loan to the
National Gallery, London.

The Florentine Medici family derived their vast wealth from directing one of the major banking concerns in Europe. Throughout the sixteenth century, their banking interests secured that wealth, enabling them to be great patrons of the arts. Florence was a republic for most of the century, but the Medici led the city's independent *comune.* They supported the arts, enriched the city's coffers, and managed, most of the time, to have the support of the Florentine citizenry. Many of the early Medici strove for the good of the city.

Unfortunately, with the accession of Francesco I (ruled 1574–87), the golden age of the Medici was supplanted by "corruption and negligence of public affairs [and] reckless and disastrous fiscal policies."[8] Family scandals and atrocities abounded: Francesco's sister, Isabella, was strangled by her husband, Paolo Giordano Orsini (who earlier had fought in the pope's service against the duke of Alba); Pietro, Francesco's brother, "spent his time in orgiastic pursuits, which vilified him in the eyes" of the Florentines[9] and then he murdered his wife, Eleanor. The notoriety accompanying Francesco's rule only increased after his wife, the Archduchess Joanna of Austria died (1548–78; sister of Maximillian II, and thereby a Hapsburg, it was through this connection that Anguissola may have come into the duke's employ). Prior to his marriage Francesco had been having an affair (which continued

172

throughout his marriage) with Bianca Capello (1548–87), a Venetian, whom he married three months after Joanna's death. [Sacchi mentions (p. 8) a portrait, now lost, done by Anguissola that he thought was of Bianca Capello.] None of this sat well with the Florentines, who remembered the wonderful days of Lorenzo de' Medici, "the Magnificent."

Francesco was moody, melancholy, undisciplined, introverted, and arrogant. Although Cosimo I had tried to prepare his son to administer Florence's government in a responsible way, Francesco turned everything over to his ministers. Instead, he devoted time to pleasurable pursuits and his passion for alchemy and chemistry. Attempting to manufacture Chinese porcelain and imitation jewelry, he was the first to experiment with both these commodities, which would later prove to be valuable to Florence's history and economy. These experiments eventually led the way for the establishment of the Doccia porcelain factory and the Opificio delle Pietre Dure (precious stone works), both of which are still in existence.

Francesco patronized the arts lavishly and commissioned Vasari's successor, Bernardo Buontalenti, to design his *studiolo* (little study) in the Palazzo Vecchio where he conducted his experiments. He also was responsible for establishing the Uffizi Gallery, as part of his wish to create a public museum. The gallery then had studios for young artists. Although Anguissola alludes to having done work for Francesco in her letter, the works have not come down to us.

After her marriage to Orazio, she sent Francesco another letter:

> To His Serene Highness
> Grand Duke of Tuscany
>   My husband, Orazio, is coming to pay homage to your Serene Highness and to offer himself as one of your servants, as we are obliged to do. I beg your Serene Highness that among other favors I have received from you, that you will accept and favor him. I am most confident in you Serene Highness's benevolence, being your most affectionate servant.
>   I remain praying God that your Serene Highness will have many long and happy years. From Pisa, 14 January 1580.
>   Your servant, Sofonisba Lomel[l]ina et Anguissola[10]

If someone was in the employ of a ruler, it was customary, upon marriage, for her or his new spouse to "pay one's respects." So Orazio went to Florence to meet Francesco. How long he stayed is unknown, but most likely it was a brief visit. While in Florence, he may have bought his new bride some embroidered silks or velvets, as the city was renowned for its magnificent textiles.

After resting in Pisa, the newly married couple traveled to Cremona (as mentioned in Sofonisba's letter of 18 December 1579) to visit her family. It is conceivable that Sofonisba accompanied Orazio to Florence (although her letter was written from Pisa and she does not mention accompanying him), and from there they traveled to Cremona. It would have made good traveling sense to continue on to her birthplace together, stay through the dead of winter and then go to Genoa, the home of the Lomellini family.

Orazio's ancestors originated in Germany, and a branch moved to Lombardy in the twelfth century. There, they were an important political force in Lombardy's *comune*. Later, they emigrated to Genoa, and by 1528 (the same year that Admiral Andrea Doria liberated the Genoese from the French), they had set up a business as innkeepers. The family prospered as part of the new merchant-nobility and became involved in charitable works for the community. The Lomellini contributed several senators, prelates, bishops—one Giovanni Battista took part in the Council of Trent—archbishops, and cardinals to Genoa's thriving community. In 1533, they became dukes, and as the city was also an important port, several of the family became commanders of ships.

Genoa was a vital commercial port. Both the Lomellini and Doria families were prominent in the city's political and naval affairs. The most illustrious member of the Doria family was Admiral Andrea Doria (1466–1560). In 1528, he ensured Genoa's freedom from French political intrigue by allying himself with Charles V. The emperor in return, guaranteed the city's liberty by having the Genoese as allies and dependent upon the Hapsburg empire. The admiral fought for Charles V against the French who were allies of Süleyman, the Magnificent. The city was thus assured of its republican form of government, and Admiral Doria became both its most important leader and the most famous naval commander of the period.

Orazio's father, Niccolò, married Nicoletta Spinola (the daughter of Giorgio) and they had five children: Gironima, Lorenzo, Maria, Perretta, and Orazio.[11] No dates of birth, marriage, or death have been found for the family. As the Lomellini were both merchants and nobility, Orazio's education was assured. When he was about ten, he probably went to stay with another nobleman's family as Amilcare had done. It is possible that he stayed with Lomellini relatives, while putting the finishing touches on his academic and professional training, perhaps even with one of the Lomellini who was involved in shipping, as that became his career.

When Orazio and Sofonisba moved to Genoa, she became part of a large family network. It must have been gratifying for her to be surrounded by a new family rather than hundreds of courtiers. Orazio had his own palazzo on the Carubeo Auri Genue (Street of Gold),[12] and Sofonisba became the lady of her own palazzo, overseeing its daily running. She also kept up her correspondence with the Spanish royal family and in 1583, she interceded on Orazio's behalf when she wrote to King Philip. The letter, discovered by this author in Castle Simancas, is the only one known that is written entirely in her own hand (see plate 1).

Sacred Catholic Royal Majesty

With Orazio Lomellino, my husband, I wrote to your Majesty, begging you to allow me the grace of recommending my husband to you who wishes a favor granted. Again, I repeat my request to remind your Majesty to favor him speedily in what he asks. I am confident in the usual benevolence and generosity of your Majesty towards his subjects, among whom I am your most affectionate servant. I hope to receive this favor from your royal hands in which happiness I depend. I shall put this favor among many I have received from your Majesty. With humility and reverence, I kiss your hand, praying God to keep you for a long and happy life. From Genoa, 14 October 1583.

Your humble and faithful servant,
Sofonisba Lomellina et Anguissola[13]

What Orazio needed from the king remains a mystery, but evidently it was important enough to warrant Sofonisba's letter. Perhaps it was related to Orazio's shipping interests.

While Orazio was at sea, Sofonisba had ample time to devote to painting. Her studio at the palazzo became a gathering place for the nobility and other artists. The city was out of the mainstream of Italian art, and Anguissola's fame as a court portraitist to the Spanish king naturally drew artists to her.

During the 1580s and 1590s, Anguissola divided her time between painting for the nobility and painting religious themes, which she had not done since her days with Bernardino Campi (when, of course, she had far fewer demands on her time).[14] It is also conceivable, now that her reputation was firmly established, she felt she could paint subjects usually reserved for male painters. However, there also may have been a more compelling reason for her to do so. Over a fifteen-year period she had lost people who had meant a great deal to her: Lucia in 1565, Queen Isabel in 1568, her father in 1573, and Don Fabrizio in 1579. She had witnessed death in the case of the queen and Don Fabrizio. The pain must have been deep.

In 1582, Anguissola turned fifty, quite an advanced age then. Religion played a major role in sixteenth-century life, and it was an important force in Anguissola's life as well. She had lived at Philip's court where devotion to the Church was fanatic and legendary. Her age and life experiences may have drawn her more deeply into religion, and the desire to paint religious themes would have resurfaced.

It is known that Anguissola did numerous religious paintings, although many are now lost. Lancetti mentions a *Saint Francis* done by Anguissola and given to the Capuccine order,[15] and Sacchi notes two others: *Lot with His Daughters* and *Saint John the Baptist in the Desert.*[16] Bonetti states that in 1587 Anguissola painted a *Mystical Marriage of Saint Catherine,* and Sacchi also mentions it.[17] Another painting, *Saint Catherine della Ruota* (now lost), was done for the duke of Alba.[18]

The name Catherine belonged to numerous saints. Saint Catherine, who may have lived in Alexandria in the fourth century, was sent to her death on a spiked wheel by order of Emperor Maxentius. She was a patron saint of women students and scholars;[19] Saint Catherine of Genoa (Catherine Fieschi, 1447–1510) was venerated in Genoa shortly after her death (although not canonized until 1746); and Saint Catherine of Siena (1347–80) dedicated her life to acts of charity and trying to heal the divisions in the Church. She was a Dominican tertiary (i.e., from the third order of Saint Dominic). It was this third Saint Catherine who, in 1368, at twenty-one, had a vision in which she was mystically married to Christ. This incident became a popular theme in Renaissance art.

Anguissola's *Mystical Marriage of Saint Catherine* (1587) may have been done to commemorate the attributes of her sister, Minerva, who was considered a Latin scholar. Minerva, by this date, already may have died, and the painting may have been a memorial. The whereabouts of these religious works are unknown.

In 1588, Anguissola painted *Madonna Nursing Her Child* (Museum of Fine Arts, Budapest, see plate 100). The painting had been attributed to Luca Cambiaso until it was cleaned in 1967, revealing Anguissola's signature: "[Sof]onisba Lomel[l]ina Anguissola P[inxit] 1588."[20] This is one of only two known paintings on which the artist signed her married name.

PLATE 100. Sofonisba Anguissola. *Madonna Nursing Her Child,* 1588. Oil on canvas, 30 5/16 x 25 in. (77 x 63.5 cm). Museum of Fine Arts, Budapest.

PLATE 104. Sofonisba Anguissola. *Holy Family
with Saints Anne and John*, 1592. Oil on canvas,
48 7/16 x 42 15/16 in. (123 x 109 cm). Lowe
Art Museum, University of Miami, Coral Gables,
Florida, gift of Mrs. Forbes Hawkes, 1952.

Cambiaso (1527–85) was a Genoese painter trained by his father, Giovanni, who saw to it that his young son kept to his art studies by hiding his clothes and shoes. Luca collaborated on numerous murals in Genoa with his father, whom he surpassed in talent.

Genoa's splendor lay in its architecture, much of which was built by the Doria family. Galeazzo Alessi (1500–72), who was a pupil of Michelangelo, built the Palazzo Sauli in 1555 as well as many other Genoese churches and palaces; his student, Lurago, built the Palazzo Municipio in 1564. Cambiaso painted prolifically and decorated many of Genoa's churches. The monumental murals he created eventually laid the foundation for a Genoese style that would last into the next century.

In 1575, Cambiaso went to Florence and Rome to study the works of Raphael and Michelangelo. There, he absorbed the latter's monumentality. He returned to Genoa and worked there from 1580 to 1583. After Anguissola left Spain, King Philip invited Cambiaso to the Escorial in 1584 to complete frescoes for San Lorenzo's choir ceiling. Philip was so pleased that he rewarded Cambiaso by paying him seven thousand ducats, the highest sum ever paid an artist up to this time.

It is likely that Anguissola saw some of Cambiaso's works in the churches around Genoa. He left hundreds of drawings as well, covering a broad spectrum of subjects. Today he is best remembered for the scope of his sketches, which he apparently dashed off with tremendous rapidity.

The incorrect attribution of Anguissola's work to Cambiaso is significant. Before Cambiaso left for the Escorial, he was working in Genoa. Anguissola's studio in Genoa was a gathering place for artists, and she was the best-known artist in the city. Both she and Cambiaso had established reputations. It is quite conceivable that they met and discussed the ongoing artwork that Philip was commissioning at the Escorial. Cambiaso may have enlisted Anguissola's help in obtaining a position with King Philip, who was always interested in adding more religious works to his vast collection. It is possible that Anguissola encouraged the king to invite Cambiaso to Spain; she would have been in the ideal position to have done so. She understood the king's wishes, and Cambiaso certainly would have wanted a recommendation from a painter who had been in the king's service for so many years.

Anguissola's *Madonna Nursing Her Child,* done in 1588 while she was in Genoa, is painted in vibrant Venetian colors. Mary looks down lovingly at her son who is partially wrapped in a blanket. This painting also takes on the element of a devotional work, thereby combining the larger meaning of Christ's life and message with the intimate, personal experiences of mother and child with which the viewer could identify. (These two elements can also be seen in Anguissola's *Holy Family with Saints Anne and John,* see plate 104.) The handling of the child's anatomy shows that Anguissola had an understanding of the nude body. As a woman painter, this would have been the only acceptable nude that she could have done. Both figures are solidly executed. The oval shape of the painting accentuates the roundness of both Mary's figure and that of the infant Jesus, which are more in keeping with Bernardino Gatti's style. Together their bodies form oval and pyramidal shapes. The Mannerist influence of Michelangelo has been adapted in the Christ child's elongated body and the S–curves of the composition.

PLATE 101. Bernardino Campi. *Saints Cecilia and Caterina*, 1566. Chapel of Saints Cecilia and Caterina, San Sigismondo, Cremona.

Symbolic of Nature's bounty, the nursing child was portrayed from ancient times, with its origins most probably in Egypt. Ancient goddesses suckled "their divine offspring as far back as discovered civilization,"[21] and votive statues remain of Isis and Horus. Stories abound of Amaltheia nursing Zeus and Hera Heracles, whose milk created the Milky Way. This theme was then adopted by the early Christians—with one of the earliest portrayals in the catacombs of Santa Priscilla in Rome in the second century—known as *Maria Lactans* (Mary Nursing).

However, in Christian iconography, whether Mary's breast was bared or not depended upon the Church's fluctuating view of a woman's body. Early in Church history, while there were still strong ties with ancient holistic goddess traditions of the Ancient Near East, a woman's nudity (even partial) was still viewed positively and "milk symbolized in an ever more pronounced way this cluster of ideas, uniting new life and paradise."[22] By the mid-sixteenth century, however, the Church changed its view to one stressing "Purity's alliance with modesty and shame at the naked female body's beauty. . . . It became indecorous for the Virgin to bare her breast."[23] Renaissance artists followed papal dictates, as their reputations and livelihood depended upon acceptance of their portrayals of this theme.

PLATE 102. Sofonisba Anguissola. *Portrait of a Soldier*, 1580–85. Oil on canvas, 39 3/8 x 31 1/2 in. (100 x 80 cm). Accademia Carrara, Bergamo.

PLATE 103. Sofonisba Anguissola. *Portrait of a Nobleman and His Son*, 1580s. Oil on copper, 6 5/16 x 4 15/16 in. (16 x 12.5 cm). Pinacoteca Nazionale, Siena.

It is therefore quite interesting that Anguissola chose to portray Mary nursing her son in a tender and maternal way: smiling, breast bared, and her son, his eyes partially closed, in a nursing reverie. This painting then had a dual purpose: a religious work that portrayed an intimate maternal scene, rather than a distant icon to whom a family or individual could not relate.

The year in which Anguissola painted this picture was the year Sánchez Coello died and King Philip's Armada was defeated. The king had set out to invade England and remove Queen Elizabeth from her throne. Although the reasons for the war were complex, two issues were central: one economic and one religious. Elizabeth—a Protestant ruler—had tacitly been sanctioning the piracy and privateering of her English ships, which had been seizing Spanish galleons loaded with treasures from the Americas.

By the 1580s, Philip was the most powerful king in Christendom. He had consolidated his authority on the Iberian Peninsula and, several years after the death of his nephew, King Sebastian of Portugal, he invaded the country (with the help of the duke of Alba) and claimed it as his rightful inheritance. Grandiosely, he thought that England, too, should be his.

The undertaking was a catastrophe from the beginning. Secluded in his rooms at the Escorial, Philip endeavored to direct the war. It was an impossible situation. He was too far away, and he gave command of the Armada to the duke of Medina Sidonia, Don Alonso Perez de Guzman, who was totally lacking in naval skills. By the time the Armada (with its thirty thousand men and fleet of one hundred thirty ships) reached the English Channel, it was doomed. Outmaneuvered by Sir Francis Drake's lighter English ships, the Armada suffered horrendous shipboard fires and eventual shipwrecks on the Scottish and Irish coasts.

Word traveled quite fast when there was war, especially since Genoa was a major seaport. Sofonisba, on hearing that the king was at war, would have been in close touch with the royal family and probably wrote to Isabella Clara Eugenia.

The Armada was defeated in September, and by the beginning of the new year, some degree of normalcy must have returned to Genoa. Sofonisba also continued to keep in touch with her own family in Cremona. Now that she was in Italy, a journey to Cremona was not as difficult as one from Spain had been. She may have taken a trip to Cremona either with or without Orazio (depending on his sailing schedule) to visit family, friends, and her teacher.

Bernardino Campi was still alive (he died in 1591). A visit from his internationally recognized pupil would have brought great pleasure to the elderly painter. Sofonisba would have shared with him discussions of other artists' techniques as well as glimpses of the Spanish royal family. She and her teacher may have visited San Sigismondo, on the outskirts of Cremona. Bernardino had been commissioned by that church to do an extensive amount of painting for its interior: *Saints Cecilia and Caterina* (in the chapel dedicated to them, see plate 101), signed and dated 1566; *Saint Jerome* (see plate 66), done the same year; and the vault of the chapel of *Saints Filippo and Giacomo* (see plate 15). Sitting in the tranquil church interior with the sun streaming through the windows (as it still does today), or talking in the garden of the cloister, teacher and student would surely have spent happy hours discussing family, their own careers, and the changes in art that had occurred since Sofonisba was a young girl mixing paints in Bernardino's kitchen.

It is possible that Sofonisba's mother, Bianca, died about this time.[24] There is a document dated 13 May 1589, from notary Raffaele Tartesio stating that "Sofonisba gives to her brother the annual pension of 800 [lire] which had been assigned to [her from King Philip] for life."[25] Years before, Sofonisba had given the money to Amilcare and, on his death, she may have had these payments sent to her mother. Upon her death, the pension then went to Asdrubale. He is noted as living near the Church of San Vincenzo in Cremona. Sofonisba may have visited her brother about this time. Asdrubale apparently had not married, and brother and sister could comfort one another.

When she returned to Genoa, Anguissola continued to take on new commissions, and *Portrait of a Soldier* (Accademia Carrara, Bergamo, see plate 102) dates from this time.[26] The identity of this nobleman, done in oil on canvas, is unknown. It shows Anguissola's coloring and characteristically fine costume details in the starched ruff and armor and also contains her "square-U" delineation in the gentleman's left hand and fingers. The angularity of his right little finger is almost identical to that of Don Carlos's left little finger (see plate 81).

Another portrait that also dates from about this period is *Portrait of a Nobleman and His Son* (Pinacoteca Nazionale, Siena, see plate 103). The painting had been attributed to an anonymous sixteenth-century north Italian artist by the museum. Based upon style and coloring, it is here attributed to Anguissola (and this is supported by the museum).

This beautiful oil on copper oval can be dated to the latter part of the century: the style of the nobleman's starched and pleated ruff (they became increasingly larger with wider pleats towards the last twenty years of the century) places it about 1580–85. He is wearing a black velvet doublet with gold buttons down the front and satin cut-and-slashed sleeves. He is portrayed here with a young boy of about ten, who is probably his son. The boy wears a plain linen ruff edged in *punto in aria* lace. Portions of the upper part of his light brown-mustard-colored doublet and white-striped silk chemise are visible. His auburn hair is worn short.

Although Anguissola's characteristic hands are not part of this composition, the meticulous attention to the costume details and the coloring of both faces indicates her work, as visible in the soft peach facial tones outlined in a pale brown. Further, even in this formal portrait, there is an indication of family warmth, as the boy's head and shoulders are placed on the father's left, close to his heart. This might indicate that the child is his first-born son. It appears that part of his left arm—had the rest of it been part of the portrait—would have been placed around his son.

While Anguissola continued to do polished, courtly portraits, she also pursued religious themes. In 1592, she painted *Holy Family with Saints Anne and John* (Lowe Art Museum, Coral Gables, Florida, see plate 104). It is oil on canvas, and on the piece of paper near the dog's head, she inscribed: "Sofonisba Lomel[1]ino et Anguissola pinsit 1592."

The composition has similarities to her *Madonna Nursing Her Child* in its pyramidal arrangement and elongation of the figures. The Christ child's body and Mary

PLATE 106. Lavinia Fontana. *Portrait of a Lady with a Lap Dog*, 1590s. Walters Art Gallery, Baltimore.

and Anne's arms are attenuated but not exaggerated, as in many of Parmigianino's works. Mary's face is done with the same gentle roundness. Both women are smiling, giving a great warmth to the scene. The composition's *contrapposto* is done tastefully and subtly, thus maintaining an overall harmony. Finally, Anguissola's "square U" is evident in both St. Anne's and Mary's fingers.

The dog curled up in the lower left corner harks back to the sleeping dog in Anguissola's *Portrait of Massimiliano Stampa* (see plate 61). Symbol of melancholy, it might have been incorporated into the painting to commemorate the death of Bianca Ponzone Anguissola. Here, Anguissola has blended themes of new life and death in a harmonious way, and the maternal theme of this painting is therefore emphasized and deepened.

Anguissola's religious paintings had evolved from the thin, attenuated figures she had copied from Campi thirty years earlier when her *Pietà* (see plate 23) and *Holy Family* (Accademia Carrara, Bergamo, see plate 105)[27] were both painted within a few years of each other before she left for Spain. She copied her teacher's style both in composition and the shape of the figures. When she resumed painting religious subjects, her figures were more solidly constructed and had a gentle, human quality. In a lifetime of painting and experience, her style naturally had matured and also given her a deeper connection to her faith.

During the last decade of the sixteenth century, Anguissola's palazzo continued to be a mecca for artists.[28] It must have been unusual for those Genoese artists (who did not have the same access to art studies as painters in Florence, Venice, or Rome) to have an internationally acclaimed woman painter in their midst. Whatever difficulties or prejudice that had existed at the beginning of her career now had abated.

PLATE 107. Barbara Longhi. *Madonna with Sleeping Child.* Walters Art Gallery, Baltimore.

Her home might have been an early forerunner of the eighteenth-century salon, where an educated woman hosted a gathering of the best of Genoese culture.

Along with her family responsibilities, commissions, and her own work, Anguissola also found time to teach. Raffaele Soprani (more well known for his lives of Genoese painters than for his own paintings) says that she took under her wing Francesco Piola (1565–1600), a minor painter who lived in Genoa. Soprani goes on to say, erroneously, that Anguissola's artistic ideas were "formed in Genoa."[29] Perhaps his fervor as a Genoese went a bit too far. Nothing is known about Piola's studies with his illustrious teacher.

It is possible that, besides teaching Piola, Anguissola had contact with other women artists in northern Italy whose careers were on the rise. Anguissola's work was well known all over Italy, and her sketches and life were used as a role model. Indeed, she was important to those few talented women, including Lavinia Fontana (1552–1614), Barbara Longhi (1552–1638), and Fede Galizia (1578–1630), who chose painting as a career.

Lavinia Fontana's studies began with her father, Prospero (1512–97), who "was one of the leading painters in Bologna."[30] Prospero received his early art training in Genoa and then worked in Florence and Rome before returning to Bologna. Lavinia's earliest recorded works date from 1575 when "she produced a steady stream of . . . portraits, small religious works, mythologies, and, after 1589, altarpieces in Bologna . . . and Rome."[31]

In 1589, Fontana was commissioned by King Philip to do a *Holy Family* for the Escorial. It seems likely that Anguissola's stay in Spain paved the way for the king to commission this work. Undoubtedly, Fontana knew of Anguissola, and through her father's teacher, Perino del Vaga (1500/02–47), had connections in Genoa. So, it is possible that she traveled there to meet Anguissola. Frederick Hartt calls Vaga "the only gifted artist"[32] (ignoring Anguissola's later Genoese accomplishments) in Genoa, where he fled in 1528 after the sack of Rome. Lavinia Fontana was twenty years younger than Anguissola and, by the 1590s, "had what might be called a normal successful artistic career, which remained a rare phenomenon until the late eighteenth century." She was adept at "a considerable range of subject matter and was the first to carry out a substantial number of public commissions."[33] She gained fame in her youth as a portrait painter of many of Bologna's aristocracy and was noted for the great care that she paid to costume details (see plate 106). She was summoned to Rome by Pope Gregory XIII (whose portrait she painted) to do a larger-than-life-size work, *The Stoning of St. Stephen*. Fontana was the first woman to maintain workshops in both Rome and Bologna. Subsequently, she was elected to Rome's prestigious Academy and was charging as much for her works as was Anthony Van Dyck. Harris and Nochlin state that without Fontana's pioneering works the later achievements of Artemisia Gentileschi would not have been possible.

Barbara Longhi of Ravenna is less well known than Fontana, in part because her works were produced locally and her reputation remained regional. In this century, her life and works have received very little attention. She came from a family of painters. Her father, Luca Longhi (1507–80), was a Mannerist painter, and her brother Francesco Longhi (1544–1620) was both a poet and painter. She trained with her father, with whom she served as both his assistant and model.

Inspired by Parmigianino and Coreggio, she "produced a series of small Madonna and Child compositions (see plate 107) that were, according to Vasari, 'unique for their purity of line and soft brilliance of color.'"[34] Although only fifteen of her works are known today, during her thirty-year career, she painted portraits, biblical themes, and devotional works, mostly of the Madonna and Child. She imbued these small devotional pieces with a warmth that brought together a sense of intimacy between the work and the viewer.

Fede Galizia also was the daughter of an artist. Her father, Nunzio, was a miniaturist who worked both in his native city, Trent, and in Milan. Before she was twenty, Fede (whose name means "faith"), had gained an international reputation as a portraitist who also did religious works (including commissions from several Milanese churches) and numerous still-life paintings. She is considered one of the pioneers of that genre. Nochlin and Harris state that "it is even possible that Nunzio Galizia was inspired to train his daughter by the example of Sofonisba."[35] One of Fede Galizia's earliest patrons, Jesuit historian and scholar Paolo Morigia (see plate 108), wrote that she showed "clear and evident signs of becoming a truly noble painter."[36] Even if Galizia was exploring a new genre, it was not appreciated or valued as highly as portraiture or religious themes. Further, she was a woman, and that was still a considerable handicap. It would take another half a century before the Dutch still lifes—and Rachel Ruysch's magnificent and accurately executed floral arrangements—were accepted artistic fare.

If Anguissola was a source of inspiration for Galizia as a young artist, Galizia may have wanted to visit Anguissola and learn directly from her (although no connection between them is currently known). Anguissola's sketches had been known since the early 1550s and were passed around in artistic circles all over Italy. Both Fontana and Galizia would have known some of them and routinely copied them as part of their art studies.

There is also a story that Titian "agreed to instruct the granddaughter of his friend Paolo di Ponte, Irene di Spilimbergo [1541–59] . . . who had been orphaned of [her] father and been sent to live in her grandfather's house."[37] When she was eighteen, she went to paint early one morning, caught a chill, and died.

> A collection of poems, written by every eminent Venetian contemporary on the occasion of her death, was published in 1561. In the introduction it is said that 'having been shown a portrait by Sofonisba Anguissola, made by her own hand, presented to King Philip of Spain, and hearing wondrous praise of her in the art of painting, moved by generous emulation, she was fired with a warm desire to equal that noble and talented damsel' [*valorosa donzella*] .[38]

Finally, Artemisia Gentileschi (1593–1652/53) was a budding artist in 1609 when Anguissola was still in Genoa.

> Van Dyck and Artemisia Gentileschi may both have known Sofonisba in Genoa as well, if Soprani is correct. . . . But certainly Artemisia would have known her by reputation, if not in person. No obvious connection exists between the art of Anguissola and Gentileschi, and there is no evidence that Artemisia had a special interest in other women artists, yet it remains fascinating to imagine what a conversation might have been like between Europe's two most illustrious female painters of the time.[39]

Gentileschi refused to be confined to portraits (although she did many) and was a pioneer in portraying biblical women as dramatic, heroic figures. One of her well-known biblical themes is *Judith and Maidservant with the Head of Holofernes* (Detroit Institute of Arts, Detroit, see plate 109), a subject that she painted many times. Anguissola also painted a work known as *Judith with the Head of Holofernes,* now lost but known from a nineteenth-century source.[40] Barbara Longhi also painted the same subject. It is quite conceivable that both Longhi and Gentileschi knew of Anguissola's rendition, or possibly had even seen it, and that it became a source of inspiration for their own works.

Gentileschi's father, Orazio (1563–1638), was a follower of Caravaggio; and by the third decade of the seventeenth century, Artemisia's "presence in Genoa led to Genoese Caravaggism."[41] She was Caravaggio's only female follower and one of the most important painters of the Baroque.

Although there is no concrete connection between Gentileschi and Anguissola, there is a strong one between the latter and Caravaggio. Anguissola's sketch of Asdrubale, *Asdrubale Being Bitten by a Crab* (see plate 39) was the source of Caravaggio's *Boy Being Bitten by a Lizard* (see plate 37). Copies of the sketch had been circulating for the previous forty years, and Caravaggio is known to have painted two versions, both done about 1596–97, and based on Anguissola's work.

In the Lombardian painting tradition that explored emotions and opposites,

FIDES GALLICIA VIRGO PVDICISS·ÆTAT·SVÆ·ANN·XVIII OPVS HOC·
PAVLI MORIGII SIMVLACRVM, ANN·72 GRATI ANIMI ERGO EFFINXIT
ANNO 1596

PLATE 108. Fede Galizia. *Portrait of Paolo Morigia*, 1596. Pinacoteca Ambrosiana, Milan.

capturing someone in a moment of pain was a common theme by the end of the century. The psychological drama of Caravaggio's sensuous youth, whose bare shoulder is twisted in pain as the lizard bites his middle finger, is beautifully posed against the backdrop of a still-life composition of flowers and fruits. "Caravaggio is recorded as saying it took as much skill to paint flowers as figures."[42] The skill required to depict nature with scientific accuracy was expected of sixteenth-century artists. Caravaggio's drops of water on the leaves and touches of light on the vase enhance the depiction of nature, which, nonetheless, is subservient to the larger theme of emotion.

A man with a violent temper, Caravaggio was imprisoned on several occasions. In July 1605, he fled to Genoa after assaulting a notary. He even may have met Anguissola during the month that he was there (she is known to have been living in Genoa at the time). She certainly knew of this promising young artist who led a tempestuous existence. The following year, in an argument over a tennis match wager, Caravaggio killed his opponent. Again, he fled. In July 1610, when some of his "enemies caught up with him, slashing his face so badly that he was almost unrecognizable . . . [he] then boarded a boat for Rome, where his pardon was being negotiated by Cardinal Gonzaga. Upon landing, he was mistakenly identified and thrown into prison for two days. He then resumed the trip on foot, caught a fever, and within a few days died as miserably as he had lived."[43] He was thirty-eight.

Anguissola's position as a role model may also have extended to women musicians. It is conceivable that her two self-portraits at the clavichord (see plates 44 and 82) may have circulated in Italy as sketches or engravings and also become a source of inspiration to women who were pursuing a musical profession in singing, playing an instrument, or composing. Music was part of a noblewoman's education, and especially within the confines of the court, became much more accessible to women during the sixteenth century. This easily observable change was important not only socially but also musically, for the increased participation of women in professional music-making had wide repercussions in the monuments of late-sixteenth- and early-seventeenth century music that have come down to us. . . . The crucial steps in this change occurred around 1580 in the closely connected courts of Florence, Mantua, and Ferrara.[44]

Duke Alfonso d'Este at Ferrara "established a pioneering group of singing ladies with his court[45] in June 1581, shortly after Anguissola had returned to Italy. He had a passion for poetry and music, "which then led to a subtle but important shift in the function of music for women within the court."[46] Hiring "women singers in the guise of ladies-in-waiting"[47]—an idea he may have borrowed from Philip II when the king brought Anguissola to the Spanish court—proved an overwhelming success. These singing ladies, known as *concerto di donne,* spread quickly throughout northern Italian courts, including that of Francesco [I] de' Medici and his second wife, Bianca Capello (whose portrait Anguissola had painted).

These talented women came from either the wealthy merchant class or families of well-known poets. Laura Peverara from Mantua belonged to a merchant family; Anna Guarini and Tarquinia Molza both had relatives who were poets. Anna's father, G. B. Guarini, was both a poet and court secretary; Tarquinia's uncle was the poet Francesca Maria Molza. These women were part of the *concerto di donne* at the court

PLATE 109. Artemisia Gentileschi, c. 1625. *Judith and Maidservant with the Head of Holofernes.* Detroit Institute of Arts, Detroit, gift of Mr. Leslie H. Green.

in Ferrara. In Mantua, singer Claudia Cattaneo married Claudio Monteverdi in 1599. She was the daughter of Giulio Caccini, who was the music director of the court of Francesco de' Medici, and later became part of the *capella di musica* in Mantua. Since Anguissola had worked for Francesco, it is conceivable that she knew Claudia Cattaneo and Monteverdi.

The most well-known woman composer during this time was Madalena Casulana who wrote madrigals that "appeared in the anthology *Il Desiderio* in Venice in 1566" and "were the first compositions by a woman to be published anywhere."[48] In 1568 and 1570, she had published two complete books of madrigals for four voices. Her works were published again in 1583 and 1586. Within this same time, three other woman were also composing madrigals: in Parma, Paola Massarenghi; in Ferrara, Vittoria Aleotti; and Cesarina Ricci di Tingoli. Thus, by "1600 it was possible for a father of quite modest background to educate his daughter directly for a career in music, without the pretense that music had entered simply as part of the education of the aspiring woman courtier."[49]

Anguissola, as the epitome of the multi-talented courtier/artist, may have given many Italian women the impetus to pursue their musical careers in an environment that was more accepting of their capabilities than half a century before.

Anguissola's life continued its routine until she received word that King Philip had died on 13 September 1598, at the age of seventy-one. He was buried in the Escorial next to other members of his family. It is probable that Anguissola received a letter from Isabella Clara Eugenia. Whatever his flaws were as a monarch, Anguissola knew him over a span of thirty-eight years as her patron and, in his own way, her friend. Even after she left Spain, he continued sending her a pension. She must have been saddened to read the news. It is quite conceivable that she wrote to Isabella Clara Eugenia to express her condolences, especially as the two were to be in close correspondence the following year. It was the passing of an era.

The next year, 1599, Anguissola received word from Isabella Clara Eugenia that she was to be married to her cousin, the Archduke Albert of Austria. Before Philip's death, the king had wanted to see his daughter settled and married; she was over thirty, quite old for anyone let alone a princess, still to be unmarried, and was considered "the greatest catch since Elizabeth of England."[50] Since the archduke was also a cardinal, he had to receive papal dispensation in order to marry Isabella. Albert was one of Philip's trusted rulers: Philip had appointed him viceroy of Portugal in 1583, and later governor of the Netherlands.

As part of her dowry, Philip bestowed upon his daughter the Netherlands. It was one of the king's wiser decisions. Isabella Clara Eugenia then became a sovereign, ruling jointly with Albert; their reign brought a period of peace to a country that had been fraught with religious and political bloodshed for decades.

On her way to her wedding, the infanta stopped in Genoa to have Sofonisba paint her betrothal portrait. As De Soressina Vidoni wrote in the nineteenth century, "Isabella wrote to Sofonisba and gave her assurances of affection for the sweet memories that she had for her services and virtues, and [Isabella had Sofonisba] paint her portrait."[51]

Sofonisba had been keeping in touch with the infanta during the almost twenty years since she had left Spain. Despite the distance and passage of time, there was a great bond of affection between the two women. There were other court painters at the Escorial who could have painted Isabella, but it speaks volumes of their friendship and the infanta's trust in Sofonisba that she went to Genoa to have this special portrait done. Unfortunately, the location of this painting is not known.

Isabella made the same arduous trip (in reverse) that Sofonisba had taken thirty years before: she left the Escorial and journeyed to Barcelona. From there, she took a ship to Genoa. It is quite possible that Orazio's ship took Isabella from Barcelona to Genoa. Sofonisba may have felt that having her husband in command of the infanta's ship would insure a safe voyage, as he had a reputation as an excellent captain.

The reunion of the infanta and her favorite painter—who had been such a source of companionship after Queen Isabel's death—was a joyous occasion. The city of Genoa greeted this Hapsburg princess in the regal fashion befitting her station. Her father had been welcomed in Genoa fifty-one years before, but his taciturn personality did not endear him to the Italians. Philip's daughter was different. Her personality and capabilities won friends—just as her mother had done upon her arrival in Spain. There were rounds of festivities and elegant feasts at several palazzi.

Sofonisba knew of Isabella's arrival months ahead of time. She would have ordered new gowns, and perhaps even sent to Florence for a new bolt of silk to be given to the infanta as a wedding gift. Surely, she would have reminisced about her days in Madrid shopping for silk for Queen Isabel. And now Isabel's daughter would be her honored guest. It was customary for the local nobility to entertain and put up visiting royalty; and most probably, Orazio and Sofonisba would have gladly welcomed the infanta at their own palazzo. After living in Philip's palaces for so many years, Sofonisba would surely have been very happy to extend her own hospitality to Isabella.

The royal visit probably lasted for a few weeks while the infanta sat for her portrait, and then the future archduchess of the Netherlands left for Milan. Although Sofonisba and Isabella continued to correspond, it was the last time they would see each other. As Isabella Clara Eugenia left by coach for Milan with her huge retinue, Sofonisba must have been flooded with memories of the little infanta she had so lovingly taken care of so long ago in Spain. Now grown up, and well educated, she was off to the Netherlands. Even after Albert's death (1621), Isabella Clara Eugenia continued to rule judiciously. Philip would have been pleased with his daughter's administrative acumen.

This was the last year of a century filled with political disasters and artistic triumphs. The art created during these one hundred years was some of the greatest ever produced. Anguissola was part of it. At the turn of that century, art was undergoing a period of transition.

Anguissola must have been thankful for her iron constitution, a valuable gift from her long-lived Anguissola and Ponzone relatives. Despite the hazards of illness, ever-present plague, and death at an early age (especially for many women), she was in good health. Sofonisba could look forward to the beginning of a new century with Orazio.

PLATE 110. Sofonisba Anguissola. *Self-Portrait*,
c. 1610. Oil on canvas, 37 x 29 1/2 in.
(94 x 75 cm). Gottfried Keller Collection,
Bern, Switzerland.

X

THE TWILIGHT YEARS

When I drew her [Anguissola's] portrait, she gave me
several hints: not to get too close, too high, or too low.
—Sir Anthony Van Dyck. Italian Sketchbook

s the new century began, Anguissola turned sixty-eight. She and Orazio had been married twenty years, and their lives in Genoa had been filled with a rich combination of his sailing adventures and her art. According to Pietro Selvatico, writing in 1870, it "was then [in Genoa] that a great opportunity opened up for Sofonisba where she could display sumptuous and aristocratic customs acquired at the Spanish court"[1] when she entertained at the Lomellini palazzo. Further, Bonetti says that she was still sought out by artists who wished to "admire her work and consult with her."[2] Although she did not keep up the same pace, Anguissola was still actively painting in Genoa. Her portraits, spanning half a century, documented many of the Spanish and Italian clergy and nobility.

On 22 September 1605, in Genoa, notary Agostino Romairone drew up for Anguissola a document called *fides vitae*. Literally, it was a certificate to prove that she was still alive. Due to her advanced age, she needed it in order to be able to cash her stipends from King Philip II which his son, Philip III continued to send her.[3] A similar document was drawn up by the same notary on 6 December.[4]

Anguissola still kept her close ties with Asdrubale (although no letters are known from this period), and in the spring of 1606, she wrote to King Philip III to request that he transfer her pension to her brother. Now fifty-five, Asdrubale must have been going through some financial difficulties and probably asked his sister for help. On 8 June, King Philip III sent Anguissola a letter giving his official permission for the pension transfer.[5] Philip's approval was only the first step in the bureaucratic process, as the paperwork dragged on until the end of the year. The governor of Milan, Count de Fuentes, approved the transfer on 15 September[6] and another document was drawn up at the Lomellini palazzo. Finally, on 9 December, the Milanese senate "ratified the transmission of the pension."[7] With all this red tape, Anguissola still had to continue signing *fides vitae* documents periodically so that Asdrubale

193

could cash her pension.[8] It is possible that she may even have made another trip to Cremona during this decade, especially if Asdrubale was having problems. Anguissola also may have had another reason in traveling to Cremona at this time. The Franciscan monk composer Lodovico da Viadana (?1560–?1627) was in Cremona from 1602–8 at San Luca. She may have known his music and played it, and while there may have painted his portrait.

Although by this time Anguissola may have taken on only a few commissions, she still continued to do self-portraits. A signed *Self-Portrait,* done for King Philip III, dates from the first decade of the seventeenth century (Gottfried Keller Collection, Berne, see plate 110). On the piece of paper she holds in her right hand, Anguissola inscribed this little-known painting, "Alla Mag[esta]d Catolica besa la m[ano] . . . Anguissola" (To his Catholic Majesty, I kiss your hand, Anguissola).

Here Anguissola portrays herself in a three-quarter-length pose as the elder stateswoman of the Renaissance: seated as an elegant septuagenarian. In her left hand, she holds a book with her index finger inserted into the book, as a reminder to keep her place (perhaps to let the viewer know that it is important to Anguissola). Her right hand holds the written inscription that she displays prominently. This is her link to the new Hapsburg king, Philip III, whom she had known as an infant. (He had been born in 1578, before she left Spain.) The importance of this *Self-Portrait* and the last one she did (now at Niva, Denmark, see plate 113) document her skill and continuing interest as she portrayed herself in her seventies and eighties, by which time she had been painting for almost eighty years.

Early in the new century, Flemish painter Peter Paul Rubens (1577–1640) paid a visit to Genoa while Anguissola was still living there. Rubens, who was to become one of the greatest Flemish painters of the seventeenth century, had studied under Adam van Noort (in his studio in Antwerp) and then under Otto van Veen. In 1599 Rubens assisted in van Veen's studio when the latter was commissioned to take part in the construction of festive preparations for the triumphant entry into the city of the archdukes (as they were known) Albert and Isabella.

> On this occasion the city was decorated with lavish and elaborate temporary architecture—arches and screens—which in allegorical fashion welcomed the Archdukes and at the same time called attention to Antwerp's sad economic plight, which had been brought on by the continuing war with the northern provinces.[9]

The citizens hoped that the presence of the new Spanish governors—they arrived in Brussels on 5 September 1599—would alleviate the ongoing economic problems and bring peace. Albert was known as a capable administrator and was responsible for opening a dialogue between Flanders and the United Provinces which, subsequently, led to a formal truce and peace.

It is quite possible that Rubens met the Archduchess Isabella Clara Eugenia at this time, but it was not until 1609 that she took him into her service. In 1600, Rubens left for Italy, and while he was there "he painted for Archduke Albert some altar pictures for the Church of the Holy Cross in Rome, of which the Archduke had been cardinal."[10] Rubens also worked for Vincenzo Gonzaga, the duke of Mantua, and, while in his service, traveled to Genoa. An extremely well-educated man, fluent in many languages, "keenly interested in all aspects of the contemporary scene and well informed through an extended correspondence, he was ideally suited for services far exceeding those normally entrusted to an artist."[11]

An interesting and intimate account of Rubens's versatility was written in 1621 (during the time when Anthony Van Dyck was still at Rubens's studio) by a Danish doctor, Otto Sperling, who was visiting Antwerp and had the opportunity to visit

> the celebrated painter Rubens, and found the great artist at work. While still painting, he was having Tacitus read aloud to him, and was dictating a letter. When we kept silent so as not to disturb him with our talk, he himself began to talk to us, while still continuing to work, to listen to the reading and to dictate the letter, answering our questions and thus displaying his astonishing powers. After that he told one of his servants to show us every part of his splendid house, in which we were shown Greek and Roman antiquities, which he possessed in great quantity. We saw there also a large hall which had no windows but was lit through an opening in the ceiling [this was on the floor above the large studio]. In this hall were a number of young painters, all at work on different pictures, for which Rubens had made the drawings in chalk indicating the tones here and there. . . . [12]

During his visit to Genoa, Rubens may have met Anguissola. When he returned to Antwerp in 1608 (due to the death of his mother), he became "confidential advisor"[13] to Isabella. It was a post that he held for many years, and "as her special envoy he made trips to Spain, England, and Holland, carrying out delicate diplomatic missions."[14] In this capacity, Rubens returned to Genoa and may have contacted Anguissola through his association with Isabella—perhaps even bringing letters from her. Anguissola would have been happy to receive firsthand news of the archduchess as well as up-to-date information on the artistic happenings in the north. His fresh approach to color and his portrayal of both mortal men and the gods (infusing them with human qualities) were part of his rejection of Mannerism and his own way of striking out in new artistic directions. Anguissola would have been interested in hearing his views of northern art techniques.

> [Upon his return to Antwerp, Rubens's] 'fame had already spread far and wide, and the Archdukes Albert and Isabella, who wished to be painted by him, appointed him court painter and bound him by chains of gold lest he return to Italy, whither the high prices paid for his pictures might attract him.'[15]

The archduchess, who had inherited her generosity from her parents, gave Rubens a gold necklace depicting the archdukes. He was paid five hundred florins a year, and any other commissions from his royal patrons were paid to him over and above his regular salary. He was exempted from paying taxes or registering his pupils with the painter's Guild of St. Luke. This generous salary enabled Rubens to live between his two homes in Antwerp and Brussels. Eventually, he was knighted by King Charles I of England (Mary, Queen of Scots's grandson) and given noble standing by the king of Spain.

With Rubens, the new generation of the Hapsburgs continued a pattern of paying their favorite artist in a lavish way and entrusting him with responsibilities other than artistic ones. Isabella Clara Eugenia had seen that practice firsthand from

her father and mother: Sofonisba had been an intimate of her mother, Isabel, and Philip (after Isabel's death) continued entrusting the care of their daughter to his noble Cremonese court painter.

The role and responsibility of the artist had changed significantly under Hapsburg patronage. With the building of the Escorial, which housed his vast art collection, Philip II had become the greatest patron of the century. By the end of his forty-two-year reign, his collection included the entire spectrum of sixteenth-century art: sculpture, architecture, an enormous library, maps, religious paintings and relics, and portraits. He was an exacting master and kept detailed notes on precisely what he wanted in each work of art—especially the religious ones—he commissioned. In portraiture, however, Titian's and then Anguissola's unusual position at court, the rapport the king had with his court painters (including Coello), and Philip's noted generosity, all paved the way for a more elevated status for artists in the next century.

Philip's tastes also were passed on to his daughter and son-in-law. From the time Albert was eleven (in 1570), he was sent to Philip's court for his education which, naturally, included exposure to his uncle's artistic tastes. As an adult, Albert "understood and keenly appreciated the works of artists and architects."[16] Albert and Isabella, raised together at the Spanish court, brought that appreciation to their own court in the Netherlands when they became joint rulers. After Philip II's death, Hapsburg patronage continued in northern Europe with the archdukes' patronage of Anguissola, Rubens, and Van Dyck, as well as in Spain under Philip III, the great patron of

PLATE 112. Peter Paul Rubens. *Portrait of Isabella Clara Eugenia*, c. 1618. Prado Museum, Madrid.

Velásquez. Now as the last survivor of Mannerism, a style that had spanned a great portion of the sixteenth century and now was supplanted by the Baroque, Anguissola continued to be viewed and treated with the respect due her by a new generation of painters.

Sometime about 1618 (before Sofonisba and Orazio moved to Palermo), Isabella probably wrote to Sofonisba to tell her that Rubens had recently completed two portraits (Prado Museum, Madrid) of her and the archduke. In the separate canvases, Rubens portrayed them each seated in front of a balcony, a curtain pulled back to show a view of two castles in the countryside. Albert is wearing a large, pleated ruff, and the Order of the Golden Fleece hangs from a gold chain around his neck (see plate 111). His solemn face appears careworn. Isabella, too, though painted in all her regal opulence, seems tired (see plate 112). Both had inherited Philip's predilection for long hours, working long into the night on state matters, and it shows in these paintings. The archduchess is wearing an elaborate gown with ropes of pearls on her bodice, a jeweled pointed tiara, and an extremely wide ruff and the matching cuffs that were so popular. Rubens also painted for the archduchess a copy of the *Portrait of Queen Isabel* based on the canvas done by Anguissola about 1563–65.

By the time she was in her late eighties, Sofonisba and Orazio had traveled on occasion to Palermo, as he "owned extensive properties in Sicily."[17] Sofonisba may already have been experiencing difficulties with her eyesight, and she would have cut back on all but perhaps a few commissions in order to spend time working on her

PLATE 113. Sofonisba Anguissola. *Self-Portrait*,
c. 1620. Oil on canvas, 38 5/8 x 30 11/16
in. (98 x 78 cm). Nivaagaards Art Museum,
Niva, Denmark.

own painting. Orazio may have suggested moving permanently to Palermo (about 1620), as the winters would be warmer, and it might give them an opportunity for a quieter life. Sofonisba most likely wrote to Asdrubale and Isabella to let them know of the impending move to Palermo. Preparing for another move would have consumed many months of Sofonisba and Orazio's time. Furniture, clothes, art, and navagational supplies would all have to be carefully packed for the sea journey.

Palermo had social and economic ties with many of the Genoese nobility, and "among the commercial colonies located in Sicily and Palermo, the strongest and most favorite of the Sicilian monarchy were the Genoese."[18] They had been on the island since the Middle Ages and, from the days of Charles V, they had prospered and become powerful nobles.

The Genoese community in Palermo was affluent. In 1576 they acquired the old church of San Luca and on its site, under the architectural design of Giorgio di Fazio, built San Giorgio dei Genovesi. It was completed three years later and became the gathering place for the Genoese community. Orazio's Palermitani ancestors had been instumental in helping the Genoese community back on its feet after the expenses were paid for the building of San Giorgio.

It was not Sofonisba's first trip to Palermo, and she may have been delighted to see the new church and how much the city had grown. As the Moncadas were important members of the city, so, too, were the Lomellini. So Orazio and Sofonisba would have been greeted warmly by friends and family upon their arrival. The Lomellini were no doubt happy to have such an important couple in their midst.

Life in Palermo may have reminded Sofonisba of her days with Don Fabrizio. However, in comparison to Paternò, Palermo was more cosmopolitan, but the pace would have been slower and easier than in Genoa. Unpacking and settling into a slower routine—especially if they had moved there during the hot summer months—would have taken time.

Sometime about 1620, Anguissola began work on her *Self-Portrait* (Nivagaards Art Museum, Niva, Denmark, see plate 113). Against a plain background, the painter has seated herself in a three-quarter-length pose. She is simply dressed with a long shawl pulled over her shoulders. Her delicate hands still show her characteristic "square-U" delineation. As an octogenarian, Anguissola portrays herself in all her frailty: her gray hair is tucked neatly under her coif, and her eyes appear unbalanced, as if she were having trouble seeing in the mirror she used. It probably was the last painting she attempted with her failing vision. Anguissola also is reported to have "executed miniatures and taught others how to paint them in Palermo,"[19] but no record of them remains.

In 1927, Nicodemi attributed this portrait to Van Dyck,[20] but recent attribution by Karen Petersen has given it rightfully back to Anguissola.[21] Van Dyck's hallmark were his elegant long, slender, tapering hands—which often had a boneless, translucent quality—not Anguissola's "square-U," so evident in this self-portrait.

In 1621, Sofonisba and Orazio received word that Archduke Albert had died at sixty-two. Born the year that Sofonisba left for Spain, he had spent his married life as a good administrator of the Netherlands. Now Isabella, without the comfort of children (they had never had any), would have to govern alone. It was something she would do very well until her own death in 1633. Discarding the opulent court dress-

PLATE 114. Copy after Anthony Van Dyck. *Portrait of Isabella Clara Eugenia.* Monasterio de las Descalzas Reales, Madrid.

es she had worn since she was a small child, the archduchess now wore only the simple mourning costume of Terciaria Francescana.[22] In a copy after Van Dyck of a full-length *Portrait of Isabella Clara Eugenia* (Monasterio de las Descalzas Reales, Madrid, see plate 114), she wears a Franciscan girdle around her waist. This was the first time in Isabella's life that she had been portrayed in unadorned fashion, with just a large shawl covering her head that trails to the floor. Van Dyck is known to have painted several versions of this portrait.

By the early 1620s, Anguissola was in retirement. She was having difficulty with her eyesight. For a woman who had seen nine decades, and whose life revolved around art for eight of them, painting now was to be enjoyed as a spectator. She and Orazio spent their days quietly in courtly pursuits: visiting noble relatives, attending occasional festivities, and listening to music. Music had been one of Sofonisba's great loves since her childhood. Now, she could listen and perhaps sit at the clavichord once in a while.

Sometime in June 1623, Sofonisba received word that Asdrubale had died on 16 May.[23] He was seventy-two, and he was her last link with her own family. She must have sensed that her time was very close, too.

In the spring of the following year, Anthony Van Dyck received an invitation from Emmanuele Filiberto (1588–1624), prince of Savoy, to come to Palermo to have the artist paint his portrait.

Van Dyck had studied under Rubens but, prior to that (at the age of fifteen), he was already an established painter and had been "received as a master into the Guild of St. Luke."[24] A "Mozart with the brush,"[25] his facility for painting costume details was noted during his own lifetime. It was due, in part, to his childhood exposure to, and appreciation of, ornate textiles: his father was a wealthy silk merchant and his mother was a well-known embroideress. By the middle of 1620 (while in Rubens's studio), Van Dyck had already exhausted the artistic milieu in Antwerp and entered the earl of Arundel's service in England. Although his initial trip there was brief, it was in England that he was able to see for the first time the Italian masterpieces of the Renaissance. He then realized that he had to journey to Italy to see them first hand.

Returning to Antwerp briefly (to obtain permission to travel and probably get a letter in introduction from the archduchess to Anguissola), Van Dyck traveled to Genoa, arriving there in November 1621, the same year he painted his *Self-Portrait* (Metropolitan Museum of Art, New York, see plate 115). While in the city, he stayed with Lucas and Cornelius de Wael (distant relatives of his mother). Both brothers were art dealers and painters who had moved from Antwerp and had settled in Genoa. It was there (if not directly from the archduchess herself) that Van Dyck surely would have heard stories about Anguissola. Bonetti says that Cornelius de

PLATE 115. Anthony Van Dyck. *Self-Portrait*, 1621. The Metropolitan Museum of Art, The Jules Bache Collection, 1949. (49.7.25), New York.

PLATE 117. Anthony Van Dyck. *Portrait of Sofonisba Anguissola*, 1624. Galleria Sabauda, Turin.

Wael knew of her "presence in Genoa."[26] Pietro Selvatico says erroneously that Van Dyck met her in 1620 in Genoa (when, in fact, Van Dyck was in England). Unfortunately, Walter Liedtke's 1984 article for the Metropolitan Museum of Art's *Bulletin* totally ignores Anguissola's existence there:

> Like Rubens twenty years earlier, Van Dyck found in Genoa aristocratic patrons who were suited to and in need of his abilities. The city had distinguished families who lived in magnificent style (as Rubens demonstrated in his book, *Palazzi di Genova*), but it did not have a *worthy* [italics added] portraitist.[27]

Whenever Anguissola and Van Dyck actually first met (perhaps prior to his dated notes in his *Italian Sketchbook)*, it is apparent that Van Dyck knew of Anguissola's work, as she was the leading portraitist in Genoa before she moved to Palermo.

When Van Dyck arrived in Palermo in May, the plague had just broken out in the city. It was still raging in early July 1624 when he contacted Anguissola. On 12 July, Anguissola received the twenty-five-year-old painter at the Lomellini palazzo. Van Dyck kept a notebook, now known as his *Italian Sketchbook* (British Museum, London, see plate 116), throughout his stay in Italy. As Christopher Brown, the painter's most recent biographer, states, "it is the sketchbook of a working painter, not an antiquarian."[28] Van Dyck was not interested in Roman antiquities (as other

PLATE 118. Anthony Van Dyck. *Portrait of Sofonisba Anguissola,* 1624. Lord Sackville Collection, Knole, Kent.

PLATE 116. Page from Anthony Van Dyck's *Italian Sketchbook*, describing his visit to Sofonisba Anguissola, 12 July 1624. Department of Prints and Drawings, British Museum, London.

visiting artists had been), but rather sketching the people around him during his travels. Whereas the rest of the notebook is filled with sketches, on the day that he met with Anguissola, he not only sketched her but wrote a full-page diary entry (in poor Italian). It is the only page in his *Sketchbook* that is accompanied by text:

> Portrait of Signora Sofonisba Anguissola, painter, done from life at Palermo on July 12, 1624, when she was 96 [sic] years old, still with a good memory, quick spirit and kind. Although her eyesight was *weakened* [italics added] through age, it was a great pleasure for her to have pictures placed in front of her, and while she then placed her nose very close to the painting with a lot of effort, she managed to recognize some of it. She enjoyed that very much. When I drew her portrait, she gave me several hints: not to get too close, too high or too low so the shadows in her wrinkles would not show so much. She also talked to me about her life and that she was a wonderful painter of nature. Her greatest sorrow was not to be able to paint any more because of her failing eyesight. Her hand was steady, without any trembling.[29]

Brown says that "Sofonisba must have held Van Dyck spellbound as she told stories of Philip II and his courtiers."[30]

Seventeenth- and eighteenth-century sources usually refer to Anguissola as "blind," but Van Dyck's notes clearly state that she had some—as he states, "weakened"—vision left. It is possible that she had cataracts, which would probably explain her partial, dimmed vision.

Van Dyck's sketch of Anguissola would be the basis for several portraits of her, and it seems probable that he met with her several times to work on these portraits. It is most likely that he started them in Palermo and finished them in Genoa. Nicodemi, in his 1927 article, mentions the *Portrait of Sofonisba Anguissola* (Gualino Collection, Galleria Sabauda, Turin, see plate 117). Fournier-Sarlovèze's 1899 article also discusses this portrait[31] which shows Anguissola's left eye partially closed.[32] It is quite apparent from the portrait that Van Dyck heeded Anguissola's advice: he softened the lines of age, making her appear somewhat younger, as she rests on a pillow with elegant, tapered hands—typical Van Dyck style—clasped. Still noticeable, however, is the problem with her left eye.

Another *Portrait of Sofonisba Anguissola* was discovered in 1988 in the Lord Sackville Collection (Knole, Kent, see plate 118). The painting is in poor condition. Of Van Dyck's known paintings of Anguissola, it is this one that most closely resembles the sketch of her in his *Italian Sketchbook*. It was probably the last portrait of Anguissola done from life. It is also quite evident that Van Dyck has captured the problems with her vision, as her eyes are not clear: her left eye is red and inflamed and the pupil is somewhat opaque.

Anguissola is portrayed dressed in a black velvet gown with a simple starched collar and a white linen scarf over her head. She appears more weary than in her own self-portrait done a few years before. Van Dyck "was exceedingly sensitive to psychological subtleties and, apparently, to the particular viewers a portrait might have. . . . National character, too, is sensed in the disposition of each of his sitters: one is received differently in a Genoese palace than . . . an English country house."[33] As-

PLATE 119. Anthony Van Dyck. *Portrait of Emmanuele Filiberto*, 1624. By permission of the Governors of Dulwich Picture Gallery, London.

drubale's death and the trauma of the plague in Palermo as well as her age had taken their toll on Anguissola. Van Dyck's sympathetic portrait captured it all. It is certainly a more somber portrait than her own. The plague must have been uppermost in both their minds, and Van Dyck may have asked if Anguissola could recommend a doctor in Palermo. Perhaps she suggested Dr. Fabricio Valguernero, whose name is written in his *Italian Sketchbook*.

During the crisis, Van Dyck also painted the *Portrait of Emmanuele Filiberto* (Dulwich Picture Gallery, London, see plate 119). The prince of Savoy died on 3 August in Palermo, shortly after this portrait was completed. He may have been a victim of the plague. In addition to the prince's portrait, Van Dyck was to profit inadvertently from the outbreak of pestilence. Two days after meeting with Anguissola, the supposed remains of St. Rosalie, the patron saint of Palermo, were discovered; it brought hope to a beleaguered city.

Van Dyck was commissioned to paint the altarpiece *The Madonna of the Rosary* for Palermo's Oratorio del Rosario (where it remains). The altarpiece, finished in Genoa in 1627 and sent back to Palermo, shows St. Rosalie interceding on behalf of the plague-stricken city. Van Dyck also painted two other smaller canvases of St. Rosalie during June and July.

It was Van Dyck who established the iconography of St. Rosalie [as the saint had rarely been represented before]. He painted two positions: in one the saint is kneeling, eyes raised to heaven, interceding for the inhabitants of Palermo; the other [at the

PLATE 120. Anthony Van Dyck. *St. Rosalie Interceding for the Plague-stricken of Palermo*, 1624. The Metropolitan Museum of Art, Purchase, 1871. (71.41), New York.

PLATE 121. Anthony Van Dyck. *The Lomellini Family*, c. 1625. National Gallery of Scotland, Edinburgh.

Metropolitan Museum of Art, New York, see plate 120] shows her being borne up to heaven by angels.[34]

The plague continued to rage throughout the city unabated. Van Dyck was forced to shorten his stay, fleeing the city in September with his incomplete canvases and sailing for Genoa. Settling there, he established himself as the foremost painter of the Genoese aristocracy. With a letter of introduction, probably from Orazio and Sofonisba, Van Dyck painted "the great Lomellini family portrait"[35] of Giovanni Francesco, son of the doge, Giacomo Lomellini, and relatives of Orazio (National Gallery of Scotland, Edinburgh, see plate 121). In this family portrait, the woman is the central focus: with her two children on the left and her husband, dressed in armor, on the right. The other man probably is her brother. The elaborate background—curtain, arch, and statue of Venus—is typical of Van Dyck's work. He was much in demand for the elegance of his portraits and had a "gift for the depiction of lace, satin, and velvet, while flattering his sitters . . . and making them seem even more remote than they were in life."[36]

Anguissola's meeting with Van Dyck was to be the last artistic contact she would have, as she had little more than a year left to live. She spent that time with Orazio, to whom she was devoted, as noted by several of her early biographers. Whatever their usual routine may have been, everything must have been severely curtailed, as the plague continued raging. It eventually wiped out half of the city's population.

The following year, sometime in the early part of November, Sofonisba Anguissola died in her ninety-third year. She was buried on 16 November 1625 in Palermo's San Giorgio dei Genovesi—the church the Lomellini family helped to build. The last of the Mannerist painters may have been another victim of the plague—as was Titian. Only her burial date is recorded.[37]

ANGUISSOLA'S TOMB INSCRIPTION

SOPHONISBAE UXORI AB ANGUISSOLAE
COMITIBUS DUCENTI ORIGINE[M] PARENTU[M]
NOBILITATE FORMA EXTRAORDINARIISQUE
NATURAE DOTIBUS IN ILLUSTRES MUNDI MULIE
RES RELATAE AC IN EXPERIMENDIS HOMINUM
IMAGINIBUS ADEO INSIGNI
UT PARE[M] AETATIS SUAE
NEMINE[M] HABUISSE SIT AESTIMATA
HORATIUS LOMELLINUS
INGENTI AFFECTUS MAERORE DECUS
HOC EXTREMUM ET SI TANTAE MULIERI EXIGUUM
MORTALIBUS VERO MAXIMU[M]
DICAVIT 1632

PLATE 122. Tomb of Sofonisba Anguissola, dedicated in 1632. San Giorgio dei Genovesi, Palermo.

EPILOGUE

After Anguissola's death, there remained three people whose lives had touched hers: Orazio, the Archduchess Isabella Clara Eugenia, and Van Dyck. After Van Dyck fled Palermo and settled in Genoa, he became the leading portraitist of the city's aristocracy. His cool delineation of his sitter's slightly elongated figures combined with meticulous attention to costume detail became the height of artistic fashion in Genoa. By the time he left there, his artistic style was set. It is conceivable that his visits with Anguissola may have had some indirect effect on his technique. They both shared an intense interest in rendering costume details precisely. That he bothered to commit to writing details of his 12 July visit to Anguissola—he had not done so on any other page of his *Italian Sketchbook*—speaks of the considerable interest and value that he placed on what she had to say.

When Van Dyck returned to Antwerp, Isabella Clara Eugenia appointed him court painter. It seems quite probable that the archduchess would have wanted to hear all the details of Van Dyck's visit with Anguissola, and he may have brought back one of his portraits of Sofonisba for her. While he remained there, he painted Isabella frequently, and many portraits were dispatched as diplomatic gifts. He revolutionized portraiture wherever he traveled: in Genoa, Antwerp, and later in England—his greatest triumph—where his style was imitated for the next two hundred years. His untimely death in 1641, at forty-one, cut short a brilliant career.

Isabella Clara Eugenia died during the night of November 30/1 December 1633, in Brussels. Governing alone since her husband's death twelve years earlier, she followed in her father's and husband's rigid path, immersing herself in the day-to-day affairs of governing and working late into the night, a routine that was only broken by time devoted to prayer and religious works for the needy. She had inherited Philip and Albert's strong monastic bent. It was one of the Hapsburg traits, the other being ardent patronage of the arts. Both Rubens and Van Dyck grew prosperous in her employ.

Orazio's final years remain, for the most part, obscure. It is known that he participated in Palermitani politics, and he was elected a senator from 1630 to 1631. In 1632, on the centenary of Sofonisba's birth, Orazio erected a marble tomb in her memory in San Giorgio dei Genovesi (see plate 122). He had the following epitaph carved on her tomb:

> To Sofonisba, my wife, whose parents are the noble Anguissola, for beauty and extraordinary gifts of nature, who is recorded among the illustrious women of the world, outstanding in portraying the images of man, so excellent that there was no equal in her age. Orazio Lomellino, in sorrow for the loss of his great love, in 1632, dedicated this little tribute to such a great woman.

Sofonisba Anguissola stood as the pioneering model for late sixteenth- and early-seventeenth-century women artists. The increasing complexity of her many portraits of herself and her family, commissioned works, and religious paintings showed that women were equally capable of experimenting with new and difficult compositions. Anguissola's sketches and probably numerous copies of them continued to circulate into the early seventeenth century. Her substantial financial remuneration (as well as costly gifts, dowry, and a lifelong pension) and the widespread reputation generated by her success and fame would also serve to encourage other women to pursue a professional career.

Her legacy, however, was not only her international reputation and example. Adapting to the constraints of being unable to study in a workshop environment, she turned that potential liability into an asset with the encouragement of a sympathetic teacher and a large family who were at ease when they sat for her. Capturing this informality led her, albeit inadvertently, to pioneer genre painting and explore psychological intimacy three-quarters of a century before it became an accepted and popular vehicle for the Dutch and Flemish.

Anguissola was also an important link in the dissemination of north Italian art to Spain. While Titian contributed enormously to both the art collections of Charles V and Philip II, he never lived in Spain. Anguissola's daily presence and intimacy with the royal family for twenty years had a direct impact on art there. Indeed, her few collaborative efforts with Sánchez Coello brought Italian techniques directly to a Spanish artist. Her work with him also may have been an important factor in his daughter, Isabel, becoming a painter, although much archival research remains to be done on her life.

Anguissola's noble status and importance as a court painter paved the way for the seventeenth-century Hapsburgs to elevate their court painters and entrust them with other important court duties. Her position at Philip's court probably paved the way for the knighting of Rubens and Van Dyck: their ennoblement was not mere coincidence. Living in Italy, Spain, and Sicily and actively participating in her chosen field for eight decades also brought her influence to regions outside the mainstream of sixteenth-century art.

Hers was a rich and full life. She had a tenacious spirit combined with artistic gifts and received early contemporary recognition and commissions—all this despite the Renaissance masculine bias that women lacked intelligence and creativity. Now that the historical record has been enhanced, may *"la bella pittrice"* take her rightful place once more in the history of Renaissance art.

ENDNOTES

CHAPTER I: THE ANGUISSOLAS: A NOBLE FAMILY'S BEGINNINGS

1. Peter Burke. *Culture and Society in Renaissance Italy* (N.Y.: Charles Scribner's Sons, 1972), 257.

2. Peter Lavin. *Renaissance Italy: 1464–1534* (London: B. T. Batsford, 1966), 39.

3. The Council of Trent, which met on and off between 1545 and 1563, had two important claims: first, to state clearly Catholic doctrine (this dated back to 1517 when Martin Luther had first urged Church reform), as the Protestant view was markedly different; and second, to institute much-needed reform. It was one of the most important councils in the history of the Church and "played a major role in revitalizing the Church in many parts of Europe." See, Ernest Graf. *A History of the Council of Trent* (St. Louis, 1957), 277. Specifically, under the Council of Trent, reforms included statements condemning indulgences, regulations on ordination and religious orders. For the first time clerics' responsibilities included regular record keeping (for births, marriages, and deaths) and new rules on the procedures for a marriage ceremony.

4. These documents were drawn up by a notary who was part of what might be termed a new class of "professional men" (which also included doctors, lawyers, and university teachers). Some notaries had a university education; others did not. They were what Burke called "the lay equivalent of the clergy" (p. 237). Notaries performed many duties that today are part of a lawyer's practice.

5. Carlo Bonetti. "Nel centenario di Sofonisba Anguissola" *Archivio Storico Lombardo*, 5 (1928), 288.

6. Bonetti, 289, 300.

7. Lavin, 39.

8. Bonetti, 289.

9. Cremona. Archivio di Stato. Archivio ala Ponzone, busta 57.

10. Cremona. Archivio di Stato. Archivio Notarile. Notaio Giovanni Pietro Comenducci, f. 135, atto 31 July 1534.

11. Cremona. Archivio di Stato. Archivio Notarile. Notaio Giovanni Pietro Comenducci, f. 26–28, atto 4 May 1536.

12. Cremona. Archivio di Stato. Archivio Notarile. Notaio Giovanni Pietro Comenducci, f. 336, atto 6 December 1537.

13. Cremona. Archivio di Stato. Archivio Notarile. Notaio Giovanni Pietro Comenducci, f. 342–344, atto 30 December 1537.

14. Cremona. Archivio di Stato. Archivio Notarile. Notaio Giovanni Pietro Comenducci, f. 251–254, atto 9 June 1546.

CHAPTER II: A CHILD AT LAST

1. A search in the archives and churches in Cremona and Milan in 1983 and 1988 did not turn up any documentary evidence relating to a birth date for Sofonisba Anguissola. Documents from San Giorgio (the parish of the Anguissola family) still remain from the sixteenth century. However, a number of them were stolen in the 1970s, thus leaving gaps in what remained of the family's history. According to Marianne Haraszti-Takács, Sofonisba was born at the late date of 1540. This date cannot be substantiated. Between 1546 and 1549 Sofonisba and Elena were studying under Campi. Although Sofonisba was considered extraordinary at an early age, a birth date of 1540 would have made her six when she started her studies with Bernardino Campi, which seems highly unlikely, given her noble status. See Marianne Haraszti-Takács, "Nouvelles données relatives à la vie et à l'oeuvre de Sofonisba Anguissola" *Bulletin du Musée Hongrois des Beaux-Arts* 8 (1968) 67.

2. Donald Armstrong. *The Reluctant Warriors* (N. Y.: Thomas Y. Crowell, 1966), 55.

3. Armstrong, 55.

4. See Christiane Klapish-Zuber, *Women, Family, and Ritual in Renaissance Italy* (Chicago: University of Chicago Press, 1985); Margaret L. King, "Book Lined Cells: Women and Humanism in the Early Italian Renaissance," in *Beyond Their Sex: Learned Women of the European Past*, Patricia H. Labalme, ed. (N.Y.: New York University Press, 1984); and Joan Kelly-Gadol, "Did Women Have a Renaissance?" in *Becoming Visible: Women in European History*, Renate Bridenthal and Claudia Koonz, eds. (Boston: Houghton Mifflin, 1977).

5. Burke, 208.

6. Germaine Greer, *The Obstacle Race* (N.Y.: Farrar Straus Giroux, 1979), 182.

7. Giovanni Battista Zaist, *Notizie istoriche de' pittori, scultori ed architetti cremonese* (Cremona, Italy: Banco Popolare di Cremona, 1976), Reprint of 1774, 227.

8. Filippo Baldinucci, *Notizie dei professori dei disegno*, vol. II (Florence, 1846), 621.

9. Raffaelo Soprani, *Le vite de' pittori, scultori, et architetti genovesi* (Genoa, 1674), 411.

10. According to noted Florentine paleographic scholar, Gino Corti, both Amilcare's Italian grammar and spelling had serious errors, even considering that in the sixteenth century there was neither a codification of the Italian language nor any dictionaries (until late in the century).

11. Black silk embroidery done on a white ground was known in England as far back as Chaucer's day. It became popular both in Spain and England when Catherine of Aragon married Henry VIII in 1504. See Mary Gostelow, *Blackwork* (N.Y.: Van Nostrand Reinhold, 1976).

CHAPTER III: EARLY ART STUDIES

1. Burke, 40.

2. Howard Hibbard. *Michelangelo* (N.Y.: Harper Row, Icon, 1974), 41.

3. Frederick Hartt. *A History of the Italian Renaissance*, 2nd ed. (N.Y.: Harry N. Abrams, 1979), 573.

4. Hartt (1979), 573.

5. Federico II Gonzaga (1500–40) was the first duke of Mantua, and succeeded his father, Francesco, as marchese of Mantua in 1519. He fought against Francis I's mercenary troops at Pavia and supported Charles V, who rewarded him by raising the city's status from marquisate to a duchy in 1530.

6. Hartt (1987), 224.

7. Lavina Teerlinc's successor, Nicholas Hilliard (1547–1619) is the English miniaturist who is generally remembered. He was Teerlinc's student. As yet, no biography has been written on Teer-

linc, and she deserves scholarly attention. For a discussion of her work, see Roy Strong. *Artists of the Tudor Court: The Portrait Miniature Rediscovered, 1520–1620* (London: Thames and Hudson, 1983). Flemish painter Caterina van Hemessen (1528–after 1587) worked from 1556–58 at the Spanish court of Mary of Hungary. Her brief career lasted only into her twenties. Only ten of her paintings have survived.

8. Zaist (1774), 228.

9. Burke, 45.

10. Jacques Maroger, *The Secret Formulas and Techniques of the Masters* (N.Y.: The Studio Publications, 1948), 190.

11. Lionello Venturi, *Catalogo della collezione Gualino* (Milan: Bestetti e Tumminelli, 1926), 924, 926.

12. Mina Gregori, in I *Campi: e la cultura artistica cremonese del Cinquecento*, catalogue (Milan: Electa, 1985), 177.

13. Charles Petrie, *Philip II of Spain* (London: Eyre and Spottiswood, 1964), 50; and Giulio Bora, "Note cremonesi II, L'eredità di Camillo e i Campi" *Paragone* 28 (1977), 57.

14. Bora (1977), 64–65.

15. Zaist, 192.

16. Pietro Torriti. *La Pinacoteca Nazionale di Siena: I dipinti dal XV al XVIII secolo* (Genoa: Sagep, 1978), 247.

17. As early as 21 October 1546, Gatti's name appears on a contract to paint an arch in San Sigismondo. See Cremona, Archivio di Stato. Archivio Notarile. Notaio Giovanni Pietro Comenducci, f. 1005, atto 21 October 1546.

18. Avery, Catherine B., ed. *The New Century Italian Renaissance Encyclopedia* (N.Y.: Appleton-Century-Crofts, 1972), 276.

19. Zaist, 228. Earlier mention of Gatti's presence in Cremona in 1546 (see above, endnote 17) and that he knew Amilcare Anguissola would make these dates, when Sofonisba studied with him, very plausible.

20. *I Campi* catalogue (1985), 180.

CHAPTER IV: ROME AND MICHELANGELO

1. Zaist, 234–235. Interestingly, the term nun derives from the word "nonne, a nurse, because in antiquity priestesses were practitioners of the healing arts." See, Barbara G. Walker, *The Woman's Encyclopedia of Myths and Secrets*(San Francisco: Harper and Row),731.

2. Eleanor Tufts, *Our Hidden Heritage: Five Centuries of Women Artists* (N.Y.: Paddington Press, 1974), 22.

3. It has been listed in the Borghese collection since "1693, and thus noted in the *Inventory* of that year: a small painting on wood from an unknown hand with a nun who holds a crucifix in one hand, and in the other a lily." See, Paola della Pergola, *Galleria Borghese: I dipinti,* 2 vols. (Rome: Istituto Poligrafico dello Stato, 1955), Vol. I, 75.

4. George Ferguson, *Signs and Symbols in Christian Art* (London: Oxford University Press, n.d.), 33.

5. Although no dating is now visible on the canvas, Giovanni Morelli, writing in 1892, stated that when he saw the painting of Elena as a novitiate, it was in Lord Yarborough's "collection in London, signed and dated 1551." This, of course, would support this author's dating given here. See, Giovanni Morelli, *Italian Paintings: Borghese and Doria Pamphili, Rome, Vol. I* (London: John Murray, 1892), 197. In 1983, when the author examined this painting, there was no trace of either a signature or date.

6. *Gli Uffizi catalogo generale* (Florence: Centro Di, 1979), 791. The Vasari Corridor, located above the Uffizi Gallery, is closed to the general public. The corridor was begun in l559 by Giorgio Vasari. When he died in 1574, Francesco I de' Medici had Bernar-

do Buontalenti and Alfonso Parigi complete the Uffizi's third floor, creating an art gallery and establishing a studio for young artists.

7. Private discussions in August 1988 with San Diego Police Department forensic document examiners, Charles R. Principe and Sandy Wiersema, regarding letters written by Anguissola proved inconclusive as to which hand she used. There is also an etching based on the Uffizi *Self-Portrait* reproduced in De Soresina Vidoni (which may have been reversed in printing) where Anguissola also holds a brush in her left hand. See Bartolommeo De Soresina Vidoni, *La pittura cremonese* (Milan: Della Società Tipografica de' Classici Italiani, 1824), 26. As a comparison self-portrait, see that of *Antonio Moro* in the Uffizi Gallery (catalogue number 151776). Here, the artist portrays himself with brushes in his right hand. The painting in the Zeri Collection, although attributed to Anguissola and showing the artist holding brushes in her right hand, is not consistent with either her facial features or the "square-U" in other portraits that she did during this period. Further, her eyes are not looking directly at the viewer, as she does in all her self-portraits; and her jaw is far too square (again not consistent with her other self-portraits).

8. Margaret Swain, *The Needlework of Mary Queen of Scots* (N.Y.: Van Nostrand Reinhold, 1973), 17. Mary, while frequently denied quill and paper, was never without threads and needles for her many needlework projects.

9. Swain, 17.

10. John Pope-Hennessey, *The Portrait in the Renaissance*, The A. W. Mellon Lectures in the Fine Arts, 1963. Washington, D.C., National Gallery of Art (N.Y.: Bollingen Foundation, 1966), 124.

11. The dome originally had been started by Bramante (1444–1515) and was continued by Antonio da Sangallo the Younger (c. 1485–1546), his carpenter-assistant turned architect. Michelangelo had accepted the commission of St. Peter's from Pope Paul III but refused any payment, saying he was doing it for the "love of God." See, Frederick Hartt, *Michelangelo* (N.Y.: Abrams, 1964), 63.

12. Charles de Tolnay, *The Complete Works of Michelangelo* (N.Y.: Reynal, n.d.), 56.

13. De Tolnay, (n.d.), 59.

14. E. H. Ramsden, *The Letters of Michelangelo* (Stanford, CA: Stanford University Press, 1963), vol. 2, xliv.

15. John Addington Symonds. *The Life of Michelangelo*. 2 vols. (N.Y.: Charles Scribner's Sons, 1893), vol. 2, 340.

16. Florence. Biblioteca Mediceo Laurenziana. Archivio Buonarroti, VI 35. I am deeply indebted to the well-known paleographic scholar, Dr. Gino Corti, Villa I Tatti, Florence, for his gracious assistance in translating and discussing the grammar of these two letters. See also author's note, Chapter II, note 10.

17. Florence. Biblioteca Mediceo Laurenziana. Archivio Buonarroti, VI 36. The envelope to this letter also survives and is addressed to Michelangelo in Rome.

18. Symonds, 344. Symonds, too, discusses (p. 340) Michelangelo's kindness to pupils and friends.

19. De Tolnay (1941), 118.

20. Giovanni Papini, *Vita di Michelangelo nella vita del suo tempo* (Milan: Garzanti, 1950), 57.

21. Iris Cheney, "Francesco Salviati's North Italian Journey" *The Art Bulletin* XLV (December 1963), 251.

22. Iris Cheney. *Francesco Salviati: 1510–63*. New York University dissertation (Ann Arbor, Mich., 1963), 337.

23. Baldinucci (1681), 622–623.

24. Cavalieri met Michelangelo in 1532. Their friendship and cultural interests brought a quick bond and his "Messer Tommao [as Michelangelo called him] remained entirely devoted to him." See, Ramsden, vol. 2, xliv.

25. Vasari, *Vite* (1568), 2 (third part), 174.

26. De Tolnay (n.d.), 456.

27. De Tolnay, "Sofonisba Anguissola and her Relations with Michelangelo" *J. of the Walters Art Gallery* 4 (1941), 117–118. This letter is also quoted in: Papini, 574–75 and Lancetti, 258.

28. Florence. Archivio di Stato. Mediceo del Principato 3281, f. 262r.

29. De Tolnay (1941), 117–118.

30. Information on conservation work which may have been done on this sketch was not available from the museum.

31. The information on this oil painting was graciously supplied by Dr. Alessandra Mottola Molfino, director of the Poldi Pezzoli Museum, Milan. Her assistance during my research has been very much appreciated.

32. Ramsden, vol. 2, xxxix–xl.

33. Annibale Caro. *Delle Lettre Famigliare*, 3 vols. (Bassano, Italy, 1782), vol. 1, 118. Author's translation. This letter is also quoted in Lancetti, 251.

CHAPTER V: EARLY PORTRAITS

1. Cassandra Fedele. *Epistolae et orationes*. Cited in King, 76. I am indebted to Christiane Klapish-Zuber for pointing out this reference and for her valuable comments on the status of sixteenth-century women in private conversations during the summer of 1989.

2. King, 75.

3. Bruno Molajoli, *Notizie su Capodimonte catalogo delle gallerie e del museo* (Naples: L'Arte Tipografica, 1958), 38. The museum does not have any information on this restoration other than the date.

4. The *clavicordo* originated in the fifteenth century and the "earliest existing specimens are generally Italian and date from the first half of the sixteenth century." The "case is oblong and the strings are stretched horizontally so as to cross the back ends of the keys" with a range of four octaves. See, Eric Bloom, ed., *Grove's Dictionary of Music and Musicians*, 5th ed. (N.Y.: St. Martin's Press, 1970), vol. 1, 336. The spinet, however, is "a wing-shaped instrument typically of English make, with a compass of four to five octaves." Bloom, vol. 2, 7.

5. Adolfo Venturi, *Storia dell'arte italiana*, vol. 9, *La pittura del Cinquecento* (Milan: Ulrico Hoepli, 1933), 929–30.

6. Unfortunately, further information on the change in attribution was not available from the museum.

7. Alfredo Puerari, *La pinacoteca di Cremona* (Florence: Sansoni, n.d.), 147.

8. I am extremely grateful to Dr. Ardea Ebani, director of the Museo Civico ala Ponzone, Cremona, for her gracious help over the years and for permission to remove these two paintings from exhibition in order to examine them. The museum did not have any information on possible past conservation of these paintings.

9. Vasari (1568), 561.

10. Baldinucci (1681), 624.

11. Baldinucci (1681), 624.

12. Claude Lulier, "Sofonisba Anguissola et ses soeurs," M. Fournier-Sarlovèze, ed., *Artistes Oubliers* (Paris: Librarie Paul Ollendorff, 1902), 21. The subtitle of this article is "Amateurs of the Sixteenth Century."

13. For a further discussion on the importance of oriental carpets in Renaissance painting, see John Mills, *Carpets in Painting* (London: National Gallery, 1983).

14. Private communication with painter Michael Bergt who specializes in Renaissance painting techniques. I am extremely appreciative to him for spending time discussing sixteenth-century painting techniques.

15. These gold link chain necklaces also can be seen in the *Portrait of Three Children* (Lord Methuen Collection, Wiltshire). In 1988, similar sixteenth-century chain necklaces were sold at Christie's, New York. See Ilya Sandra Perlingieri in *Gold and Silver of the Atocha and Santa Margarita*, Christie's Catalogue June 14–15, 1988 (N.Y.), 172–173, 257.

16. Blackwork, also known as "Spanish work," reached its greatest popularity in Spain between 1530 and 1560. Since Cremona, in mid century, was part of Philip's empire, it would have been readily available. See Gostelow.

17. A. Venturi (1933), 922.

18. Giorgio Nicodemi, "Commemorazioni di artisti minori: Sofonisba Anguissola" *Emporium* (1927), 227.

19. Bernard Berenson, *Lorenzo Lotto* (N.Y. Phaidon, 1956), 147.

20. Soprani, 412. Author's translation.

21. Robert B. Simon, "The Identity of Sofonisba Anguissola's Young Man" *J. of the Walters Art Gallery*, 44 (1986), 117–122.

22. Simon, 120.

23. Private communication with Renaissance painting techniques expert, Frank Redelius, July 1989.

24. Redelius, 1989.

CHAPTER VI: JOURNEY TO MILAN

1. Caro, vol. I, 118–119. Author's translation.

2. Soprani mentions (p. 413) that Amilcare accompanied Sofonisba to Milan after she came to the duke's attention in 1558.

3. William S. Maltby, *Alba: A Biography of Fernando Alvarez de Toledo, Third Duke of Alba, 1507–82* (Berkeley: University of California Press, 1983), 21. Alba inherited a tradition (from his father and grandfather) where he was not only the king's soldier but where he also "had a moral obligation . . . to advise the crown" (p. 70).

4. Maltby, 16.

5. Maltby, 16.

6. I am indebted to Don Jesus Aguirre Ortiz de Zárate, the current duke of Berwick y Alba and his archivist, Don José Manuel Calderón, for their generous assistance in permitting me to research in the duke's private archives. This new information in this chapter was found during research in the Casa de Alba Archives, Palacio Liria, Madrid. See Dukes of Berwick y Alba, *Discurso* (Madrid, 1924), *Cartas de Pago*, unedited, 1541–86, caja 211–1.

7. Casa de Alba Archives, Palacio Liria, Madrid. *Inventory of 1682*, p. 106, number 980, mentions *Santa Catalina della Ruota* by Sofonisba Anguissola, as well as two other untitled paintings by her hand.

8. Baldinucci (1681), 108.

9. David Loth, *Philip II of Spain* (London: Routledge and Sons, 1932), 71.

10. Maltby, 83.

11. Petrie, 78.

12. Maltby, 113.

13. Antonia Fraser, *Mary Queen of Scots* (N.Y.: Delacorte Press, 1969), 86. This book is one of the most beautiful yet scholarly works ever published on Mary's life. It has been a great source of inspiration.

14. Fraser, 91.

15. Simancas. Archivo General de Simancas. Papeles Estado Milano, Leg. 1210, f. 190.

16. Simancas. Archivo General de Simancas. Papeles Estado Milano, Leg. 1210, f. 153.

17. A. Venturi, 922.

18. George Francis Hill, *Portrait Medals of the Italian Renaissance* (London: Philip Lee Warner, 1912), 3.

19. Fraser, 155.

20. Fraser, 155.

21. In private discussions with the staff of the Department of Medals, British Museum, it was mentioned that Leoni possibly may have done this medal.

22. Milan. Archivio di Stato. Registri delle Cancellerie Spagnole. 22 August 1559, XXII, II, c. 104v. Each city issued its own coinage. The scudi or gold crown was issued from 1533 on. It had sixty-nine and twelve one-hundredths grains of twenty-four karat gold. Cellini designed the Florentine scudi that was commissioned in 1533 by Alessandro de' Medici.

23. Baldinucci (1681) vol. III, 627.

24. Kax Wilson. *A History of Textiles* (Boulder, Colo.: Westview Press, 1979), 148.

CHAPTER VII: JOURNEY TO SPAIN

1. Loth, 143.

2. Augustín G. Amezúa y Mayo, *Isabel de Valois: Reina de España* (1546–1568). 3 vols. (Madrid: Graficas Ultra, 1949), vol. I, 121.

3. Baldinucci (1681), 627.

4. Carl Justi. *Micellaneen aus Drei Jahrhunderten Spanishen Kunstlebens* (Berlin, 1908), 12.

5. Loth, 142.

6. 15 January 1561, cited in Hector de la Ferrière, *Lettres de Catherine de' Médicis*. 3 vols. (Paris: Imprimerie Nationale, 1880), vol. I, 163–164.

7. Petrie, 112.

8. Loth, 144.

9. E. Lafuente Ferrari. *El Prado: Del Romantico al Greco* (Madrid: Aguilar, 1967), 250.

10 . Fraser, 43–44.

11. Amezúa y Mayo, vol. I, 261.

12. Amezúa y Mayo, vol. I, 262.

13. Federico Sacchi. *Notizie pittoriche cremonese* (Cremona, 1872), 16.

14. Baldinucci (1681), 628. Also, see Milan, Archivio di Stato. Famiglie 6, "Anguissola," 15 December 1562.

15. Milan, Archivio di Stato. Famiglie 6, "Anguissola," January 1563.

16. Milan. Archivio di Stato. Famiglie 6, "Anguissola," January 1563.

17. Lafuente Ferrari, 241; see also Francisco Javier Sánchez Canton. "Los pintores de los Austrias" *Boletín Sociedad Española de Excursiones* 22 (June 1914), 152.

18. Bonetti (1928), 292.

19. Simancas. Archivo General de Simancas. Casa y Sitios Reales, Leg. 395, 24 September 1560.

20. Simancas. Archivo General de Simancas. Casa y Sitios Reales, Leg. 40, f. 333, June 1560.

21. Simancas. Archivo General de Simancas. Casa y Sitios Reales, Leg. 40, f. 351.

22. Lancetti, 254; Vasari (Milanese edition, 1878), 500; and Baldinucci, vol III, 628.

23. Madrid. Biblioteca Nacional. Mss. fond. fr. vol. 3902, f. 86; and also cited in Amezúa y Mayo, vol. III, 169.

24. Vasari (Milanesi edition, 1878), 500.

25. Tufts, 23. This English version quoted by Tufts is from the Hinds translation of Vasari's *Vite* (London, 1927).

26. This was acquired by the Brera in 1848. My deepest appreciation goes to Dr. Maria Teresa Binaghi Olivari, Director of Art History, Pinacoteca di Brera; Milan, for her unstinting encouragement and gracious help over these many years of my research.

27. Bartolommeo de Sorisina Vidoni. *La pittura cremonese* (Milan: Dalla Società Tipografi de' Classici Italiani, 1824), 106.

28. Lancetti, 255. A recent attribution to Anguissola (formerly given to Alonso Sánchez Coello) by Maria Kusche of a *Portrait of Juana* (Isabella Stewart Gardner Museum, Boston) mentioned in this letter cannot be substantiated. Both the coloring and Juana's hands are not characteristic of her work. See Maria Kusche, "Sofonisba Anguissola en España, ritratista en la corte de Filipo II junto a Alonso Sánchez Coello y Jorge de la Rua" *Archivo Español de Arte* LXII, 28 (1989), 391–420. In this article, Kusche also erroneously attributes several other paintings to Anguissola.

29. Argote de Molina states that this portrait is by Anguissola. See Gonzálo Argote de Molina, *Descripción del Bosque y Casa Real de El Pardo* (1916 Reprint), 36.

30. René Huyghe, ed., *Larousse Encyclopedia of Renaissance and Baroque Art* (N.Y.: Excalibur Books, 1966), 231.

31. George Kubler and Martin Soria, *Art and Sculpture in Spain and Portugal and Their American Dominions: 1500–1800* (Baltimore, Penguin, 1959), 205.

32. Lafuente Ferrari, 241–242. I am most grateful to Dr. Joanna Woodall, Courtauld Institute of Art, London, for sharing her dissertation on Moro with me as well as her recent research on Mary Tudor. See Joanna Woodall. "An Exemplary Consort: Antonio Moro's Portrait of Mary Tudor." *Art History* 14, 2 (June 1991): 192–224; dates on Moro are from: Joanna Woodall. *The Portraiture of Antonis Mor.* PhD dissertation, London University, Courtauld Institute of Art, 1989.

33. See Part III: "Isabel Sánchez Coello," in Cristobal de Castro, *Mujeres del Imperio* (Madrid: Espasa-Calpe, 1941), 143–159.

34. Kubler and Soria, 207.

35. C. J. Holmes, "Sofonisba Anguissola and Philip II" *Burlington,* 26 (1915), 181–187.

36. Holmes, 181.

37. Roy Strong, *Tudor and Jacobean Portraits* (London: HMSO, 1969), 248.

38. Simancas. Casa y Sitios Reales. Leg. 41, f. 9; also cited in Amezúa y Mayo, vol. I, 264; and Pedro Beroqui, *Tiziano en el Museo del Prado* (Madrid, 1946), 106.

39. I am very appreciative of the assistance of Carmen Bernis, noted authority on sixteenth-century Spanish costume, who discussed costume details with me. Private communication, Madrid, May 1988.

40. *Prado Museum* catalogue (Madrid, 1985), 611. This was listed as a full-length portrait in 1636 in the Alcázar de Madrid.

41. Baldinucci (1681), 628; also, Soprani, 414.

42. Petrie, 155.

43. Petrie, 157.

44. Petrie, 163.

45. Alaistair Smart, *The Renaissance and Mannerism in Northern Europe and Spain* (N.Y.: Harcourt Brace Jovanovich, n.d.), 210.

46. Lafuente Ferrari, 235. See also Mariana Jenkins.*The State Portrait: Its Origins and Evolution* (N.Y.: College Art Association, 1947).

47. Kubler and Soria, 206.

48. Harold Wethy, *The Paintings of Titian.* Vol. II: *The Portraits* (London: Phaidon Press, 1971), 4.

49. Wethy, 5.

50. Wethy, 6.

51. William Stirling-Maxwell, *Annals of the Artists of Spain,* 4

vols. (London: John C. Nimmo, 1891), vol. I, 231. A later copy (possibly nineteenth century) of this portrait is at Goodwood House, Chichester.

52. This diagnosis is put forth here for the first time. I am extremely grateful to Dr. Lincoff for his medical opinion, in order to diagnose some of Sofonisba's ophthalmic problems. Personal interview, San Diego, 13 February 1984.

53. See Amezúa y Mayo, vol. II, 483 ff; also Martha Freer Walker. *Elizabeth de Valois*, 2 vols. (London: Hurst and Blackett, 1857), vol. II, ch. 4 and 5.

54. Amezúa y Mayo, 485.

55. Bonnie S. Anderson and Judith P. Zinser. *A History of Their Own: Women in Europe from Prehistory to the Present*, 2 vols. (San Francisco: Harper and Row, 1988), 39.

56. Simancas. Papeles Estado Francia. K. 1511, f. 124.

CHAPTER VIII: THE 1570S IN SPAIN

1. Loth, 199.

2. M. J. Rodríguez-Salgado, et al., *Armada: 1588–1988,* catalogue (London: Penguin, 1988), 88, 90.

3. Francesco Sánchez Canton, "Los pintores de cámera de los reyes de España" *Boletín de la Sociedad de Excursiones* 22 (June 1914), 149. See also, *Armada* catalogue, 90–92.

4. Kubler and Soria, 205–206.

5. *Armada* catalogue, 89.

6. *Armada* catalogue, 89.

7. Baldinucci (1681), 630; Lancetti, 33. Soprani states (415) that Sofonisba was the infanta's tutor.

8. Zaist, 231.

9. Adolfo Venturi is the only one who mentions (p. 923) erroneously that Don Fabrizio was the brother of Francesco II and states, incorrectly, that he was prince of Palermo when, in fact, he was prince of Paternò. King Philip II conferred that title on him on 8 April 1565. See A. Mango De Casalgerado, *Nobilità di Sicilia* (n.d.), 455. In recent correspondence with Armand de Fluvia, heraldic advisor, Catalunya Society of Genealogy, and a specialist on the Moncada family, he writes that the only Fabrizio listed is the *son* of Francesco de Moncada, prince of Paternò, and his wife, Caterina Pignatelli. They were married in Palermo. Private correspondence, Barcelona, 5 September 1991. Litta lists seven children (without any dates): Fernando, Giulia, Cesare, Camillo, Fabrizio, Giovanna, and Lucrezia. See Pompeo Litta. *Famiglie celebri italiane*. 2nd series, vol. II (Napoli: Libreria Detken and Rocholl, 1905), 75.

10. John C. Shideler, *A Medieval Catalan Noble Family: The Montcadas 1000–1230* (Berkeley: University of California Press, 1983), ix.

11. Shideler, ix.

12. Shideler, ix. The Catalan spelling of the family's name is Montcada.

13. Madrid. Archivo Historico Nacional. Consejo, Cámera de Castilla Patronato, Lib. 251, f. 178. I am very grateful for the courteous assistance of Señora Doña Carmen Crespo, the director, Archivo Historico Nacional, Madrid.

14. This document does not specifically mention by date the two others it is supposed to supersede. See Madrid. Archivo Historico Nacional. Consejo, Cámera de Castilla Patronato, Lib. 251, f. 107, 108, 127.

15. Madrid. Archivo Historico Nacional. Consejo, Cámera de Castilla Patronato, Lib. 251, f. 178, 179. Philip did not sign his name on this document. As was his custom he signed it "El Rey" (the King). I am indebted to Dr. Tom Case, Chair, Department of Span-

ish and Portuguese, San Diego State University, for his assistance in translating this document.

16. Bonetti (1928), 298. According to these documents Elena was still alive in 1578.

17. Bonetti, 290, 298.

18. Baldinucci (1681), 635, erroneously mistakes Europa's work for Anna Maria's, which is signed. It has been commonplace for historians to confuse the six sisters' identities and works.

19. Anne Sutherland Harris and Linda Nochlin, *Women Artists: 1550–1950*. Catalogue, Los Angeles County Museum of Art (N.Y.: Alfred A. Knopf, 1976), 110, fn. 11. There also may be another connection to Anguissola knowing the Gonzaga family. Caterina Anguissola Gonzaga (from the Piacenza branch of the family) married Luigi Gonzaga (dates are unknown), and it is possible that through this other branch of the Anguissola family she met the Gonzagas. See Maria Buti Bandini, *Poetesse e scritrici* (Rome, 1941), vol. I, series VI, 139.

20. Baldinucci (1681), 631.

21. Petrie, 168.

22. Petrie, 168.

23. I am grateful for the kind assistance of archivist Don José Manuel Calderón, Casa de Alba, Palacio Liria, Madrid.

24. *Alonso Sánchez Coello,* catalogue (Madrid: Prado Museum, 1990), 154.

25. Amezúa y Mayo, vol. III, 414 ff.

26. Swain, 31.

27. F. Sacchi, 13–14.

28. Smart, 212. Also see Kubler and Soria, 204, who call Morales "the greatest native Mannerist painter Spain produced."

29. Smart, 209.

30. Personal interview with Federico Zeri, Mentana, 3 June 1983.

31. *Armada* catalogue, 90.

32. *Armada* catalogue, 90.

33. *Armada* catalogue, 89.

34. Conservation of numerous works by Sofonisba Anguissola and the mounting of a major international exhibition (which would then bring together her scattered oeuvre, alongside those of her sisters and Sánchez Coello) would enable a more detailed comparison to be carried out.

35. *Armada* catalogue, 90.

36. Bonetti (1928), 298.

37. Bonetti (1928), 298.

38. R. Prete Natale Battilana, *Geneologie delle famiglie nobili di Genova* (Genoa: Fratelli Pagano, 1825), vol. I, 14.

39. Papini says, in passing, that Sofonisba had children, but does not give any documentation. See Giovanni Papini, *Vita di Michelangelo nella vita del suo tempo* (Milan: Garzanti, 1950), 575. A portrait in the Tel Aviv Museum, Jerusalem, lists a painting erroneously titled, *Self-Portrait of Sofonisba Anguissola and Her Son*. The boy portrayed is about six years old. The woman's costume dates from the end of the century, when Sofonisba was in her sixties. Further, the woman in the Tel Aviv portrait, who appears in her thirties, does not look like any of Sofonisba's self-portraits. Her hands are not done in the artist's characteristic "square-U". Stylistically, this painting looks more like the work of Lavinia Fontana.

40. Bonetti (1928), 298, 304–305.

41. *Decurione* was the title given to the ten men who ran Cremona's government. The city was still using Latin titles for the men who held office. See also, G. B. di Crollalanza, *Dizionario Storico-Blasonico delle famiglie nobili e notabili italiane* (Bologna: Arnaldo Forni, 1977), vol. II, 147.

42. Bonetti (1928), 304–305. Author's translation.

43. Tenoghi, *Iconografia italiana degli uomini e delle donne celebri* (Milan: Antonio Locatelli, 1836), 3.

CHAPTER IX: THE RETURN OF AN ILLUSTRIOUS DAUGHTER

1. Lancetti, 257. Author's translation. Stirling-Maxwell also stated (pp. 228–229) that "she was entertained with so galant a courtesy by the captain, Orazio Lomellini, one of the merchant princes of the 'proud city', that she fell in love out of sheer gratitude."

2. Zaist, 231.

3. Greer, 185.

4. Florence. Archivio Mediceo, 731, f. 79. I am indebted to Dr. Gino Corti for discovering these four letters from Anguissola to Francesco I. Author's translation.

5. Florence. Archivio Mediceo, 731, f. 120. Author's translation.

6. Florence. Archivio Mediceo, 731, f. 136. Author's translation.

7. Baldinucci, 632.

8. Marcel Brion, *The Medici: A Great Florentine Family* (N.Y.: Exeter Books, 1969), 196.

9. Brion, 197.

10. Florence. Archivio Mediceo, 731, f. 83.

11. Battilana, 14.

12. Rosanna Sacchi, "Documenti per Sofonisba Anguissola" *Paragone* 8, vol. 457 (March 1988), 88.

13. Simancas. Papeles Estado Genova, Leg. 1417, f. 97. Author's translation.

14. There is a painting of the *Infant Jesus* (Monasterio de las Descalzas Reales, Madrid), done, according to the museum, in the 1560s and currently attributed to Anguissola. However, there is insufficient provenance information to support this as her work. Stylistically, the painting is inconclusive.

15. Lancetti, 258.

16. F. Sacchi, 19–20.

17. Bonetti (1928), 292, F. Sacchi, 19.

18. Fundación Casa de Alba, Palacio de Liria, *Inventory 1682*. "Ruota" means wheel, referring to the spiked wheel of fire on which St. Catherine was martyred.

19. St. Catherine of Alexandria is on the liturgical calendar for 17 November. A fourth Catherine, St. Catherine of Bologna (1413–63) was patron of painters. She was maid of honor to Catherine d'Este and later abbess of the Poor Clares in Bologna. She was canonized in 1712. Her liturgical date is 9 March. Since most of the religious works dating from this period relate to the various St. Catherines, the name may have had some special significance for Anguissola.

20. Haraszti-Takács, 53–67.

21. Marina Warner, *Alone of Her Sex: The Myth and Cult of the Virgin Mary* (N.Y.: Vintage/Random House, 1976), 193.

22. Warner, 195.

23. Warner, 203.

24. An incomplete nineteenth-century archival entry (copied from a sixteenth-century source, no longer extant) lists "Bianca, the wife of Amilcare Anguissola" as deceased in 1600. See Cremona. Archivio di Stato. Comune, Raccolta Araldica, Sommi-Picenardi, Famiglia Ponzone, vol. 47, f. 133.

25. Bonetti (1928), 298–299.

26. The museum acquired this painting in 1804.

27. Anguissola's *Holy Family* is signed in the lower left, "Sofonisba Anguissola Adolescens P[inxit] 1559." A second painting, similar in composition, is also known: *Holy Family with Saints Giovanni and Francesco*, signed in the lower left, formerly in the Cavalieri Collection, Milan. Its current location is unknown.

28. Corrado Ricci, *Art in Northern Italy* (N.Y.: Charles Scribner's Sons, 1911), 250.

29. Soprani, 415. Piola is also mentioned by Delondres, 33; A. Venturi, 923; and Zaist, 233.

30. Sutherland Harris and Nochlin, 111.

31. Sutherland Harris and Nochlin, 111.

32. Hartt, 3rd ed., 561.

33. Sutherland Harris and Nochlin, 111–112.

34. Liana De Gerolami Cheney, "Barbara Longhi of Ravenna" *Woman's Art Journal*, 9 no. 11 (Spring/Summer 1988), 16.

35. Sutherland Harris and Nochlin, 116.

36. Morigia was also aware of the creative accomplishments of several women musicians in Italy. In 1595, he noted that many Milanese "convents of nuns devoted themselves to music" both instrumental and vocal. See Jane Bowers "The Emergence of Women Composers in Italy, 1566–1700" in *Women Making Music: The Western Art Tradition 1150–1950* (Urbana, Ill.: University of Illinois Press, 1986), 125.

37. Greer, 182.

38. Greer, 182–183.

39. Mary D. Garrard, *Artemisia Gentileschi* (Princeton: Princeton University Press, 1989), 58.

40. F. Sacchi, 334.

41. Elsa Honig Fine, *Women and Art* (Montclair, N. J.: Allenheld and Schram, 1978), 14.

42. Greer, 228.

43. *The Art of Caravaggio* catalogue, 200. Recent discovery of letters "documenting Caravaggio's last days" show that he probably died of pneumonia and not malaria. See *J. of Art*, 4, no. 10 (Dec. 1991): 1, 6.

44. Anthony Newcomb, "Courtesans, Muses, or Musicians? Professional Women Musicians in Sixteenth-Century Italy" in *Women Making Music: The Western Art Tradition, 1150–1950*, 92–93. Very little research has been done on these gifted women. Their contributions to music deserve scholarly attention. I am indebted to Oneil Cormier Jr. for bringing both Viadana's compositions and Renaissance women musicians to my attention.

45. Newcomb, 92.

46. Newcomb, 96.

47. Newcomb, 96.

48. Jane Bowers, "The Emergence of Women Composers in Italy, 1566–1700" in *Women Making Music: The Western Art Tradition, 1150–1950*, 116.

49. Newcomb, 101.

50. Loth, 282.

51. De Soresina Vidoni, 107.

CHAPTER X: THE TWILIGHT YEARS

1. Pietro Selvatico, "Sofonisba Anguissola e Antonio van Dyck" in *L'arte nella vita degli artisti* (Florence: G. Barbèra, 1870), 362–363.

2. Bonetti (1928), 293, and also cited in Lancetti, 259.

3. R. Sacchi, 87.

4. R. Sacchi, 88.

5. Milan. Archivio di Stato. Famiglia 6, Anguissola, doc. XVI–XVIII. 8 June 1606.

6. R. Sacchi, 89.

7. R. Sacchi, 89.

8. R. Sacchi, 89.

9. Christopher Brown, *Van Dyck* (New York: Cornell University Press, 1982), 14.

10. L. Klingenstein, *The Great Infanta: Isabel, Sovereign of the Netherlands* (New York: G. P. Putnam's Sons, 1910), 181.

11. Julius S. Held and Donald Posner, *Baroque Seventeenth and Eighteenth Century Art* (Englewood Cliffs, N. J.: Prentice-Hall and Harry N. Abrams, n.d.), 197.

12. Cited in Brown, 25.

13. Held and Posner, 197.

14. Held and Posner, 197.

15. Brown, 16.

16. Klingenstein, 180.

17. Brown, 82.

18. Roberto Patricolo, *San Giorgio dei Genovesi e le sui epigrafi* (Palermo, Sicily: Stampatori Tipolitografi Associati, 1977), 5. Author's translation.

19. Sutherland Harris and Nochlin, 107, fn. 9.

20. Giorgio Nicodemi, "Commemorazione di artisti minori: Sofonisba Anguissola" *Emporium* vol. LXVI (1927), 232–33.

21. Petersen, 26.

22. According to Señora Maria Luisa Rurana, Monasterio de las Descalzas Reales, Madrid, after Albert's death, Isabella never wore a nun's habit as sometimes has been erroneously stated (e.g., see Held and Posner, 204). See Luis Carandell, *El Pais Semanal*, No. 580, 22 May 1988, 87. Klingenstein states (p. 185) that Isabella wore the "gray habit of the nuns of the . . . Poor Clares."

23. Cremona. Archivio di Stato. Comune. Raccolta Araldica Sommi–Picenardi. Vol. 76, Famiglia Anguissola, f. 117.

24. Brown, 12.

25. Walter A. Liedtke, "Anthony Van Dyck" *Metropolitan Museum of Art Bulletin* vol. XLII, no. 3 (Winter 1984/85), 6.

26. Bonetti (1928), 293.

27. Liedtke, 23.

28. Brown, 70.

29. Nicodemi, 232.

30. Brown, 82.

31. Nicodemi, 233.

32. M. Fournier-Sarlovèze, "Van Dyck et Anguissola" *Revue de l'art ancien et moderne,* vol. VI (1899), 315.

33. Liedtke, 24.

34. Brown, 81.

35. Brown, 89.

36. Brown, 85–86.

37. It is listed in the register of Santa Croce, Palermo. See also, Herbert Cook, "More Portraits by Sofonisba Anguissola" *Burlington*, vol. 26 (1915), 228.

SELECTED BIBLIOGRAPHY

Adriani, Gert. *Anton Van Dyck Italienishes Skizzenbuch*. Vienna: 1940.

Aglio, Giuseppi. *Le pitture e le sculture della città di Cremona*. 1794. Reprint. Cremona: Arnaldo Forni, 1979.

Agulló Cobo, Mercedes. *Noticias sobre pintores Madrileños de los siglos XVI y XVII*. Madrid: University of Granada, 1978.

Amezúa y Mayo, Augustín G. *Isabel de Valois: 1546–68*. 3 vols. Madrid: Grafica Ultra, 1949.

Anderson, Bonnie S. and Judith P. Zinser. *A History of Their Own: Women in Europe From Prehistory to the Present*. 2 vols. New York: Harper and Row, 1988.

Argote de Molina, Gonzalo. *Discurso a la Monetería: La Descripción del Bosque y Casa Real del Pardo*. Seville, 1582.

Arnold, Janet. *Patterns of Fashion, c. 1560–1620*. New York: Drama Books, 1990.

Aznar, José Camon. *La pintura Española del siglo XVI*. Vol. 24 of *Summa Artis Historia General del Arte*. Madrid: Espasa-Calpe, 1970.

Baldinucci, Filippo. *Opere*. Milan: 1808–12.

———. *Notizie dei professori dei disegno*. Vol. 2. Florence: 1681.

Berenson, Bernard. *Italian Pictures of the Renaissance: Central Italian and North Italian Schools*. 3 vols. London: Phaidon, 1968.

———. *North Italian Painters of the Renaissance*. New York: G. P. Putnam's Sons, 1907.

Beroqui, Pedro. *Tiziano en el Museo del Prado*. Madrid, 1949.

Binaghi Olivari, Maria Teresa, and Alessandra Mottola Molfino. *I pizzi: moda e simbolo*. Milan: Electa Editrice, 1977.

Bloom, Eric, ed. *Dictionary of Music and Musicians*. 5th ed. vols. 2 and 8. New York: St. Martin's Press, 1970.

Boccaccio, Giovanni. *Concerning Famous Women*. Translated by Guido A. Guarino. New Brunswick, N.J.: Rutgers University Press, 1963.

Bowers, Jane, and Judith Tick. *Women Making Music: The Western Art Tradition, 1150–1950*. Chicago: University of Illinois Press, 1986.

Brion, Marcel. *The Medici: A Great Florentine Family*. New York: Exeter Books, 1969.

Brown, Christopher. *Van Dyck*. Ithaca, N.Y.: Cornell University Press, 1982.

Burke, Peter. *Culture and Society in Renaissance Italy: 1420–1540*. New York: Charles Scribner's Sons, 1972.

Butazzi, Grazietta. *Il costume in Lombardia*. Milan: Electa Editrice, 1977.

Campi, Antonio. *Cremona fedelissma città e nobilissima colonia di Romani*. 1585. Reprint. Cremona: Annaldo Forni, 1974.

Caro, Annibale. *Delle lettere famigliari*. 3 vols. Bassano, Italy: 1782.

———. *Lettere inedite*. 3 vols. Milan: 1830.

Cheney, Iris. *Francesco Salviati*. 2 vols. Ann Arbor, Mich.: University Microfilms International, 1984.

Ciardi, Roberto Paolo. *La raccolta Cagnola: dipinti e sculture*. Pisa: Editizione de Comunità, 1965.

Cook, S.A., et al. *The Cambridge Ancient History*. Vol. 8, *Rome and the Mediterranean*. Cambridge: Cambridge University Press, 1954.

Danvila, A. *Felipe II y el Rey Don Sebastian*. Madrid: 1954.

De Castro, Cristobal. *Mujeres del Imperio*. Madrid: Espace-Calpe, 1941.

Defourneaux, Marcelin. *Daily Life in Spain in the Golden Age*. New York: Praeger, 1966.

De la Ferrière, Hector. *Lettres de Catherine de' Médicis*. 3 vols. Paris: Imprimerie Nationale, 1880.

Della Pergola, Paola. *Galleria Borghese*. Vol. 1, *I dipinti*. Rome: Istituto Poligrafico dello Stato, 1955.

De Maulde la Clavière, R. *The Women of the Renaissance: A Study of Feminism*. New York: G. P. Putnam's Sons, 1901.

De Soresina Vidoni, Bartolommeo. *La pitture cremonese*. Milan: Dalla Società Tipografi de' Classici Italiani, 1824.

De Tolnay, Charles, et al. *The Complete Works of Michelangelo*. New York: Reynal, n.d.

Di Castelgerardo, A. Mango. *Nobilità di Sicilia*. 1915. Reprint. Bologna, n.d.

Durant, Will. *The Renaissance: A History of Civilization in Italy From 1304–1576*. N Y.: Simon and Schuster, 1953.

Emanuele e Gaetani, F. M. *Della Sicilia nobile*. Bologna: Forni Editore, n.d.

Engass, Robert, and Jonathan Brown. *Italy and Spain: 1600–1750, Sources and Documents*. Englewood Cliffs, N.J.: Prentice Hall, 1970.

Ferrari, Maria Luisa. *Il tempo di San Sigismondo a Cremona*. Milan: Cassa di Risparmio delle Provincie Lombarde, 1974.

Fine, Elsa Honig. *Women and Art*. Montclair, N.J.: Allenheld and Schram, 1978.

Fraser, Antonia. *Mary Queen of Scots*. New York: Delacorte, 1969.

Fredericksen, Burton B., and Federico Zeri. *Census of Pre-Nineteenth-Century Italian Paintings in North American Public Collections*. Cambridge: Harvard University Press, 1972.

Freedberg, Sydney. *Painting in Italy: 1500–1600*. Middlesex, England: Harmondsworth, 1971.

Freer, Martha Walker. *Isabel de Valois*. London: Hurst and Blackett, 1857.

Garrard, Mary D. *Artemisia Gentileschi*. Princeton, N.J.: Princeton University Press, 1989.

Gaye, Giovanni. *Carteggio inedito d'artisti dei secoli XIV, XV, e XVI*. Vol. 3: 1501–1672. Florence, 1840.

Goldscheider, Ludwig., ed. *Unknown Renaissance Portraits: Medals of Famous Men and Women of the XV and XVI Centuries*. London: Phaidon Press, 1952.

Gostelow, Mary. *Blackwork*. New York: Van Nostrand, 1976.

Greer, Germaine. *The Obstacle Race*. New York: Farrar, Straus and Giroux, 1979.

Haraszti-Takács, Marianne. *Spanish Genre Painting in the Seventeeth Century*. Budapest: Akadémiai Kiadó, 1983.

Hartt, Frederick. *History of Italian Renaissance Art*. 2d ed. New York: Harry N. Abrams, 1979.

———. *History of Italian Renaissance Art*. 3d ed. New York: Harry N. Abrams, 1987.

———. *Michelangelo*. New York: Harry N. Abrams, 1981.

Held, Julius, and Donald Posner. *Seventeeth and Eighteenth Century Art: Baroque Painting, Sculpture, Architecture*. Englewood Cliffs, N.J.: Prentice-Hall/Harry N. Abrams, 1979.

Hildebrandt, Hans. *Die Frau als Kunstlerin*. Berlin: Rudolf Mosse, 1928.

Hill, George Francis. *Portrait Medals of the Italian Renaissance*. London: Philip Lee Warner, 1912.

Hymans, Henry. *Antonio Moro: son oeuvre et son temps.* Brussels: G. Van Oest, 1910.

Jaffe, Michael. *Van Dyck Antwerp Sketchbook.* 2 vols. Cedar Rapids, Iowa: MacDonald, 1966.

Jenkins, Marianna. *The State Portrait: Its Origins and Evolution.* New York: College Art Association, 1947.

Justi, Carl. *Miscellaneen aus Drei Jahrhunderten Spanishen Kunstlebens.* Berlin, 1908.

Kagan, Richard, ed. *Spanish Cities in the Golden Age: The Views of Anton van den Wyngaerde.* Berkeley: University of California Press, 1989.

Kelly-Gadol, Joan. "Did Women Have a Renaissance?" In *Becoming Visible: Women in European History,* edited by Renate Bridenthal and Claudia Koonz. Boston: Houghton Mifflin, 1977.

King, Margaret. See Labalme.

Klapisch-Zuber, Christiane. *Women, Family and Ritual in Renaissance Italy.* Chicago: University of Chicago Press, 1985.

Klingenstein, L. *The Great Infanta Isabel: Soverign of the Netherlands.* New York: G. P. Putnam's Sons, 1910.

Kubler, George, and Martin Soria. *Art and Architecture in Spain and Portugal.* Baltimore: Penguin Books, 1959.

Kusche, Maria. *Pantoja de la Cruz.* Madrid: Editorial Castalia, 1964.

Labalme, Patricia, ed. *Beyond Their Sex: Learned Women of the European Past.* New York: New York University Press, 1984.

Lafuente Ferrari, E. *El Prado: Del Romantico al Greco.* Madrid: Aguilar, 1967.

Lamo, Alessandro. See Zaist.

Lancetti, V. *Biografia cremonese.* Milan, n.d.

Lavin, Peter. *Renaissance Italy: 1464–1534.* London: B. T. Batsford, 1966.

Litta, Pompeo. *Famiglie celebri italiane.* 2d series. Naples: Libreria Detken e Rocholl, 1905.

Lomazzo, Giovanni Paolo. *Tratto dell'arte de la pittura.* Milan, 1584. Reprint. Hildesheim: Georg Olms, 1968.

Loth, David. *Philip II of Spain.* London: George Routledge and Sons, 1932.

Luzio, Alessandro. *La galleria dei Gonzaga: venduta all'Inghilterra nel 1627–28.* Milan: Casa Editrice L. F. Cogliati, 1913.

Maltby, William S. *Alba: A Biography of Fernando Toledo, Third Duke of Alba 1507–82* Berkeley: University of California Press, 1983.

Maroger, Jacques. *The Secret Formulas and Techniques of the Masters.* New York: The Studio Publications, 1948.

Mario, Alberto. *Teste e figure.* Padua, 1877.

Morelli, Giovanni. *Italian Painters.* Vol. 1, *Borghese and Doria Pamphili in Rome.* London: John Murray, 1892.

Nadal, Santiago. *Las cuatro mujeres de Filipe II.* Barcelona: Ediciones Mercedes, 1944.

Pacheco, Francisco. *Arte de la pintura. 1638.* Reprint. Madrid: Instituto de Valencia de Don Juan, 1956.

Panni, Antonio Maria. *Distinto rapporto delle dipintura che trovansi nelle Chiese della città e soborghi di Cremona. 1762.* Reprint. Cremona: Banco Populare di Cremona, 1976.

Papini, Giovanni. *Vita di Michelangelo nella vita del suo tempo.* Milan: Garzanti, 1950.

Patricolo, Roberto. *San Giorgio dei Genovesi e le sue epigrafi.* Palermo: Stampatori Tipografi, 1977.

Petersen, Karen, and J. J. Wilson. *Women Artists: Recognition and Reappraisal from Early Middle Ages to the Twentieth Century.* New York: Harper Colophon Books, 1976.

Petrie, Sir Charles. *Philip II of Spain.* London: Eyre and Spottiswoode, 1964.

Pigler, A. *Katalog der Galerie Alter Meister.* 2 vols. Tübingen, Germany: Verlag Ernst Wasmuth, 1968.

Pope-Hennessey, John. *The Portrait in the Renaissance.* The A.W. Melon Lectures in the Fine Arts, 1963. National Gallery of Art, Washington, D.C. New York: Bollingen Foundation, 1966.

Raven, Susan, and Alison Weir. *Women of Achievement.* New York: Harmony Books, 1981.

Ramsden, E. H., ed. *The Letters of Michelangelo.* 2 vols. Palo Alto, Calif.: Stanford University Press, 1963.

Ricci, Corrado. *Art in Northern Italy.* New York: Charles Scribner's Sons, 1911.

Roblot-Delondre, Louise. *Portraits d'infantes, XVI siècle.* Paris: G. Van Oest, 1913.

Sacchi, Federico. *Notizie pittoriche cremonese.* Cremona, 1872.

Scotti, Orazio Anguissola. *La famiglia Anguissola.* Piacenza: T. E. P. Gallarati, 1976.

Selvatico, Pietro. "Sofonisba Anguissola e Antonio Van Dyck." In *L'arte nella vita degli artisti. Racconti storici.* Florence: Barbèra, 1870.

Shideler, John C. *A Medieval Catalan Noble Family: The Montcadas 1000–1230.* Berkeley: The University of California Press, 1983.

Signori, Ettore. *Cremona.* Bergamo: Istituto Italiano d' Arte Grafiche, 1928.

Smart, Alaistair. *The Renaissance and Mannerism in Northern Europe and Spain.* New York: Harcourt Brace Jovanovich, 1972.

Soprani, Raffaelo. *Le vite de' pittori, scultori, ed architetti genovesi.* Genoa, pub. 1674.

Stone, Donald, Jr. *France in the Sixteenth Century: A Medieval Society Transformed.* Englewood Cliffs, N.J.: Prentice-Hall, 1969.

Swain, Margaret. *The Needlework of Mary Queen of Scots.* New York: Van Nostrand Reinhold, 1973.

Symonds, John Addington. *Life of Michelangelo.* 2 vols. New York: Charles Scribner's Sons, 1893.

Tenoghi, M. *Iconografia Italiana degli uomini e delle donne celebri.* Milan: Antonio Locatelli, 1836.

Tufts, Eleanor. *Our Hidden Heritage: Five Centuries of Women Artists.* New York: Paddington Press, 1974.

Vasari, Giorgio. *Le vite de più eccellenti pittori, scultori, ed architettori.* 8 vols. 1568. Reprint, edited by Gaetano Milanese. Florence: Casa Vasari, 1878.

———. *Le vite de' più eccellenti pittori, scultori, ed architettori.* 8 vols. Florence. 2nd ed. 1568.

Vecellio, Cesare. *Vecellio's Renaissance Costume Book.* New York: Dover, 1977.

Venturi, Adolfo. *Storia dell'arte italiana.* Vol. 9, pt. 6, *La pittura del Cinquecento.* Milan: Ulrico Hoepli, 1933.

Von Pastor, Ludwig. *The History of the Popes.* London: Routledge Kegan Paul, 1967.

Walker, Barbara. *The Woman's Encyclopedia of Myths and Secrets.* San Francisco: Harper and Row, 1983.

Wethey, Harold. *The Paintings of Titian.* London: Phaidon Press, 1971.

Wilson, Kax. *A History of Textiles.* Boulder, Colo.: Westview Press, 1979.

Woodall, Joanna. *The Portraiture of Antonis Mor.* Ph.D. dissertation, Courtauld Institute of Art, University of London, 1989.

Zaist, Giovanni Battista. *Notizie istoriche de' pittori, scultori, ed architetti cremonesi. 1774.* Reprint. Cremona: Banco Populare di Cremona, 1976.

Zeri, Federico. *Italian Paintings in the Walters Art Gallery.* 2 vols. Baltimore: 1976.

CATALOGUES

Alonso Sánchez Coello y el retrato en la corte de Filipe II. Madrid: Museo del Prado. June/July 1990.

Catalogo sommario della Galleria Doria Pamphili in Roma. Rome: 1965.

Chambers, David, and Jane Martineau, eds. *Splendors of the Gonzaga.* London: Victoria and Albert Museum, 1981.

De Pantorba, Bernardino. *A Guidebook of the Prado Museum.* Madrid: Editorial Gran Capitan, 1950.

Gli Uffizi: Catalogo Generale. Florence: Centro Di, 1979.

Harris, Ann Sutherland, and Linda Nochlin. *Women Artists: 1550–1950.* Los Angeles County Museum of Art. New York: Alfred A. Knopf, 1976.

I Campi e la cultura artistica cremonese del Cinquecento. Cremona: Museo Civico, Milan: Electa, 1985.

Mauro, Natale. *Catalogo Museo Poldi Pezzoli: I dipinti.* Milan: Electa Editrice, 1982.

Modigliani, Ettore. *Catalogo della pinacoteca di Brera.* Milan: Presso la Pinacoteca di Brera, 1950.

Molajoli, Bruno. *Notizie su Capodimonte, catalogo delle gallerie e del museo.* Naples: L'Arte Tipografia, 1958.

Puerari, Alfredo. *La pinacoteca di Cremona.* Florence: Sansoni, n.d.

———. *Mostra di antiche pitture dal XIV al XIX secolo.* Cremona, 1948.

———. *Museo Civico di Cremona.* Milan: 1960.

Rodríguez-Salgado, M. J., *Armada: 1588–1988.* National Maritime Museum, Greenwich. London: Penguin Books, 1988.

Shapley, Fern Rusk. *Paintings from the Samuel H. Kress Collection, Italian Schools, XVI to XVIII Century.* London, pub. 1973.

The Age of Caravaggio. The Metropolitan Museum of Art, New York. New York: Electa International, 1985.

The Stirling Maxwell Collection, Pollok House. Glasgow Museums and Art Galleries. Glasgow, 1977.

The Story of Christmas. December 13, 1968–January 9, 1969. New York: Finch College, 1968.

Strong, Roy. *Artists of the Tudor Court: The Portrait Miniature Rediscovered, 1520–1620.* London: Victoria and Albert Museum, 1983.

Torriti, Piero. *La Pinacoteca Nazionale di Siena: I dipinti dal XV al XVIII secolo.* Genoa: Sagep, 1978.

Torselli, Giorgio. *La galleria Doria.* Rome: Fratelli Palombi, 1969.

Venturi, Lionello. *Catalogo della collezione Gualino.* Milan: Bestetti e Tumminelli, 1926.

PERIODICALS

Binaghi Olivari, Maria Teresa. "Sofonisba Anguissola: L'autoritratto del Poldi Pezzoli e la sua carriera artistica." *Le domeniche al museo Poldi Pezzoli* (1977–78): 1–23.

Bonetti, Carlo. "Nel centenario di Sofonisba Anguissola." *Archivio Storico Lombardo* 55 (1928) : 285–306.

———. "Sofonisba Anguissola: 1531–1625." *Bollettino Storico cremonese* II (1932): 109–152.

Bora, Giulio. "Note Cremonese I: l'eredità di Camillo e i Campi." *Paragone* 28 (May 1977): 49–74.

Borea, Evelina. "Caravaggio e la Spagna: osservazioni su una mostra a Siviglia." *Bolletino d'Arte* 59 (January–June 1974): 47–48.

Cheney, Iris. "Francesco Salviati's North Italian Journey." *The Art Bulletin* XLV (December 1963): 337–49.

De Tolnay, Charles. "Sofonisba Anguissola and her Relations with Michelangelo." *J. of the Walters Art Gallery* 4 (1941): 115–118.

Di Giampaolo, Mario. "Aspetti della grafica Cremonese per San Sigismondo: da Camillo Boccacino a Bernardino Campi." *Antichità Viva* 13, no. 16 (November–December 1974) : 19–31.

Fournier-Sarlovèze, M. "Van Dyck et Anguissola." *La Revue de l'Art* 6 (1899): 316–320.

Frimmel, Theodor. "Einige Werke der Sofonisba Anguissola." *Blätter für Gemäldekunde* (1905): 38–42.

Frizzoni, Gustavo. "La pietra tombale di Sofonisba Anguissola." *Rassegna Bibliografica dell'Arte* 12 (1909): 53–55.

Haraszti-Takács, Marianne. "Nouvelles données relatives à la vie et à l'oeuvre de Sofonisba Anguissola." *Bulletin du Musée Hongrois des Beaux-Arts* 31 (1968): 53–67.

Holmes, C. J. "Sofonisba and Philip II." *Burlington* 26 (1915): 181–187.

Kuhnel-Künze, Irene. "Zur Bildniskunst der Sofonisba und Lucia Anguissola." *Pantheon* 20 (1962): 83–96.

Liedtke, Walter A. "Anthony van Dyck." *The Metropolitan Museum of Art Bulletin* XLIV, 3 (Winter 1984–85).

Longhi, Roberto. "Indicazioni per Sofonisba Anguissola." *Paragone* 157 (1963): 50–52.

Lulier, Claude. "Sofonisba Anguissola et ses Soeurs." In *Artistes Oubliées.* Paris: Librairie Paul Ollendorff, 1902.

Millar, Oliver. "A Van Dyck Sketchbook." *Apollo* 86 (July 1967): 73.

Mulcahy, Rosemary. "Two Letters by Alonso Sánchez Coello." *Burlington* CXXVI (1984): 775–77.

Nicodemi, Giorgio. "Commemorazione di artisti minori: Sofonisba Anguissola," *Emporium* (1927): 222–33.

Perlingieri, Ilya Sandra. "Lady in Waiting: Rediscovering the Forgotten Brilliance of an Illustrious Renaissance Painter." *Art & Antiques* (April 1988): 67–71, 116–119.

———. "Strokes of Genius." *Ms.* (September 1988): 54–57.

———. "Sofonisba Anguissola's Early Sketches." *Woman's Art J.* 9, no. 2 (Fall 1988/Winter 1989): 10–14.

Rey, Garcia. "Nuevas noticias para la biografía del pintor Alonso Sánchez Coello." *Boletín de la Sociedad Española de Excursiones* 35 (1926–27): 199–208.

Roblot-Delondre, Louise. "Argote de Molina et les tableaux du Pardo." *Revue archaelogique* 16, no. 4 (1910): 52–70.

Rooses, M. "Les années d'étude et voyage de Van Dyck." *L'Arte Flammande et Hollandais* 7 (1907): 5–15.

Sacchi, Rosanna. "Documenti per Sofonisba Anguissola." *Paragone* 8, vol. 457 (March 1988): 73–89.

Sanchèz-Canton, Francisco Javier. "Los pintores de camara de los Austurias." *Boletín de la Sociedad Española de Excursiones* 22 (June 1914): 147–50.

Simon, Robert B. "The Identity of Sofonisba Anguissola's Young Man." *J. of the Walters Art Gallery* 44 (1986): 117–122.

Tufts, Eleanor M. "Sofonisba Anguissola, Renaissance Woman." *Artnews* 6 (October 1972): 50–53.

ARCHIVES

England
British Museum, London
Victoria and Albert Museum, London
Witt Library, Courtauld Institute of Art, London.
France
Bibliothèque Nationale, Paris
Italy
State archives (Archivio di Stato) were consulted in the following cities: Arezzo, Brescia, Cremona, Ferrara, Florence, Mantua, Milan, Pisa, Rome, and Siena, as well as the Biblioteca Apostolica Vaticana and Archivio Segreto (Rome).
Sicily
Archivio di Stato, Palermo
Spain
Biblioteca Nacional, Madrid
Archivo Historico Nacional, Madrid
Archivo General, Castle Simancas, Simancas
United States
Frick Art Reference Library, New York
J. Paul Getty Center for the Study of Art and the Humanities, Malibu, Calif.

INDEX

CREDITS

Plates 15, 27, 28, 92, 101, E. Fazoli, Cremona; plates 52, 54, Photographic Library, Villa E. Tatti, Florence; plates 6, 103, 108, 114, 122, Ilya Sandra Perlingieri

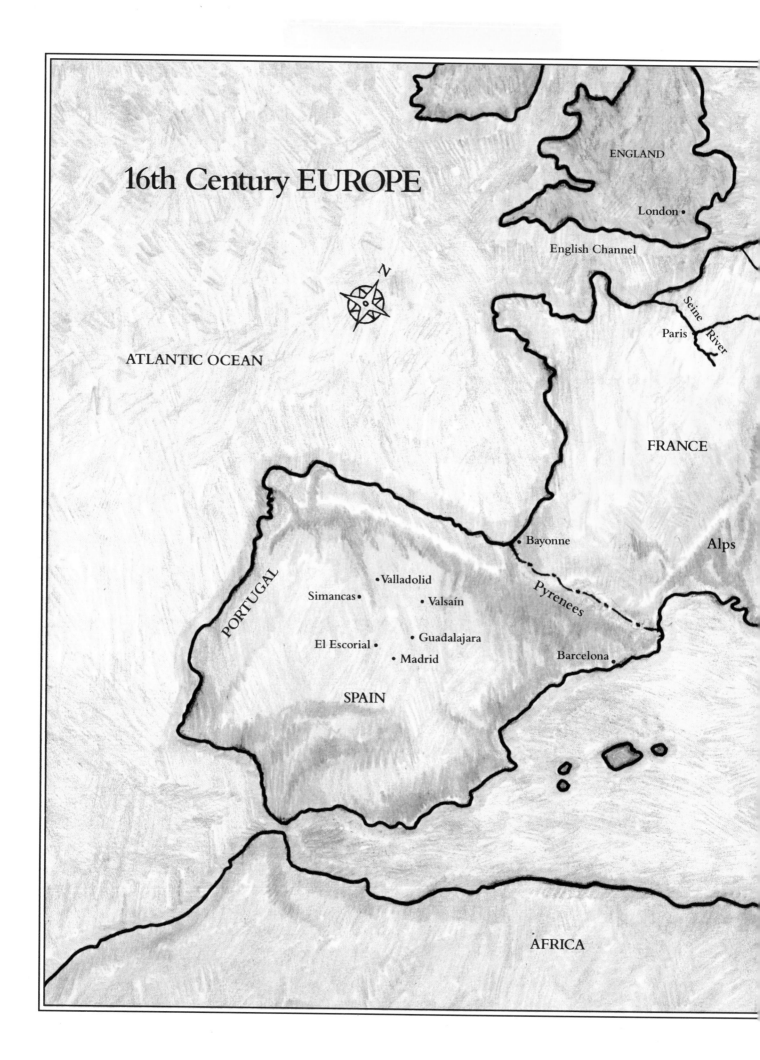

16th Century EUROPE

ENGLAND

London •

English Channel

ATLANTIC OCEAN

Paris •

Seine River

FRANCE

Alps

Bayonne •

Pyrenees

PORTUGAL

• Valladolid

Simancas •

• Valsaín

Barcelona •

El Escorial •

• Guadalajara

• Madrid

SPAIN

AFRICA